Reading and Teaching with Diverse Nonfiction Children's Books

NCTE Editorial Board

Reading and Teaching with Diverse Nonfiction Children's Books

Representations and Possibilities

Edited by

Thomas Crisp
Georgia State University

Suzanne M. Knezek
University of Michigan–Flint

Roberta Price Gardner
Kennesaw State University

National Council of Teachers of English
340 N. Neil St., Suite #104, Champaign, Illinois 61820
www.ncte.org

Staff Editor: Bonny Graham
Manuscript Editor: The Charlesworth Group
Interior Design: Jenny Jensen Greenleaf
Cover Design: NIMBUS Inc.

NCTE Stock Number: 39974; eStock Number: 39981
ISBN 978-0-8141-3997-4; eISBN 978-0-8141-3998-1

Library of Congress Cataloging-in-Publication Data

Names: Crisp, Thomas, 1980- editor. | Knezek, Suzanne M., 1964- editor. | Gardner, Roberta Price, 1968- editor.
Title: Reading and teaching with diverse nonfiction children's books : representations and possibilities / edited by Thomas Crisp, Suzanne M. Knezek, Roberta Price Gardner.
Description: Champaign, Illinois : National Council of Teachers of English, [2021] | Includes bibliographical references and index. | Summary: "Argues for the importance of including in K-8 classrooms high-quality diverse books that accurately and authentically represent the world students live in and explores the ways in which engaging with diverse nonfiction children's literature provides opportunities to counter constricted curricula and reposition the possibilities of pedagogical policies and mandates through centering the histories, lives, and cultures of historically marginalized and underrepresented people"—Provided by publisher.
Identifiers: LCCN 2021014587 (print) | LCCN 2021014588 (ebook) | ISBN 9780814139974 (trade paperback) | ISBN 9780814139981 (adobe pdf)
Subjects: LCSH: Reading (Elementary)—United States. | Children's literature—Study and teaching (Elementary)—United States. | Multiculturalism in literature—Study and teaching (Elementary)—United States. | Multicultural education—United States. | Culturally relevant pedagogy—United States. | Teaching—Social aspects—United States.
Classification: LCC LB1573 .R2782 2021 (print) | LCC LB1573 (ebook) | DDC 372.40973--dc23
LC record available at https://lccn.loc.gov/2021014587
LC ebook record available at https://lccn.loc.gov/2021014588

For Matty and Buddy.
—T. C.

For Mom and Dad, my sisters and brothers, and Gracie.
Always.
—S. M. K.

To Morris R. Gardner Jr. and Autumn.
—R. P. G.

Contents

Foreword

My mother, Mun Kyau Hew Au, the youngest of eight children, grew up in the plantation town of Pāʻia, Maui. She and her siblings spoke Hakka, a variety of Chinese, as their first language, becoming fluent in English once they entered school. Her oldest brother, Chong Meo Hew, loved books and filled the house with them. Not surprisingly, my mother was an avid reader throughout her life.

One of the stories Mom and her sisters liked to tell was about a visit that a teacher, recently arrived from the American continent, paid to their family home in the 1930s. It's likely that this was the first time the teacher (let's call her "Miss Jones") had been to the home of a Chinese family. When Miss Jones entered the house, she immediately noticed all the books. After noting how happy she was to see such a collection, Miss Jones asked in a puzzled voice, "But who reads all these books?"

That punchline always evoked hearty laughter from family members, as we have more than our fair share of bookworms. In the 1950s, when my brother, sister, and I spent the summers in Pāʻia with our grandparents, we entertained ourselves for hours in the upstairs sitting room by working our way through the bookcases. These were stuffed with old books, the ones Miss Jones would have seen, by authors such as Robert Louis Stevenson, Rudyard Kipling, and Howard Pyle. These books—and Miss Jones's assumptions—reflected the strength of colonialism in Hawaiʻi. The classics of the era before World War II presented the view of the world that the plantation power structure wished to impose on Asian and Native Hawaiian workers, a Eurocentric view in which our families' history, perspectives, and contributions were rendered invisible.

These memories of Pāʻia came to mind as I was reading the chapters in this much-needed edited volume. The authors' clear-eyed writing caused me to reflect both on the progress we have made in seeking equity in schools and on the long road yet to be traveled. Even today, how often do we as educators unknowingly send students the message that books and reading belong to some and not to others? That the works of authors from some groups are to be taken seriously, while the works of authors from other groups are not—if they have even been published at all? That some perspectives are strong and true, while others are suspect and easily dismissed?

When I think back to my time as a public elementary school student in what was then the Territory of Hawaiʻi, what strikes me most is what we were *not* taught about the history of our islands. We were not taught that Polynesians, using noninstrument navigation, had been sailing between Hawaiʻi and other far-flung groups of islands for hundreds of years prior to the arrival of the British in 1778. Two hundred years passed before those navigational skills were revived in Hawaiʻi, culminating in the world tour of the voyaging canoe *Hōkūleʻa* from 2013 to 2019.

We were not taught that Hawaiʻi had become part of the United States through the illegal overthrow of the Kingdom of Hawaiʻi, an upheaval instigated by American sugar planters that stripped Native Hawaiians of the right to govern their own lands. A hundred years passed before the anniversary of the overthrow was officially acknowledged by the State of Hawaiʻi, a solemn occasion for which ʻIolani Palace, the only royal residence on American soil, was draped in black.

We were not taught that tens of thousands of Japanese Americans, including community leaders from Hawaiʻi, had been imprisoned in concentration camps during World War II, for no reason other than their ethnicity. Fifty years passed before the United States government issued an apology and offered modest reparations to the Japanese Americans who had been displaced.

As these examples imply, diverse nonfiction books are critical to filling the gaping holes in what is taught in school and to leading students toward fuller perspectives. This volume serves as a valuable introduction to the many diverse nonfiction books available. It also heightens awareness of the role and power of nonfiction. Younger children tend to think of nonfiction as "real" versus "make-believe," with older ones referring to this distinction as "fact" versus "opinion." We want students to see that this is not such a hard and fast distinction, and that readily available books often present only one perspective: that of the dominant or mainstream group. We want students to recognize that there are multiple perspectives on every significant event, topic, and issue, and that they should be well informed before deciding on their own stance. Working with diverse nonfiction books helps us meet the challenge of teaching students to evaluate the credibility of sources, look at authors' positionality, analyze ideas critically, and justify their conclusions.

Engaging our students with diverse nonfiction books may be one of the most important tasks we can perform as educators committed to social justice. When we lean into this work, we help our students consider how they can contribute to changing the world for the better. And, when we lean in hard enough, we can see the way forward to a more just and compassionate society.

Kathryn H. Au, SchoolRISE
Honolulu, Hawai'i

nificance assigned to white, monolingual, heteronormative histories, subjects, and perspectives. Reading nonfiction literature, particularly diverse nonfiction, must therefore include an examination of the power dynamics and structural factors associated with that literature, such as who wrote, edited, and published it, as well as the social, cultural, racial, and political contexts in which nonfiction is produced, circulated, and read. Nonfiction children's literature continues to evolve aesthetically and ideologically, to some extent in response to larger social justice and equity-focused movements that began in the mid-1960s. Although not specific to nonfiction, organizational efforts such as the Council on Interracial Books for Children and Black Creators for Children helped to promote and publish authors and illustrators from underrepresented racial and ethnic groups.

Overall, representations of people across racial, ethnic, social, and cultural groups continue to increase due to ongoing advocacy for diverse literature; however, many of the resulting books are fiction. Policies and mandates such as Common Core State Standards (National Governors Association Center for Best Practices & Council of Chief State School Officers, 2010) and Next Generation Science Standards (NGSS Lead States, 2013) foreground the reading of nonfiction texts in K–8 classrooms in order to gain specific skill sets for analyzing information. Educational initiatives such as these have had a profound influence on the overall publication of nonfiction children's literature. And yet, the classroom inclusion of culturally diverse books (including nonfiction) is not much different today than it was more than half a century ago (Crisp et al., 2016; McNair, 2016).

Critical Analysis of Diverse Nonfiction

We agree with Harris's (1997) assertion that engaging with content related to diverse experiences and histories that are weighted down with injustice often involves introspection that can create emotional and intellectual dissonance (p. xvii). However, rather than relegating inclusion, justice, and equity to the margins (Philip et al., 2019), we situate diverse nonfiction and the critical analysis of diverse books as an integral core literacy practice that provides opportunities for educators to counter constricted curricula in PreK–8 education. It also repositions and broadens teaching, planning, and literacy instruction by centering the histories, lives, and cultures of historically marginalized people. Engaging with diverse nonfiction can prompt readers to pause and to question dominant narratives. Moreover, it can disrupt rather than define or categorize oversimplified ideas about what makes fiction *fiction*, and nonfiction *nonfiction*.

Similarly, engaging with diverse nonfiction children's literature provokes us to constantly reconsider what constitutes diversity, which, like race, is both contextual and a shifting signifier (Hall, 1996). Like *multiculturalism*, *diversity* is a term that is often redressed, reinterpreted, and diffused within various spheres, translated to mean everything and nothing all at once. Therefore, even as we admit concern about the imprecise and vague nature of the term *diversity*, we also find it important to align ourselves with organizations and movements that have similar goals (e.g., We Need Diverse Books). We therefore use the term in solidarity while still finding it necessary to articulate what we mean when we use the term *diversity*.

We view diversity as social, political, and cultural resources preserved and sustained to articulate realities and dimensions of race, class, gender, sexuality, ability, religion, nationhood, geography, and language, all of which influence readers' consciousness, engagement, and responses to literature. This description is informed by theories of critical multiculturalism, culturally relevant teaching, and critical multicultural analysis. Throughout this volume, authors employ and in some cases expand (see Chapter 2 in this volume) Rudine Sims Bishop's (1990) often-utilized metaphor, in which she described the functions of children's books as follows:

> Books are sometimes windows, offering views of worlds that may be real or imagined, familiar or strange. These windows are also sliding glass doors, and readers have only to walk through in imagination to become part of whatever world has been created and recreated by the author. When lighting conditions are just right, however, a window can also be a mirror. Literature transforms human experience and reflects it back to us, and in that reflection we can see our own lives and experiences as part of the larger human experience. Reading, then, becomes a means of self-affirmation, and readers often seek their mirrors in books. (p. ix)

Bishop's significant body of work centers African American children's literature, but has influenced children's literature research and the critical analysis of parallel cultural groups (Hamilton, 1993), "creating a critical context for examining the children's literature emanating from diverse groups in our nation" (Bishop, 2011, p. 234).

Authors in the present volume also utilize critical multicultural analysis to disrupt white heteronormative master narratives. Yenika-Agbaw (see Chapter 1) describes *critical multicultural analysis* as an analytical framework that encourages readers to examine issues of power embedded in all texts, including nonfiction literature for children. Such analysis necessarily centers the knowledge and information by and about marginalized peoples, relations, histories, and processes that have been excluded from curricula and texts (Botelho & Rudman, 2009). Engaging with nonfiction literature that addresses these omissions and oversights helps PreK–8 educators to develop and sustain their cultural competence and critical consciousness, as well as that of their students. Moreover, as authors throughout this volume note, engagement with diverse nonfiction literature provides young people with models for understanding themselves and the world in which they live.

While engaging all children with diverse nonfiction is critical, as Caraballo and Lichtenberger (2020) document, this is the kind of content with which youths of color are especially invested in engaging, particularly as they "begin to historicize their lives and see themselves and their futures as historical actors" (Gutiérrez, 2008, p. 155). We are emboldened by research that informs educators about how diverse children's books serve to enrich understandings about the ways multiple identities influence knowledge of literature and literacies. We are driven by the experiences of young people, practicing educators, and preservice educators whose pedagogical experiences, perspectives, and knowledge of diverse societies have been transformed by engagement with diverse literature. As educators and children's literature researchers, we are also informed by our own experiences and positionalities, as a heterosexual African American woman (Roberta), a heterosexual white woman (Suzanne), and a gay white man (Thomas). We echo Harris's (1997) belief in the "monumental effects" of exposure and engagement with diverse children's literature, which also reminds us of the critical need for diverse nonfiction to be a more integral and systematic component of schooling (p. xvi).

Although we often disagree with the overly scientific stance of many reading psychologists, we do find points of convergence with their assertion that content matters. For example, psychologist Daniel Willingham (2009) argues that far too many students' reading abilities are curtailed not simply because they lack discrete phonics and comprehension skills or strategies, but because the emphasis on those practices during reading instruction eclipses deep and thoughtful explorations with content knowledge. We go a step further to argue for content knowledge that is more culturally sustaining, responsive, and relevant (Gay, 2018; Ladson-Billings, 1995, 2014; Paris & Alim, 2017). Educators are uniquely positioned to help children become critical consumers of all media, including literature.

This volume brings together professional conversations about the role and function of nonfiction and informational texts in PreK–8 classrooms with ongoing discussions of diverse books and issues of representation in children's literature, including critical examinations of the quality and content of its depictions. Although there is considerable extant research on each of these topics, few scholars have focused on depictions of parallel populations and other minoritized populations specifically in nonfiction children's literature (Crisp, 2015). The authors in this edited book help to create a critical context for analysis and engagement with diverse nonfiction children's literature.

Overview of the Book

Part I of this volume provides a theoretical framework for the book. In Chapter 1, Vivian Yenika-Agbaw discusses critical multicultural analysis, a framework that interrogates critical issues such as voice and power. Yenika-Agbaw demonstrates the effectiveness of critical multicultural analysis through her examination of several nonfiction children's books.

Part II of the book includes chapters that focus explicitly on the history and trends in nonfiction children's literature about specific parallel, underrepresented, or minoritized populations. While these chapters sometimes vary in their structure and approach to their subjects, their authors provide readers with an overview of relevant texts, criteria for selecting and evaluating nonfiction literature about that particular population, points for consideration, and arguments for why it is essential that educators include these books in their classrooms, curricula, and libraries.

Obviously, and unfortunately, it is impossible for this book to be comprehensive in its inclusion of the various identities and social locations that must be represented in nonfiction children's books. For instance, two notable absences from this collection are chapters on gender and people of size. Organizing the book and selecting identities and social locations to highlight also presented problems for us as editors. While some authors take a more intersectional approach in their individual chapters, we struggled with the fact that having separate chapter topics on, for example, people with disabilities and LGBTQ+ people could reinforce oversimplified and binary understandings of identity and social location by unintentionally suggesting that there are no LGBTQ+ people with disabilities.

Further, due to the limitations of space, none of the chapters is an exhaustive discussion of its subject. It is our wish that this book will serve as a starting point, one that encourages readers to locate additional professional resources and primary sources and learn more about available books and the various populations represented in this text. Multiple bookshelves' worth of professional books can—and should—be written about each of the populations represented in this volume and the myriad other identities that have been left out. For example, we need professional resources exploring the histories and literary depictions of Latinx queer women and African American people with disabilities. We hope that our volume will help foster additional, deeper, much-needed work.

References

Bishop, R. S. (1990). Mirrors, windows, and sliding glass doors. In H. Moir, M. Cain, & L. Prosak-Beres (Eds.), *Perspectives: Choosing and using books for the classroom* (pp. ix–xi). Christopher-Gordon.

Bishop, R. S. (2011). African American children's literature: Researching its development, exploring its voices. In S. A. Wolf, K. Coats, P. Enciso, & C. Jenkins (Eds.), *Handbook of research on children's and young adult literature* (pp. 225–36). Routledge.

Botelho, M. J., & Rudman, M. K. (2009). *Critical multicultural analysis of children's literature: Windows, mirrors, and doors.* Routledge.

Caraballo, L., & Lichtenberger, L. (2020). Rethinking curriculum and pedagogy in schools: Critical literacies and epistemologies in theory and practice. In V. Kinloch, T. Burkhard, & C. Penn (Eds.), *Race, justice, and activism in literacy instruction* (pp. 53–70). Teachers College Press.

Crisp, T. (2015). A content analysis of Orbis Pictus Award-winning nonfiction, 1990–2014. *Language Arts*, 92(4), 241–55.

Crisp, T., Knezek, S. M., Quinn, M., Bingham, G. E., Girardeau, K., & Starks, F. (2016). What's on our bookshelves?: The diversity of children's literature in early childhood classroom libraries. *Journal of Children's Literature*, 42(2), 29–44.

Duke, N. K. (2000). 3.6 minutes per day: The scarcity of informational texts in first grade. *Reading Research Quarterly*, 35(2), 202–24. https://doi.org/10.1598/RRQ.35.2.1

Gardner, R.P. (2020). The present past: Black authors and the anti-Black selective tradition in children's literature. *Journal of Children's Literature*, 46(2), 8–18.

Gay, G. (2018). *Culturally responsive teaching: Theory, research, and practice* (3rd ed.). Teachers College Press.

Gutiérrez, K. D. (2008). Developing a sociocritical literacy in the third space. *Reading Research Quarterly*, 43(2), 148–64. https://doi.org/10.1598/RRQ.43.2.3

Hall, S. (1996). *Race: The floating signifier.* Media Education Foundation.

Hamilton, V. (1993). Everything of value: Moral realism in the literature for children. *Journal of Youth Services in Libraries*, 6(4), 363–77.

Harris, V. J. (1997). *Using multiethnic literature in the K–8 classroom.* Christopher-Gordon.

Kiefer, B., & Wilson, M. I. (2011). Nonfiction literature for children: Old assumptions and new directions. In S. A. Wolf, K. Coats, P. Enciso, & C. A. Jenkins (Eds.), *Handbook of research on children's and young adult literature* (pp. 290–99). Routledge.

Ladson-Billings, G. (1995). Toward a theory of culturally relevant pedagogy. *American Educational Research Journal*, 32(3), 465–91. https://doi.org/10.3102/000283120322003465

Ladson-Billings, G. (2014). Culturally relevant pedagogy 2.0: aka the remix. *Harvard Educational Review, 84*(1), 74–84. https://doi.org/10.17763/haer.84.1.p2rj131485484751

McNair, J. C. (2016). #WeNeedMirrorsAndWindows: Diverse classroom libraries for K–6 students. *The Reading Teacher, 70*(3), 375–81. https://doi.org/10.1002/trtr.1516

National Governors Association Center for Best Practices & Council of Chief State School Officers. (2010). *Common Core State Standards for English language arts & literacy in history/social studies, science, and technical subjects*. http://www.corestandards.org/assets/CCSSI_ELA%20Standards.pdf

NGSS Lead States (2013). *Next generation science standards: For states, by states*. The National Academies Press. https://doi.org/10.17226/18290

Paris, D., & Alim, H. S. (2017). *Culturally sustaining pedagogies: Teaching and learning for justice in a changing world*. Teachers College Press.

Philip, T. M., Souto-Manning, M., Anderson, L., Horn, I., J. Carter Andrews, D., Stillman, J., & Varghese, M. (2019). Making justice peripheral by constructing practice as "core": How the increasing prominence of core practices challenges teacher education. *Journal of Teacher Education, 70*(3), 251–64.

Williams. R. (1977). *Marxism and literature*. Oxford University Press.

Willingham, D. (2009, January 9). *Teaching content is teaching reading* [Video]. YouTube. https://www.youtube.com/watch?v=RiP-ijdxqEc

Yenika-Agbaw, V. (1997). Taking children's literature seriously: Reading for pleasure and social change. *Language Arts, 74*(6), 446–53.

Theoretical Foundations

literary theorist Peter Hollindale (1988) defines *ideology* as a "systematic scheme of ideas" that usually relates "to politics, or society, or to the conduct of a class or group, and regarded as justifying actions, [especially] one that is held implicitly or adopted as a whole and maintained regardless of the course of events" (p. 1).

Authors are not free from such political persuasions. Like everyone else, they are people who navigate multiple social worlds. They are people whose works, regardless of the genre, often represent their various social worlds through specific lenses (for more on this concept, see Beach & Myers, 2001; Strauss, 1978). Decisions are made regarding what to include in a piece on a subject of interest, and, although an author might have conducted thorough research to ensure the information presented on the topic is accurate, their affiliation with particular social worlds has a way of skewing how the information is represented. Hollindale (1988) discusses three kinds of ideology; however, his focus is fiction, while the present chapter is about nonfiction literature, and so my discussion will be limited to two levels: *surface ideology*, explained as one "made up of explicit social, political, or moral beliefs of the individual writer, and his wish to recommend them to children through the story" (p. 5), and *passive ideology*, which clearly reveals the "writer's unexamined assumptions" (p. 6).

Nonfiction is a complex genre with great potential to educate readers about their surrounding world and to liberate them from varying degrees of intellectual and sociocultural ignorance. Our insatiable quest for knowledge leads us to keep asking questions about our social and scientific worlds, which might enable us to further understand how our historical past has informed our modern practices and realities as a people. This is where nonfiction literature serves the reader: more so than fiction, it attempts to offer some answers in a deliberate manner. With its popularity these past years due to the rise of the Common Core State Standards (National Governors Association Center for Best Practices & Council of Chief State School Officers, 2010), there is the need to proceed with great care as we share books labeled "nonfiction" with young readers. On that note, this chapter seeks to answer the following question: How might readers be able to detect power relationships embedded in nonfiction literature for children that might result from the author's ideology?

In the remainder of this chapter, I answer this question by framing my analysis within critical multiculturalism. This is an approach all educators can utilize when selecting and evaluating books for young readers. Further, it is a framework that students can be taught to use themselves while reading all types of texts, including children's nonfiction books. Therefore, I start with a brief summary of the tenets of critical multicultural analysis (CMA) and an explanation for why it is important to mentor young readers to read nonfiction literature

I

Theoretical Foundations

A Critical Multicultural Analysis of Power Relationships in Selected Nonfiction Picturebooks

VIVIAN YENIKA-AGBAW, *Pennsylvania State University–University Park*

This chapter discusses critical multicultural analysis (CMA) and its relevance to children's nonfiction. CMA is an analytical framework that encourages readers to examine issues of power embedded in all texts, including nonfiction literature for children. The chapter presents key tenets usually associated with CMA and offers examples of ways in which educators can use these tenets to analyze children's nonfiction texts. Through this examination, power issues uncovered through the analysis are shown to be reminiscent of humanity's tenuous histories of domination and oppression.

Chapter Guiding Questions

- What is critical multiculturalism?
- What distinguishes critical multiculturalism from other forms of multiculturalism?
- How does CMA serve as an analytical framework through which readers can examine ideologies of power in children's nonfiction texts?
- How can adults help young learners become critical multiculturalists by reading and discussing children's nonfiction?

In our book *Does Nonfiction Equate Truth? Rethinking Disciplinary Boundaries through Critical Literacy* (Yenika-Agbaw et al., 2018), my coeditors and I problematize the notion of truth that is commonly associated with nonfiction. In particular, Laura Anne Hudock, Ruth McKoy Lowery, and I approached our project from the perspective of authors who are people situated in social worlds and professionals whose worldviews are shaped by sociohistorical and cultural contexts. Therefore, regardless of the degree of research that may be behind the process, the "truths" that help inform the literary/creative/informational nonfiction texts for children that authors create (the "truths" they may also pass on to readers) are steeped in ideology. Quoting from the *Oxford English Dictionary*, literary theorist Peter Hollindale (1988) defines *ideology* as a "systematic scheme of ideas" that usually relates "to politics, or society, or to the conduct of a class or group, and regarded as justifying actions, [especially] one that is held implicitly or adopted as a whole and maintained regardless of the course of events" (p. 1).

Authors are not free from such political persuasions. Like everyone else, they are people who navigate multiple social worlds. They are people whose works, regardless of the genre, often represent their various social worlds through specific lenses (for more on this concept, see Beach & Myers, 2001; Strauss, 1978). Decisions are made regarding what to include in a piece on a subject of interest, and, although an author might have conducted thorough research to ensure the information presented on the topic is accurate, their affiliation with particular social worlds has a way of skewing how the information is represented. Hollindale (1988) discusses three kinds of ideology; however, his focus is fiction, while the present chapter is about nonfiction literature, and so my discussion will be limited to two levels: *surface ideology*, explained as one "made up of explicit social, political, or moral beliefs of the individual writer, and his wish to recommend them to children through the story" (p. 5), and *passive ideology*, which clearly reveals the "writer's unexamined assumptions" (p. 6).

Nonfiction is a complex genre with great potential to educate readers about their surrounding world and to liberate them from varying degrees of intellectual and sociocultural ignorance. Our insatiable quest for knowledge leads us to keep asking questions about our social and scientific worlds, which might enable us to further understand how our historical past has informed our modern practices and realities as a people. This is where nonfiction literature serves the reader: more so than fiction, it attempts to offer some answers in a deliberate manner. With its popularity these past years due to the rise of the Common Core State Standards (National Governors Association Center for Best Practices & Council of Chief State School Officers, 2010), there is the need to proceed with great care as we share books labeled "nonfiction" with young readers. On that note, this chapter seeks to answer the following question: How might readers be able to detect power relationships embedded in nonfiction literature for children that might result from the author's ideology?

In the remainder of this chapter, I answer this question by framing my analysis within critical multiculturalism. This is an approach all educators can utilize when selecting and evaluating books for young readers. Further, it is a framework that students can be taught to use themselves while reading all types of texts, including children's nonfiction books. Therefore, I start with a brief summary of the tenets of critical multicultural analysis (CMA) and an explanation for why it is important to mentor young readers to read nonfiction literature from a critical multicultural stance, as educators make sound pedagogical decisions about a social justice curriculum to expand their literacies.

An Introduction to Critical Multicultural Analysis

CMA is understood variously, but at its core is the issue of power. This critical framework has served educators and scholars of children's literature across disciplines for decades. It enables us to carefully examine issues of power embedded in texts around several of the tenets identified by critical social theorist Stephen May (2003) within the contexts of multicultural education. CMA was repositioned in children's literature by Botelho and Rudman (2009).

In the introduction to their groundbreaking book, *Critical Multiculturalism: Theory and Praxis*, critical social theorists May and Sleeter (2010) explain why educators need to move beyond multicultural discourses that have failed to transform the curriculum to critical multiculturalism. To them, "critical multiculturalism provides the best means by which to integrate and advance . . . various critical threads," and also "gives priority to structural analysis of unequal power relationships . . . fram[ing] culture in the context of how unequal power relations, lived out in daily interactions, contributes toward its production, rather than framing it primarily as an artifact of the past" (May & Sleeter, 2010, p. 10). While their interest revolves around institutional issues of social injustice common within the formal school setting and the role of education, its focus on power relationships overlaps with those of literary scholars who strongly advocate for a critical multicultural analysis of books to dismantle unequal power in those texts.

As a result of its critical component that enhances data analysis, CMA is a theoretical framework that supports research methods such as content analysis (Johnson et al., 2017). Educators and children's literature scholars have begun embracing CMA as a legitimate approach to textual analysis. For children's literature scholar Kelley (2008), CMA is integral to the analytical process. Referencing Rudman and Botelho (2005), she breaks down the different components of the framework, noting:

> *Critical* in this sense means to analyze how power works. *Multicultural* indicates ways to consider the historical and sociopolitical dynamics that influence social practices. *Analysis* means to examine how cultural characters transpire and proliferate. (Kelley, 2008, p. 32, emphasis in original)

Obviously, CMA is an analytical framework that not only encourages readers to actively engage in the analysis process but also guides them in how to accomplish this task by having them ask simple questions. These might include the following: What power relationships are evident? What sociocultural dynamics emanate from history? How are individuals interacting? For Johnson and Gasiewicz (2017), too, CMA "is an important tool for text analysis that compels readers to examine representations of power, authenticity, accuracy, and the sociopolitical and historical context present in a narrative" (p. 29).

Like most theoretical frameworks, there are tenets typically identified with critical multiculturalism from which CMA stems. While May (2003) identifies four, including one that situates race and ethnicity as being central in the power discourse, in this chapter, I privilege his second tenet, "acknowledging (unequal) power relations" (p. 209), which states that "individuals and groups are inevitably located, and often *differentially* constrained by wider structural forces such as capitalism, racism, colonialism, and sexism" (p. 210, emphasis in original). This tenet is more expansive, and thus affords ample opportunity to examine the types of "unequal power relations" that may be embedded in the four children's nonfiction books discussed later in this chapter. Figure 1.1 summarizes key features of CMA often of relevance to children's literature scholars and educators interested in engaging this framework.

Critical Multicultural Analysis of Selected Nonfiction Texts

While each of the nonfiction picturebooks analyzed here stands by itself, my analysis takes into consideration key ideas from the CMA tenet of particular interest to me for the purposes of this study, the most compelling being the idea of a power continuum. As Kelley (2008) observes, "power can be examined on a continuum: domination, collusion, resistance, agency" (p. 33). To this power continuum, I would add *exclusion* or silencing with an attempt to render groups

---

Critical multicultural analysis . . .

- is a way of reading literary texts for re-/misrepresentations, stereotypes, and inaccuracies;
- has a history that is linked to critical multicultural education to uphold democratic values;
- acknowledges the existence of power relationships in texts for readers to actively engage;
- holds readers accountable for their roles in perpetuating inequities; and
- enables readers to read *purposefully and critically*, making connections to our sociocultural histories that have often positioned cultural groups in a power continuum.

FIGURE 1.1. CMA: A summary of key ideas of interest to literacy educators.

invisible. This is of extreme importance because this form of power manipulation may remain subtle and nuanced amidst the rich information presented on a topic by an author or illustrator. In fact, it may become obvious to readers only when they take an active stance. Such a stance often entails looking at a variety of evidence (historical, scientific, sociocultural, etc.) in order to draw and substantiate conclusions. These could range from the omission of certain groups and their contributions, the mistreatment of people or creatures because of their otherness, and scientific and technological findings skewed in favor of particular cultural groups. My analysis of these nonfiction books, therefore, is one way to engage these kinds of power manipulations.

For the purpose of this chapter, I selected four nonfiction picturebooks from a list of recently published titles. Additionally, the choices of these books were made "because of their potential to act as telling cases" (Jones, 2018, p. 169)—as example cases to illuminate subtle ideology in otherwise aesthetically appealing and intellectually engaging books. I then checked their status on Amazon.com to gauge their popularity among buyers whom I consider potential readers of these books, or who might have access to potential readers of the selected books. Under the broad genre of nonfiction, the chosen picturebooks can be subcategorized further as biographical, in the case of *Six Dots: A Story of Young Louis Braille* (Bryant, 2016), and as informational, for *Big Words for Little Geniuses* (Patterson & Patterson, 2017), *Trains* (Graham, 2017), and *Thank You, Earth* (Sayre, 2018). The nonfiction picturebooks target children of ages three to eight years old (preschool–grade 3). These are young children who might still be oblivious to the inner workings and past histories of the larger society, and their places and roles within the multiple sociocultural spaces they may occupy.

Ideologies of Cultural Dominance

To uncover power relationships embedded in these books, I begin by focusing on the rhetorical strategies the authors and illustrators use to present information deemed important on a topic. I look at the verbal and visual texts, paying attention to what information takes the spotlight and what information might be missing (or omitted), and I question why that might be so. Next, I examine the sociocultural, scientific, and technological perspectives that might have informed the selection of specific information to include in each text—in short, *what might have made this information more important from the author or illustrator's perspective?* Working only with the physical book, a cultural artifact, I do not profess to understand the author's or the illustrator's intent. I can only infer power relationships from the types of information that seem *dominant* in the book and those that are *silenced* based on historical/scientific/sociocultural evidence as mentioned earlier.

Dominance of Sighted People

Jen Bryant's (2016) picturebook biography *Six Dots: A Story of Young Louis Braille* won the 2017 Schneider Family Book Award for its portrayal of a person with a visual disability (blindness). It tells the story of Louis Braille and how he came to invent braille, an effective mode of nonverbal communication for the blind. A book on this topic is a major contribution in the field of children's literature, for it educates readers about the history of braille, including young Louis's personal struggle that led to its invention. Additionally, it expands readers' understanding of diversity beyond race, class, gender, and sexuality. There is ample research evidence to support the claims the author makes about Louis, as a sighted child who later became blind. What I consider problematic, however, in this book's portrayal of the culture of people who are blind is twofold, and concerns (1) the rhetorical strategy used in conveying the information and (2) the implied audience for the book. The front cover somewhat promises a story that will be inclusive of both readers who are blind and those without severe visual impairments, as is evidenced by the bilingual presentation of the book's title in English and in braille (though not raised, as it should have been). However, that is where the attempt ends, for the entire book talks about people who are blind using language that heightens their otherness. Braille as a legitimate language for communication is therefore simply acknowledged, for the story text is not raised, and, as such, deprives child readers who are blind and/or read braille of their rights to experience a book about a pivotal moment in their own culture's history.

This leads to the question of audience. If the picturebook is about the sociocultural histories of people who are blind, and clearly a biography of Braille, the man behind this language, why are persons with visual disabilities not given the opportunity to read it in a meaningful and personal way? Why should they wait for people who are sighted to read the story, discuss the significance of Braille's invention, and inform them that it was a milestone in human culture when it is they who use braille as their primary language of communication? This oversight of not writing the biography as a braille–English bilingual text objectifies people who are blind. In this way, I conclude that they are excluded and silenced from a discourse to which they should be at the center. They are thus dominated by the sighted population, including the author and the illustrator. Therefore, while the artists have a solid grasp of the subject matter based on their research, their positions as people who are sighted leaves them unaware of the need to include those with visual impairments in a conversation that directly concerns them.

Social Class (Upper Middle) and English Language Dominance

Susan and James Patterson's (2017) *Big Words for Little Geniuses* is a picturebook alphabet dictionary, illustrated by Hsinping Pan, that considers children "little geniuses" whose parents and caregivers should encourage them to read big words for fun. On the jacket cover, the wife and husband authors note:

> There's no **gobbledygook** in this book! Just fun big words for your **Lilliputian** genius to learn! Why should your little genius's first word be *cat* when it can be *catawampus*? Start your child off with an early love of reading with these big words that are wonderfully fun to say. (emphases in the original)

The reference to a term from Jonathan Swift's (1726/2008) *Gulliver's Travels* already gives the reader a sense of the authors' ideology regarding English literacy education, and this has to do with the valuation of the canon. The power issue here is blatant. First, there is the question of audience. While the book's Amazon.com page lists the audience as preschool to grade 1, one might wonder why children this young really need to learn big words for fun. This book made both the *New York Times* and *Smithsonian* bestselling lists in 2017. Megan Gambino (2017), an editor for the *Smithsonian Magazine*, remarks that Susan and James Patterson

> have written an alphabet book that doesn't underestimate kids' abilities to learn new words. Sure, "A is for apple," but it's also for *arachibutyrophobia* (the fear of peanut butter sticking to the roof of your mouth). And B is for bibliomania—the mission of James's fledgling children's book imprint, JIMMY Patterson, is to turn as many kids into bibliomaniacs as possible. (para. 3, emphasis in original)

We need to be mindful of the fact that, while the stated readers are very young children, an implied reader who is expected to broker this reading experience is a caregiver or an adult assumed to be of a certain educated class with a good mastery of the English language. This is the only way these adults may be able to help their children to not only learn how to pronounce the multisyllabic words in the visually playful alphabet dictionary, but to also try to have fun while learning. From the book creators' perspective, then, if the caregiver or adult lacks the appropriate background to assist their children in this way and embarrass themselves trying to pronounce these words, too bad!

On the power continuum, I see this as social class (specifically, upper middle class) dominance. Further, it silences children and families with limited proficiency in the English language and highlights their otherness. And, while the authors claim reading big words gives young children an early start to love reading, one may wonder if this is some kind of euphemism about the need to position children toward an educational path that paves the way to "Baby Ivies." For, as Victoria Goldman, author of *The Manhattan Directory of Private Nursery Schools* (2012), posits about the frenzy around having young children admitted into the right nurseries: "New York's top-tier nurseries can be feeder schools to the 'right' kindergarten, and then Trinity and Dalton, and upward to Harvard and they offer the right social element" (Goldman, 2003, para. 4). Might this be a hidden agenda for this book as well? It harkens back to the era of the canon wars, when knowledge was prescribed for children by the then US Secretary of Education, William Bennett, a coauthor of *The Educated Child: A Parent's Guide from Preschool through Eighth Grade* (Bennett et al., 1999). It is not clear how the Pattersons decided which words to feature in their text. Additionally, one may also wonder why they did not consider including words from languages other than English, since learning to read these would be fun too.

There is also what I consider parental or adult dominance, since the "little" genius would have to rely heavily on a capable adult in order to determine what kind of book to read for fun. It heightens their otherness as children. Some critics might say, "Don't adults already make these decisions about what kinds of books to buy for their preschooler?" Yes, they do, but not always with the intent of having them learn unusually complex words for fun. Therefore, while there is no doubt that the authors have adopted a novel approach to the alphabet book subgenre, with information that is accompanied by colorful images that attempt to convey the kinds of fun readers might experience, the adult authors' educated class superiority results in a lack of awareness of some children's sociocultural realities.

White Western Dominance, Non-White/Non-Western Silencing

Ian Graham's (2017) *Trains*, illustrated by Stephen Biesty, is an informational book that spotlights trains, focusing on their engineering histories—mostly in the West. Information is broken down into seven sections, with subheadings such as "Early Steam Trains," "American Steam Trains," "The Golden Age of Steam," "Diesel Replaces Steam," "Electric Trains," "Heavy-Duty Diesel Trains," "High-Speed Trains," and "Trains of the Future." Under each section, basic information is provided about the particular invention accompanied by a double-page spread image of the locomotive or train and additional information in the sidebars of scaled-down images that might be considered an addendum. The history, though purported to be from a global perspective, focuses primarily on the Western engineers' contributions to the invention and perfection of railroad transportation. Readers learn about the different parts and types of trains, the engineers behind these inventions, the technicians who operate the trains, and the passengers who travel by train ("Early Steam Trains" through to the "Trains of the Future").

From the information presented, it is clear that the locomotive was invented in Britain and then spread elsewhere, but what is not made clear is how this invention was further developed in different parts of the world other than the West. For instance, how did it develop in Asia? Also, of particular concern in regard to the history of the "American Steam Trains" is the omission of contributions to the development of the American railroad transportation industry by groups like Chinese immigrants, who constituted approximately two-thirds of the workforce. Young readers need to know important information like this to enable them to understand further the sociocultural complexities behind the transcontinental railroad, the contributions of immigrants, and the sacrifices several communities made in the process. As described on the History.com website:

> In 1865, after struggling with retaining workers due to the difficulty of the labor, Charles Crocker (who was in charge of construction for the Central Pacific) began hiring Chinese laborers. By that time, some 50,000 Chinese immigrants were living on the West Coast, many having arrived during the Gold Rush. This was controversial at the time, as the Chinese were considered an inferior race due to pervasive racism. The Chinese laborers proved to be tireless workers, and Crocker hired more of them; some 14,000 were toiling under brutal working conditions in the Sierra Nevada by early 1867. (History.com, 2019, para. 8)

Why then is information about Chinese Americans' contributions omitted in the "American Steam Train" section of *Trains*? Also, neglecting to mention how the expansionist agenda of the transcontinental railroad disrupted Native American communities is problematic, for it renders this part of history invisible.

Graham's (2017) picturebook uses a colonial lens to interpret events on this exciting topic. One might expect that, if there are gaps in history in the verbal narrative in the text, these would be filled by the visual narrative. In *Trains*, this is not so, for all of Stephen Biesty's images of workers and passengers appear to be of white people. Where the text suggests people of color, the images are scaled down so it is difficult to identify their ethnicities. For instance, in the last pages of the book, under the subheading of "Trains of the Future," the Japanese L0 Series maglev is celebrated for setting "a new speed record for trains carrying people when it reached 375 miles . . . per hour." A double-page spread image of the train accompanies the verbal text. However, the passengers all appear to be white. At the bottom of that same page, there is the Shanghai maglev, also celebrated for its speed. No passengers are shown in this scaled-down image of the train. This is how the reader exits the reading experience. Why, I wonder, are there no specific comments about the engineers behind these futuristic trains, and why are Asian passengers not featured in trains associated with their regions? We can conclude that the information projects white Western dominance and deliberately silences non-white/non-Western groups who have contributed in significant ways to the development of train engineering and railroad transportation. Very interesting, as well, is the exclusion of two continents from this global history on train transportation—Africa and South America—making it seem as though trains are not used for transportation anywhere in these continents.

Human Dominance and Silence on People's Interaction with Their Natural Environment

April Pulley Sayre's (2018) *Thank You, Earth: A Love Letter to Our Planet* is an informational picturebook for early readers that uses an epistolary format (written in the form of letters) to convey basic information about what Earth offers to human beings. From the onset, while the opening greeting might communicate a sense of gratitude, the power relationship between the human narrative voice and the planet, an object it thanks, reverberates throughout. Over successive pages, the narrative reads: "Dear Earth, . . . Thank you for water . . . mountains . . . minerals . . . plant parts we can eat . . . for being our home." Photographs that accompany the verbal text often verify or extend the information presented. From a critical multicultural stance, the reader may wonder why there is portrayal and mention of various flora and fauna only for what they offer people. It begs the following questions: Are we greater than Earth? Are we masters of Earth? Is Earth simply there to serve our needs? This may lead one to question the legitimacy of the expressed thanks. Thanking Earth for all the services it provides to humans could easily translate into thanking Earth for being there for human exploitation.

The author's note in the back of the book explains the intentions further: "This book is a thank-you note to the earth. The earth provides us with so much" (Sayre, 2018, p. 38). It offers thanks but does not hold humans accountable for their responsibility in preserving Earth. Thus, they can enjoy the services Earth renders without necessarily protecting it, even when they consider Earth "our home." In addition, there is not a single picture of a human being in this informational picturebook about Earth. If people are an integral part of Earth, should we not be featured in the book in some capacity? This nonfiction text reflects an ideology of human dominance with humans removed or separated from the rest of the planet.

Helping Young Readers Become Critical Multiculturalists

From the above analyses, it is evident that nonfiction picturebooks are not free of power issues. These books are written by authors who have been (and are) socialized in various ways, and, though they conduct research on their topics, they are selective in their presentation of specific information. Most often, the selective process of what and how information is presented is intertwined with our sociocultural histories. For this reason, readers should not expect information to be presented in a completely objective manner. All information should be suspect until readers have done further research on the topic. Educators, therefore, should help young children become savvy readers of all kinds of texts, especially nonfiction, which is often believed to espouse truths (scientific, historical, and more).

Hollindale (1988) posits that:

> In literature, as in life, we have to start from where the children are, and with their own (often inarticulate) ideology. This offends some commentators, who prefer the literature to begin where they wish the children were, or assume that easy transformations can be made by humanely open-minded critical inquiry, whether based in classrooms or elsewhere. (p. 9)

Because children occupy social worlds—some of which are governed by the same rules as those experienced by adults—they already have certain awarenesses. In order to help them learn to strategically uncover ideologies of power embedded in nonfiction literature, educators must first cultivate attitudes of reading that keep young readers alert. Such attitudes, like the ones I have shared in this chapter, are informed by research and have been translated into classroom practice in a wide range of classrooms.

My analysis of these books focused on a power continuum does not preclude the fact that each book has its strengths. However, because I am reading these books through a critical multicultural lens, the findings highlight what I posit to be problematic with each. Excluding or silencing voices is never good for any society, as it causes unnecessary pain and stifles possibilities for some children. Dialogue affords us several opportunities to be more inclusive in our discourses and practices even if the dialogue might inflict a different kind of pain. In this way, we are working together to solve a problem that places our collective humanity at the center. Children need to be aware of this very early in their educational journeys as they learn to approach any story as suspect—not the whole "truth." They must always ask, "What values are reproduced in this text?" This is why, like Hollindale (1988), I have come to accept that:

> Even if beliefs are passive and unexamined, and no part of any conscious prosely-tizing, the texture of language and story will reveal them and communicate them. The working of ideology at this level is not incidental or unimportant. It might seem that values whose presence can only be convincingly demonstrated by an adult with some training in critical skills are unlikely to carry much potency with children. More probably the reverse is true: the values at stake are usually those which are taken for granted by the writer, and reflect the writer's integration in a society which unthinkingly accepts them. In turn this means that children, unless they are helped to notice what is there, will take them for granted too. Unexam-ined, passive values are widely shared values, and we should not underestimate the powers of reinforcement vested in quiescent and unconscious ideology. (p. 6)

Although Hollindale's examples are again from works of fiction, the analysis can work for nonfiction, too.

Finally, then, as readers we need to be mindful of "unexamined assump-tions" (Hollindale, 1988, p. 6) that might reflect an author's values and belief system and so quietly seep into their works. For instance, being people who are not blind may have influenced author Jen Bryant (2016) as she and illustra-tor Boris Kulikov *re*constructed Louis Braille's biography; class privilege might have distracted Susan and James Patterson (2017) as they made decisions about the types of words to include in their alphabet dictionary; white, Western arro-gance might have muddled Graham and Biesty's (2017) historical narrative on trains; and human conceit might have fogged Sayre's (2018) heartfelt letter to Earth.

In Tables 1.1, 1.2, and 1.3, which conclude this chapter, there is information and some ideas that educators can consider as they undertake the challenge of nurturing young readers as critical multiculturalists. These are ideas that I have tried in my courses with teacher candidates who are preparing to work with young children. While not definitive, they are good places to start.

TABLE 1.1. Examples of Inquiry Strategies by Category

Book Design	Voice/Identities	Authenticity/Accuracy[a]	Power	Audience	Other
Title: How is it phrased?	Who is telling the story?	What seems authentic and how/why?	Power dynamics—between groups, cultures, creations, artifacts, etc.	Who is the primary audience? What linguistic aspects or signs convey this to you?	What else do you notice?
Peritextual features	How is the story told? Appeal of the illustrations? How are they positioned on the pages for information accessibility and entertainment appeal?	Information privileged/ omitted/ missing? Information and illustrations, how reflective of the social/ natural/ scientific worlds; historical periods?	Adult/child, scientific/layperson's local/global perspectives? Sociocultural groups, etc.	Primary and implied?	What else do you notice?
Front and back matter	Language use and font	*Front:* Does it open with an explanation? How convincing is it? Was it necessary? *Back:* How is the book advertised? What is highlighted or muted?	Gaps noticed and implications for power dynamics	Primary and implied?	What else do you notice?
Research evidence and source	Credibility of research sources	Author/illustrator's background as knowledgeable artists of nonfiction. Cultural background—insider/ outsider and measures taken to ensure accuracy and authenticity	Information omitted that is already common knowledge	Primary?	What else do you notice?
Aesthetic appeal: Alphabetic and visual language or signs	Cultural appeal of text: art/print	Language uses reflective of period/ discipline		Aesthetic appeal: Alphabetic and visual language or signs	Cultural appeal of text: art/print
Inference from the book design?	Inference from narrative and rhetorical strategies to draw conclusions?	Conclusions about authenticity and accuracy from information as presented?	Conclusions about power dynamics?	Inference about the suitability of text and audience?	What else do you notice?

[a] *Accuracy* implies factual information about the topic under discussion. Thus, with thorough research, scholars and educational researchers can verify what information on a particular subject is accurate or false without necessarily belonging to a particular sociocultural group. *Authenticity*, on the other hand, implies that information on the topic under discussion is conveyed by someone with intimate knowledge of the subject based on experiences that are rooted within the cultural spaces from which the topic emanates. It is not enough to present facts about the subject; it greatly matters *how* they are presented to convey an understanding of certain cultural norms and nuances associated with the group.

TABLE 1.2. Power in Nonfiction Literature for Children: Domination[a]

Book Title	Responses with Textual Evidence
Who is dominated and by whom?	
What forms do domination manifest in the book?	
What emotions are evoked in you on noticing forms of domination?	
How would you rethink this story to more accurately reflect … (a) the historical context? (b) the scientific reality? (c) the sociocultural reality of the context?	

[a] Adapted from Kelley's (2007) template.

TABLE 1.3. Power in Nonfiction Literature for Children/Adolescents: Exclusion

Book Title	Responses with Textual Evidence
Whose contributions are excluded from this book?	
What forms do these exclusionary practices take?	
What historical/scientific/sociocultural evidence can you locate from research to challenge information in this book?	
Other thoughts about your findings:	

Children's Books Cited

Bryant, J. (2016). *Six dots: A story of young Louis Braille* (B. Kulikov, Illus.). Knopf Books for Young Readers.

Graham, I. (2017). *Trains* (S. Biesty, Illus.). Templar Books.

Patterson, S., & Patterson, J. (2017). *Big words for little geniuses* (H. Pan, Illus.). Little Brown & Company.

Sayre, A. P. (2018). *Thank you, earth: A love letter to our planet* (A. P. Sayre, Photog.). Greenwillow Books.

References

Beach, R., & Myers, J. (2001). *Inquiry-based English instruction: Engaging students in life and literature*. Teachers College Press.

Bennett, W. J., Finn, C. E., & Cribb, J. T. E. (1999). *The educated child: A parent's guide from preschool through eighth grade.* Free Press.

Botelho, M., & Rudman, M. (2009). *Critical multicultural analysis: Windows, mirrors, and doors.* Routledge.

Gambino, M. (2017). The ten best children's books of 2017. *Smithsonian Magazine.* https://www.smithsonianmag.com/arts-culture/ten-best-childrens-books-2017-180967564

Goldman, V. (2003, January 12). The baby ivies. *The New York Times.* https://www.nytimes.com/2003/01/12/education/the-baby-ivies.html

Goldman, V. (2012). *The Manhattan directory of private nursery schools* (7th ed.). Soho Press.

History.com (2019, September 11). *Transcontinental railroad.* https://www.history.com/topics/inventions/transcontinental-railroad

Hollindale, P. (1988). *Ideology and the children's book.* Thimble Press.

Johnson, H., & Gasiewicz, B. (2017). Examining displaced youth and immigrant status through critical multicultural analysis. In H. Johnson, J. Mathis, & K. G. Short (Eds.), *Critical content analysis of children's literature: Reframing perspective* (pp. 28–43). Routledge.

Johnson, H., Mathis, J., & Short, K. G. (Eds.) (2017). *Critical content analysis of children's and young adult literature: Reframing perspective.* Routledge.

Jones, S. A. (2018). Telling cases of bilingual children's reading and writing for English-medium school: Implications for pedagogy. *Australian Journal of Language and Literacy, 41*(3), 166–176.

Kelley, J. E. (2008). Power relationship in *Rumpelstiltskin*: A textual comparison of a traditional and a reconstructed fairy tale. *Children's Literature in Education, 39*(1), 31–41. https://10.1007/s10583-006-9039-8

May, S. (2003). Critical multiculturalism. *Counterpoints, 168,* 199–212. http://www.jstor.org.ezaccess.libraries.psu.edu/stable/42977501

May, S., & Sleeter, C. E. (2010). Introduction: Critical multiculturalism: Theory and praxis. In S. May & C. E. Sleeter (Eds.), *Critical multiculturalism: Theory and praxis* (pp. 1–16). Routledge.

National Governors Association Center for Best Practices & Council of Chief State School Officers. (2010). *Common Core State Standards for English language arts & literacy in history/social studies, science, and technical subjects.* http://www.corestandards.org/assets/CCSSI_ELA%20Standards.pdf

Rudman, M., & Botelho, M. (2005). Shock of hair: Hair as a cultural theme in children's literature. *The Dragon Lode, 24*(1), 11–19.

Strauss, A. (1978). A social perspective. In N. K. Denzin (Ed.), *Studies in symbolic interaction: An annual compilation of research,* vol. 1 (pp. 119–128). JAI Press.

Swift, J. (2008). *Gulliver's travels.* Penguin. (Original work published 1726)

Yenika-Agbaw, V., Hudock, L. A., & Lowery, R. M. (2018). *Does nonfiction equate truth?: Rethinking disciplinary boundaries through critical literacy.* Rowman & Littlefield.

II

Focus Chapters

Exploring the World of Latinx Nonfiction Children's Literature

Jamie Campbell Naidoo, *University of Alabama*
Ruth E. Quiroa, *National Louis University*

One day at the library, Julio came across an article about the skulls he and his brothers had found as children. This discovery renewed Julio's pride in his ancestry. He decided to devote his medical skills to the study of the Indigenous history of Peru.

—Monica Brown, *Sharuko: El arqueólogo Peruano
Julio C. Tello/Peruvian Archaeologist Julio C. Tello*

As Latinx (a gender-inclusive reference to individuals of Latin American descent) populations continue to grow in the United States alongside negative rhetoric about this cultural group, so does the need for authentic nonfiction materials to instill students' pride—like that of Julio in this chapter's epigraph—and guide their understanding of the rich and diverse history, cultures, languages, and people of Latin America, Mexico, the Spanish-speaking Caribbean, and Latinx in the US. This chapter introduces readers to trends in Latinx nonfiction children's publishing and explores various categories of these books. Criteria for evaluating the illustrations and text of Latinx nonfiction books, as well as recommended and contentious titles, are provided to help educators find the best materials to use with their students. Instructional imaginings are also offered, to spark ideas for their use with children in both classrooms and libraries.

Chapter Guiding Questions

• What children's books with Latinx characters have you used with your students? What messages about this population do students acquire from these books? Are these messages authentic and accurate? Do they perpetuate stereotypes of the Latinx culture?

- How do you identify potential nonfiction Latinx-themed books for your classroom library and literacy curriculum? What resources do you turn to during this process and why?

- How comfortable are you in assessing the accuracy of content and images in nonfiction Latinx books? What sorts of outside research do you complete to help you ensure the books you select present the actual realities, lives, places, and histories of Latinxs?

- Think about how you use general nonfiction books with students. What about Latinx-themed nonfiction titles—how do you access or scaffold students' understandings of these books?

Given the continuing influx of diverse Latinx-origin students in US schools (Pew Research Center, 2019; United States Census Bureau, 2019), together with the political rhetoric in the United States surrounding illegal immigration, the construction of a large border wall between the United States and Mexico, and the separation of families and detainment of children at the border in unhealthy living conditions, it is imperative that students have opportunities to explore and discuss issues influencing themselves, their Latinx classmates, or the Latinx families in their community. One way to introduce these topics and open curricular space for deeper conversations is through high-quality, relevant nonfiction teaching materials that depict the diverse experiences of the Latinx population. As such, there is a strong impetus for focusing on the current status of Latinx nonfiction children's literature available today and its place in classrooms and libraries across the nation.

As each week passes, students are exposed to news media and speeches by figures in leadership roles that criminalize Latinx adults and children, painting them as untrustworthy individuals whose sole purpose is to take unjust advantage of US jobs and health benefits. Increasingly, images of Immigration and Customs Enforcement raids, detained migrant children at the US–Mexico border, and apprehensive and disillusioned Dreamers, along with conversations about sanctuary cities and the tenuous Deferred Action for Childhood Arrivals program have become commonplace. For some students, these are abstract concepts, while, for others, they are a gritty reality influencing themselves and their families and friends. Adding to this complexity, students are inundated with the message that all Latinx individuals are immigrants, when, in reality, Puerto Ricans are US citizens and many other Latinx individuals are US born.

Through educational activities and discussions that incorporate quality Latinx nonfiction children's literature, educators can provide a safe environment for students to discuss and navigate these tough topics. As authors with years of experience analyzing and using Latinx children's literature, we are deeply committed to this work. Jamie, a Latinx cultural outsider, is married to a US immigrant and is a white gay male and first-generation college student who has worked extensively with Latinx caregivers, educators, librarians, and literacy researchers. Ruth is a white, straight, first-generation college graduate whose Guatemalan American family is biracial, bilingual, and biliterate. She is a former kindergarten and bilingual (Spanish–English) second-grade educator. Our chapter describes trends in Latinx nonfiction children's literature, offers evaluation criteria, provides an overview of subcategories, suggests recommended titles, and offers ideas for using these books in both classrooms and libraries.

General Trends in Latinx Children's Books

Within the extremely small percentage of Latinx children's books published each year (Cooperative Children's Book Center, 2019), few titles are nonfiction— particularly expository nonfiction. Rather, most are realistic fiction, novels in verse, picture storybooks, and board books. In addition, the area of Latinx nonfiction children's literature is not as diverse with regard to the format or type of informational materials as is the larger field of children's nonfiction books. The dominant type of nonfiction in Latinx children's titles is the picturebook biography, followed by photo essays, holiday books, and longer biographies and memoirs. Within the past fifteen years, it has been increasingly common to see more historical nonfiction books written in poetic form and a blurring of boundaries between strictly nonfiction books and historical picturebooks and novels. This is indicative of Latinx history and culture in general, which includes elements of magical realism, rich poetic language, and storytelling as part of oral tradition. As such, books that provide informational content about a specific aspect of Latinx culture are frequently imbued with oral storytelling elements and writing in a narrative format, often including a lengthy author's note to extend main ideas and provide more information.

Many Latinx children's fiction titles today focus on a particular current topic, such as immigration or a historical event or figure. These books frequently include the aforementioned author's notes that significantly add to their informational content. For example, the historical fiction novels written by Cuban American poet Margarita Engle contain facts and endnote material that allow them to pair well with nonfiction books during instruction. Similarly, picturebooks such as *Maybe Something Beautiful: How Art Transformed a Neighborhood* (Campoy & Howell, 2016), about the work of Latinx muralist Rafael López, includes extensive back matter with links to further reading, thus serving as a springboard for lessons incorporating nonfiction books. Told from a child's perspective, this title provides readers with necessary information on López, giving a unique opportunity to explore primary sources about his work, such as his US Postal Service stamps depicting famous Latinx individuals throughout history. He also created a Mendez versus Westminster stamp, which could connect with Duncan Tonatiuh's (2014) work on the topic in *Separate Is Never Equal*; while his stamp on Celia Cruz could be paired with *My Name Is Celia: The Life of Celia Cruz/ Me llamo Celia: La vida de Celia Cruz* (Brown, 2004), the picturebook biography featuring his illustrations.

Consistent with the influx of graphic novels in the overall body of children's literature is an increase in Latinx nonfiction children's books published by small presses. Lila Quintero Weaver's (2010) *Darkroom: A Memoir in Black and White* is a prime example. This powerful work, targeted toward grades junior high and older, provides an intimate look at the author–illustrator's experience growing up as an Argentine Latinx immigrant in the Jim Crow South. The graphic format holds appeal to visual and English learners alike and can serve as a good introduction to discussing the treatment of racial groups in US history. A similar graphic novel is Elisa Amado's (2019) *Manuelito*, which profiles a thirteen-year-old asylum seeker as he flees his home in Guatemala to live with family in the US. While a work of fiction, the book is written out of the Guatemalan author's experience working with migrant children. A useful introduction positions it to provide students with greater context for the story.

The Spanish-language biography series Colección Antiprincesas, created by Argentinian magazine editor Nadia Fink, illustrated by Pitu Saá, and published by Sudestada/Chirimbote, is another graphic novel series that introduces elementary readers to Latina heroines via eye-catching, vibrant cartoon illustrations and engaging, witty text. Written as an antidote to princess stories that perpetuate gender stereotypes, these biographies celebrate strong females, including well-known artist Frida Kahlo, and Latinas lesser known to US students, such as Chilean composer–songwriter Violeta Parra, Brazilian writer Clarice Lispector, and Bolivian military leader Juana Azurduy. A strong element of these books is the accuracy with which they portray the lives of the profiled subjects. For instance, the book about Frida Kahlo discusses her bisexuality, providing opportunities for students to see a strong representation of someone from the LGBTQ+ community. Colección Antihéroes, the male version of the series, introduces readers to important Latinx figures in South American history like Argentine revolutionary Che Guevara, Argentine novelist Julio Cortázar, Uruguayan sociologist Eduardo Galeano, and Argentine folk-religious figure Gauchito Gil.

Another trend in this body of literature is the availability of nonfiction books with Latinx content via digital platforms such as Epic!, PebbleGo, and Capstone Interactive. The presence of digital titles becomes particularly important when students may not have ready access to print materials. Titles in these collections mirror content in print versions of books but may include interactive features such as the ability to have text read aloud, background reading on specific topics, videos, selection of language choices, and related curricular games. These interactive ebooks tend to be biographies, such as the PebbleGo Hispanic Americans series of seventeen titles for primary-grade students (see https://www.pebblego.com/biographies). Unfortunately, narratives in the series tend to use heavily accented American English pronunciations. Some of the other famous Latinx subjects are included in other series by PebbleGo but not represented in the Hispanic Americans series, and those subjects in the Hispanic Americans series include individuals from Spain. Another subtle form of stereotype evident in these types of series is the inclusion of male Spanish conquerors, who are labeled as "explorers"—a Eurocentric term. While their negative actions toward Native peoples are briefly mentioned, the stories of these men are overwhelmingly positive, with little attention given to their actions as colonizers.

Selection Criteria and Considerations

It is important to select high-quality nonfiction books that engage children with diverse learning styles and linguistic backgrounds and that accurately portray Latinx cultures, while also avoiding common stereotypes evidenced in books published over the years. What follows are a few recommendations for choosing the best nonfiction books with Latinx cultural content. See Figure 2.1 for a summarization of selection criteria.

Quality of Illustrations

When identifying Latinx nonfiction titles for instruction, educators should choose books with high-quality illustrations that complement the text while also normalizing and extending understanding of Latinx cultures. These images should contain strong cultural details consistent with the specific Latinx cultures described and provide contextual clues that scaffold an understandable sequence of events. For instance, the picturebook biography collection *Steps: Rita Moreno, Fernando Botero, Evelyn Cisneros* (Ada & Campoy, 2000) includes three separate biographies about notable Latinx in the arts. Each biography contains illustrations interspersed with actual photographs of the subject at various ages and a map that locates each person's country of origin. Extra details such

Illustrations/Visuals

- Do the illustrations complement the text while also extending the understanding of Latinx cultures?
- Are strong cultural details present in the illustrations and consistent with the specific Latinx culture, topic, and time period described in the text?
- Do illustrations avoid stereotypes of Latinx cultures?
- Are contextual clues embedded within the imagery of the illustrations to help scaffold a logical sequence of events?
- Do the illustrations include high-resolution photographs to reinforce the permanency of the topic?
- Are any copies of archival materials or primary sources present to add extra layers of meaning?
- Are charts, infographics, timelines, or other visual organizers used to help students better understand the content? Are these organizers presented in a way that helps students learn key concepts?
- Does the visual content of the book balance the text, providing additional information without interfering with the book's narrative or textual elements?

Text/Narrative

- Is this text's portrayal of Latinx culture historically accurate and culturally sensitive? Does it include cultural details consistent with the specific Latinx culture being described?
- Does the text avoid stereotypes and misunderstandings about the Latinx cultures?
- Is the author from the specific Latinx culture profiled? If not, have they provided evidence of research or experience working with the culture?
- Are factual details presented in a manner that is easy to understand? Are references provided in the book to support claims?
- Does the author avoid oversimplifying information for the child audience?
- How are Spanish words and phrases used within the text? Is textual redundancy avoided by naturally integrating Spanish words into the text with contextual clues that will help students determine their meaning?
- Are Spanish words spelled correctly? Do they contain the proper diacritics?
- Is a pronunciation guide for non-English terms provided in the book's front or back matter?
- Are text features such as a glossary, table of contents, and index provided to assist readers in navigating the informational content?

FIGURE 2.1. Criteria for evaluating Latinx nonfiction children's books.

as a playbill, sample artwork, and examples of dance styles are also provided. Collectively, these images give students in grades 3 to 6 additional information about each subject while also helping them understand sequential events. The inclusion of quality photographs reinforces the permanency of the profiled Latinx individual, raising their historical significance to that of non-Latinx figures of importance.

Quality of Nonfiction Writing and Spanish Text

Another important factor to consider when selecting Latinx nonfiction is the quality of writing, whether it be expository or narrative. Expository text structure can be organized using description, sequence, chronology, comparison, cause–effect, problem–solution, or a combination of these. It can also make use of creative frames within which to explain a topic. For example, Lulu Delacre's (2016) Spanish and English bilingual (a book with complete text in both Spanish and English) nonfiction poetry book *Olinguito, de la A a la Z! Descubriendo el bosque nublado/Olinguito, from A to Z! Unveiling the Cloud Forest* is a unique, colorful picturebook in poetic form, organized by the alphabet (inclusive of the "ñ"), which serves as a vehicle for young children to comprehend the text's rich vocabulary as they adventure with a zoologist in search of the olinguito, an ever-elusive new mammal discovered in 2013. Other English-based nonfiction Latinx books may include Spanish terms and phrases in problematic ways that do not enhance the realism and cultural accuracy of the topic or subject. This is because Spanish terms may be inserted in ways that serve only monolingual English educators and students, as in the literal (word-for-word) English translation immediately following the Spanish word(s), causing textual redundancy for bilingual readers. Similarly, the inclusion of a pronunciation spelling within parentheses, while useful for the non-Spanish-speaking adult, can cause younger and/or struggling readers of both English and Spanish to stumble while reading for comprehension.

Accuracy of Latinx Cultural Content

When examining Latinx nonfiction books to add to a library collection or educational instruction, it is important to consider whether the content presented about Latinx cultures is accurate. A history of cultural stereotypes and inaccuracies has been noted in the body of Latinx children's literature, including nonfiction books (Barrera & Garza de Cortes, 1997; Naidoo, 2011; Nilsson, 2005; Quiroa, 2013). Latinx cultures have been portrayed as lazy, dangerous, willful, dishonorable, untrustworthy, and unintelligent. Culturally loaded imagery such as sombreros and piñatas, or the use of broken English and hackneyed plots ("illegal" immigrants, fiestas, and drug dealers), have plagued these books. Many Latinx children's books have been created by cultural outsiders with little or no knowledge of the nuances among distinct Latinx cultures. As such, there has been a tradition of historically inaccurate and culturally insensitive educational materials and books perpetuating biases toward Latinx people.

It is important for educators and students to read broadly to avoid what Adichie (2009) identifies as misunderstandings and biases caused by exposure to a "single story" (00:03). For example, to engage with the topic of immigration and immigrants, educators can read nonfiction poetry like that of Jorge Argueta (2016) in *Somos como las nubes/We Are Like the Clouds,* Juan Felipe Herrera's (2001) autobiographical poetry in *A Movie in My Pillow/Una película en mi almohada*, and the experiences of other US Latinx immigrants portrayed in picturebook biographies like *When Angels Sing: The Story of Rock Legend Carlos Santana* by Michael Mahin (2018). Exposure to these varying life experiences of Latinx immigrants provides multiple perspectives and counternarratives that allow students to better understand this contentious and highly politicized topic in US history.

Even award-winning Latinx children's books fall victim to stereotyped imagery. For example, the 2004 Américas Award–commended fictional book *Elena's Serenade* (Geeslin, 2004) includes numerous clichéd images of a languid Mexican taking a siesta while wearing her sombrero and hanging out with her pet burro. An example of a nonfiction book that exemplifies inaccurate information about Latinx populations is *This Land Is Our Land: A History of American Immigration* (Osborne, 2016), which oversimplifies the relationships and political contexts between Mexican and white Americans during and after the Mexican American War.

The debate about who has the authority to write about a culture has been ongoing for decades. While we fully support movements such as #OwnVoices (Duyvis, 2015) to promote the publication of children's books written by underrepresented authors from within particular cultural groups, we acknowledge that cultural outsiders can successfully create books about Latinx cultures. However, they need to conduct significant research, including checking with cultural insiders, to ensure they are accurately and authentically presenting a Latinx subject and not relying on preconceived stereotypes. Whether this is easier to do with nonfiction versus fiction is debatable; however, the body of nonfiction Latinx children's literature reveals that cultural outsiders write most of its expository texts and many of its biographies.

An example of an outsider author is Jill C. Wheeler, who has written multiple, leveled series of biographies for children featuring individuals from a variety of cultural backgrounds. Her biography *Yuyi Morales* (Wheeler, 2013), part of the Children's Authors series (see https://abdobooks.com/series/156-children-s-authors), captures the creative energy of this author–illustrator's work while also sensitively addressing immigration concerns. An example of a cultural insider who also creates well-respected, culturally authentic nonfiction books is George Ancona. This author–photographer is best known for his photo essays, which examine the history, international connections, and current practices of particular aspects of Latinx cultures, such as daily life in a San Francisco community in *Barrio: José's Neighborhood* (1998) or a type of American Southwest dance in *¡Olé! Flamenco* (2010).

Overview of the Types of Latinx Nonfiction Children's Books

This section highlights some of the most common types of children's nonfiction books with Latinx content and provides examples of both noteworthy and problematic titles. It is divided into subgenres and provides a special focus on series.

Biographies and Memoirs

As previously noted, various subgenres of nonfiction books are prevalent within the body of Latinx children's literature. Most common among these are picturebook biographies for middle elementary students, which is not surprising considering that "exposure to numerous biographies in the elementary years can lay the foundation for creating a culture in which students of color aspire to high achievement because they know it is their heritage" (Gangi, 2004, p. 212). Remembering one's cultural heritage and building upon the dedication and work of previous generations is an important cultural trait of Latinx cultures, and biographies help to foster this concept.

Latinx picturebook biographies feature an array of individuals, including authors such as Gabriel García Márquez, Pablo Neruda, Gabriel Mistral, and Sor Juana Inés de la Cruz; artists like Diego Rivera and Frida Kahlo; civil rights activists such as Dolores Huerta and César Chávez; musicians such as Carlos Santana, Celia Cruz, and Tito Puentes; athletes like prima ballerina Alicia Alonso and baseball legend Roberto Clemente; and other political figures like Sonia Sotomayor, associate justice of the Supreme Court of the United States. Many of these titles cover a large span of their focal subject's life—from early childhood through adulthood, including their significant societal contributions. Susan Wood's (2016a, 2016b) *Esquivel! Space-Age Sound Artist* and *¡Esquivel! Un artista del sonido de la era espacial* are examples.

Another type of Latinx picturebook biography focuses on everyday children and their families and communities rather than on famous individuals, as evidenced in the vibrantly illustrated title *Ada's Violin: The Story of the Recycled Orchestra of Paraguay* (Hood, 2016) or in several of George Ancona's crisp photo-illustrated titles, such as *Pablo Remembers: The Fiesta of the Day of the Dead* (1993). In these examples, the children's lives serve as a vehicle to explicate specific topics in a personal way—the Paraguayan Recycled Orchestra and the Day of the Dead. Children can connect to the protagonists while learning about these topics through their lives and interactions, making them real individuals rather than people who lived long ago and far away. Many of these Latinx picturebooks or photobiographies tend to make use of narrative rather than expository writing, possibly because younger readers are often first exposed to fictional stories in narrative form at home and in school.

Memoirs and autobiographies for children created by Latinx individuals are few in number. Such titles provide a unique opportunity to explore a meaningful aspect of a person's life and can be useful in helping children better understand the impact of a specific episode or event on the overall life of a Latinx individual. A dynamic picturebook memoir is Yuyi Morales's (2018) richly illustrated *Dreamers*, which partially captures the immigration experience of this children's book author and illustrator, describing in text and illustrations the impact of the public library and Latinx children's books (as well as other books) on her life. Back matter provides additional information to help readers understand Morales's journey. *My Family Divided: One Girl's Journey of Home, Loss, and Hope* (Guerrero, 2018) is an example of a high-interest autobiography for middle grade students as it follows the life of actor Diane Guerrero (known for her role in, for example, *Orange Is the New Black*) as she describes her family's struggles with deportation, racism, and prejudice. The arresting narrative draws readers in and encourages them to become involved in social justice activities to stand up against unfair US immigration policies.

Expository Nonfiction

Although a bit sparse in annual publication numbers, expository Latinx texts in both picture and chapter book formats cover a range of themes and topics, such as flora and fauna, current world and historical events, or broad time periods. For instance, the nonfiction picturebook *Parrots over Puerto Rico* (Roth & Trumbore, 2013) makes use of colorful collage images and text that weave together the history of these near-extinct birds and their recovery that parallels that of Puerto Rico itself. Another scientifically focused title, *Not a Bean* (Martínez, 2019), chronicles the life cycle of the jumping bean moth, from the time the caterpillar hatches from an egg on yerba de la flecha seedpods and burrows its way into one of the seeds, until the time it hatches anew as a moth. The author deftly weaves Spanish-language counting words into the narrative, all of which are clearly depicted in Laura González's child-friendly, earth-tone illustrations.

In 2010, the Copiápo mining accident in Chile captured the empathy of the world, and the event is chronicled for younger students in *Buried Alive! How 33 Miners Survived 69 Days Deep Under the Chilean Desert* (Scott, 2012) and for older students in *Trapped: How the World Rescued 33 Miners from 2,000 Feet Below the Chilean Desert* (Aronson, 2011). Scott's book provides upper elementary readers with visual scaffolds, personal stories, and a sequential focus as to how events unfolded, while Aronson's text presents its middle level readers with the actual events of the accident, significant levels of background information on mining and drilling, and photos and diagrams.

Nonfiction Poetry

Nonfiction poetry is another genre that has become increasingly more common in Latinx nonfiction children's books. These titles include novels in verse, as well as thematic poetry collections written by the same poet. Many of these works blur the boundaries of traditional nonfiction by juxtaposing fictional verse with nonfiction prose. Examples of quality books in this area include works by Alma Flor Ada and F. Isabel Campoy, Margarita Engle, Pat Mora, and Francisco X. Alarcón. In Ada and Campoy's (2013) *Yes! We Are Latinos: Poems and Prose about the Latino Experience*, elementary students are introduced to biographical profiles of thirteen youth who live in America and represent diverse Latinx backgrounds. Profiles are written in verse and accompanied by nonfiction text that further explores the historical and cultural experiences referenced in each poem. Collectively, the two types of writing work together to provide a holistic view of a particular Latinx character and their cultural background, while also supplying information about politics, history, and more. The synergy between these two textual genres creates an effect similar to the pairing of a traditional nonfiction book with a historical fiction text, providing readers with both emotional and factual facets surrounding a particular time or event in history.

Margarita Engle is well respected for creating novels in verse that are mostly fictional but provide readers with a wealth of information and historical context about events in Cuba and Panama. Many of her historical fiction books contain source notes, bibliographies, or information for further reading. Her novel in verse *The Lightning Dreamer: Cuba's Greatest Abolitionist* (2015) describes the work of Cuban abolitionist and poet Gertrudis Gómez de Avellaneda via a historical fiction narrative. However, Engle also includes nonfiction elements such as a historical note, references, and excerpts of Gómez de Avellaneda's writing. This title serves as a powerful piece of informative literature that can acquaint students with an important historical figure.

Additional examples of nonfiction poetry celebrating Latinx culture, landscape, birds, and animals can be found in the works of Pat Mora and Francisco X. Alarcón. Mora's (2007) *Yum! ¡Mmmm! ¡Qué Rico! Americas' Sproutings* marries haiku and nonfiction prose to teach children about various foods indigenous to the Americas. Each two-page spread introduces a specific food via haiku and then provides a paragraph of nonfiction text describing its history. The dual texts attract students interested in poetry and/or nonfiction, providing numerous curricular opportunities to explore the haiku form or food origins. Alarcón's (2008) *Animal Poems of the Iguazú/Animalario del Iguazú* celebrates the natural beauty of the Iguazú National Park in Argentina—the waterfalls, toucans, parrots, caiman, and more. His bilingual poems are set against, and even embedded as word poems within, bright illustrations that bring the creatures and their settings alive for readers.

Series Books

Consistent with the larger body of children's nonfiction literature, Latinx nonfiction includes numerous series. Most are biographies in either English or Spanish, although a few other series are available that look at various aspects of Latinx culture or a particular Latin American country. These titles vary in quality, with some being much stronger than others. This section identifies a few of the more common series of Latinx nonfiction children's books, showcasing both exemplary and problematic titles.

Published by Lectorum and written in verse by Georgina Lázaro, the Spanish-language series Cuando los grandes eran pequeños (When the Great Ones Were Young) provides young readers with illustrated biographies about the childhoods of influential writers from Latin America and Spain. Some of the subjects include Julia de Burgos, José Martí, Sister Juana Inés de la Cruz, Pablo Neruda, Jorge Luis Borges, Gabriel García Márquez, and Rubén Darío (Lázaro, 2006, 2007a, 2007b, 2008, 2009, 2014, 2017). A notable feature of this series is that the illustrator of each title is an artist from the focal subject's country of origin.

A similar bilingual Spanish and English picturebook biography series is Personajes del Mundo Hispánico (Characters of the Hispanic World) published by Santillana/Alfaguara. Written by multiple authors, the entries in this series provide elementary children in grades 3 to 5 with information about notable individuals throughout Spanish-speaking worlds. Specific focal subjects include José de San Martín, Simón Bolívar, Gabriela Mistral, Pablo Neruda, and José Martí (Basch, 2014; Iturralde, 2014; Lázaro León, 2012, 2014; Rodríguez, 2016). Additional titles in the series are also available solely in Spanish.

Although there are other nonfiction Latinx children's literature series available, the aforementioned examples provide a good sampling of those that are the most popular and the highest quality. Considering the dearth of nonfiction books with Latinx content and the tendency for some educators to use what is readily accessible to them, in addition to exemplary titles, it is critical to identify those that miss the mark, as this assists in selecting quality books while calling attention to other titles that should be avoided. An example of a problematic, nonfiction Latinx series is Hispanic Americans: Major Minority published by Mason Crest Publishers. The writing—colloquial at times—contains grammatical errors, overgeneralizations, and inaccurate information. Multiple text boxes with identical information (e.g., such as those titled "Latinos Today" and "Latin America") are repeated throughout the volumes, as are several of the color photographs. Visually, the text of each book is printed in a font that is difficult to read, and some photographs appear dated and are blurry or pixelated. While promising extensive coverage of Latinx cultures, the series actually provides only a cursory look.

Critical Conversations and Teaching with Latinx Nonfiction Children's Books

Nonfiction and fictional Latinx children's literature can help to bring equity to the classroom curriculum, particularly when threaded throughout the academic year. In order to facilitate student engagement with these texts, educators must first delve deeply into their content, conducting close reads and researching all the resources provided to begin to fill their historical, geographical, and cultural gaps (Quiroa, 2017). A helpful starting point is the professional title *Multicultural Literature for Latino Bilingual Children: Their Words, Their Worlds* (Clark et al., 2016).

The use of Latinx nonfiction titles with children must be accompanied by critical conversations, rather than educator-imposed questions that demand rote answers. Educators can engage children in deep discussions around historical time periods, the experiences of Latinx individuals, topics like gender or social class expectations, and issues of racism and bias. Brooks (2012) notes that educators must "navigate difficult conversations" in age- and developmentally appropriate ways that consider "students' prior knowledge and experiences with regard to societal issues like injustice" (p. 97). Also crucial is educators' willingness to engage in "inquiry listening" (Martínez-Roldán, 2005, p. 30), allotting time and space for deep listening to students' dialogue around books and requesting clarification to better understand children's thinking. This is different from a simple comprehension check, "as it seeks instead to identify the rationale for students' thoughts and how they come to these ideas—all of which may involve cultural, personal, or experiential connections to texts or lessons" (Cummins & Quiroa, 2012, p. 382). Taken together, such experiences build community and establish that such discussions are essential.

Concluding Comments

Throughout this chapter, we have highlighted the various types of nonfiction Latinx children's books available, as well as important considerations when selecting titles to use with students. Although a beautiful world of nonfiction Latinx children's books exists, there is still not enough diversity in formats, reading levels, and topics. Picturebook biographies for younger children are over-represented and certain individuals are profiled repeatedly, perhaps because these are "safe subjects" that cultural outsiders can easily recognize, or because these are the "single stories" with which educators may be most comfortable. To represent the many accomplishments of Latinx individuals, including lesser-known persons, more biographies are needed at varied reading levels.

Most lacking of all are high-quality, non-series expository texts covering topics in science, the history of specific Latin American countries, and the historical and current experiences of US Latinx populations. All children deserve to see the rich tapestry of Latinx cultures within the nonfiction books they encounter in classrooms and libraries. Engagement with these books counteracts negative US media coverage of Latinx populations. They also provide a springboard for critical conversations about contemporary social and political topics, conversations that can bridge understanding between diverse groups of educators and students.

Practical Strategies

- Hold mock award ceremonies for any of the three Latinx children's literature awards (see the Book Awards section below). Allow students to read both fiction and nonfiction books that meet an award's criteria and have them vote for their favorites. When the awards are announced, students can see if their winner was chosen.
- During National Library Week, introduce students to Puerto Rican librarian Pura Belpré via a picturebook biography like *Planting Stories: The Life of Librarian and Storyteller Pura Belpré* (Denise, 2019).
- Provide students access to audiobooks and/or online ebook platforms like Epic! (https://www.getepic.com) that highlight famous Latinx individuals or various aspects of Latinx culture. Compare and contrast different versions of the same event, time period, or individual's life experiences.

- Develop classroom-based units focusing on the unique contributions of Latinxs in science and art. Units could culminate in a related family/community event highlighting the artistic and scientific accomplishments of Latinx individuals. One suggested professional book to assist educators is *Learning from Latino Role Models! Inspiring Students through Biographies, Instructional Activities, and Creative Learning* (Campos, 2016).
- Provide students with the list of criteria provided in Figure 2.1. Using those criteria, ask them to read and evaluate Latinx nonfiction books and discuss their findings together.

Ten Additional Nonfiction Books about Latinx People

1. Brown, M. (2020). *Sharuko: El arqueólogo Peruanao Julio C. Tello/Peruvian archaeologist Julio C. Tello* (E. Chavarri, Illus.; A. Domínguez, Trans.) (Spanish–English ed.). Children's Book Press.

2. Engle, M. (2017). *Bravo! Poems about amazing Hispanics* (R. López, Illus.). Henry Holt and Company.

3. Ferrada, M. J. (2021). *Niños: Poems for the lost children of Chile* (M. E. Valdez, Illus.; L. Schimel, Trans.). Eerdmans Books for Young Readers.

4. García Esperón, M. (2021). *The sea-ringed world: Sacred stories of the Americas* (A. Mijangos, Illus.; D. Bowles, Trans.). Levine Querido.

5. Hale, C. (2019). *Todos iguales/All equal: Un corrido de Lemon Grove/A ballad of Lemon Grove—y el primer caso exitoso de desegregación escolar/and the first successful school desegregation case* (C. Hale, Illus.) (Spanish–English ed.). Children's Book Press.

6. Kunkel, A. B. (2019). *Digging for words: José Alberto Gutiérrez and the library he built* (P. Escobar, Illus.). Schwartz & Wade Books.

7. Menéndez, J. (2021). *Latinitas: Celebrating 40 big dreamers* (J. Menéndez, Illus.). Henry Holt and Company.

8. Nicholson, D. M. (2016). *The school the Aztec eagles built: A tribute to Mexico's World War II air fighters*. Lee & Low Books.

9. Nickel, S. (2020). *Nacho's Nachos: The story behind the world's favorite snack* (O. Dominguez, Illus.). Lee & Low Books.

10. Rusch, E. (2019). *Mario and the hole in the sky: How a chemist saved our planet* (T. Martinez, Illus.). Charlesbridge.

Five Online Resources

1. Ada, A. F., & Campoy, F. I. (2016). *Activities for each theme* (D. Díaz, Illus.). Yes! We Are Latinos. http://yeswearelatinos.com/activities-for-each-theme (Spanish version: http://sisomoslatinos.com/actividades-para-cada-tema)

2. ¡Colorín colorado! (2019). *Hispanic Heritage Month* (English ed.). https://www.colorincolorado.org/libros-autores/calendario-de-alfabetizaci%C3%B3n/hispanic-heritage-month

3. Consortium for Latin American Studies Programs. (n.d.). *K–12 resources*. CLASP. http://claspprograms.org/pages/detail/78/K-12-Resources

4. Latin American & Iberian Institute at the University of New Mexico. (2012). *Educator's guides*. Vamos a Leer: Teaching Latin America through Literacy. https://teachinglatinamericathroughliterature.wordpress.com/teacher-resources

5. Mora, P. (2020). *Ideas and curriculum activities*. https://www.patmora.com/ideas

Book Awards

- Américas Award—see http://www.claspprograms.org/americasaward
- Pura Belpré Award—see http://www.ala.org/alsc/awardsgrants/bookmedia/belpremedal
- Tomás Rivera Mexican American Children's Book Award—see https://www.education.txstate.edu/ci/riverabookaward

Children's Books Cited

Ada, A. F., & Campoy, F. I. (2000). *Steps: Rita Moreno, Fernando Botero, Evelyn Cisneros* (I. Hernández, R. Radosh, & W. Saavedra, Illus.) (English ed.). Alfaguara/Santillana.

Ada, A. F., & Campoy, F. I. (2013). *Yes! We are Latinos: Poems and prose about the Latino experience* (D. Díaz, Illus.). Charlesbridge.

Alarcón, F. X. (2008). *Animal poems of the Iguazú/Animalario del Iguazú* (M. C. Gonzalez, Illus.) (English–Spanish ed.). Children's Book Press.

Amado, E. (2019). *Manuelito* (A. Urias, Illus.). Annick Press.

Ancona, G. (1993). *Pablo remembers: The fiesta of the Day of the Dead* (G. Ancona, Photog.). HarperCollins.

Ancona, G. (1998). *Barrio: José's neighborhood* (G. Ancona, Photog.). Harcourt Brace.

Ancona, G. (2010). *¡Olé! Flamenco* (G. Ancona, Photog.). Lee & Low Books.

Argueta, J. (2016). *Somos como las nubes/We are like the clouds* (A. Ruano, Illus.) (Spanish–English ed.). Groundwood Books.

Aronson, M. (2011). *Trapped: How the world rescued 33 miners from 2,000 feet below the Chilean Desert*. Atheneum Books for Young Readers.

Basch, A. (2014). *Conoce a José de San Martín/Get to know José de San Martín* (P. de Gaudio, Illus.) (Spanish–English ed.). Personajes del mundo hispánico series. Alfaguara/Santillana.

Brown, M. (2004). *My name is Celia: The life of Celia Cruz/Me llamo Celia: La vida de Celia Cruz* (R. López, Illus.) (English–Spanish ed.). Rising Moon Books.

Campoy, F. I., & Howell, T. (2016). *Maybe something beautiful: How art transformed a neighborhood* (R. López, Illus.). Houghton Mifflin Harcourt.

Delacre, L. (2016). *Olinguito, de la A a la Z! Descubriendo el bosque nublado/Olinguito, from A to Z! Unveiling the cloud forest* (L. Delacre, Illus.) (Spanish–English ed.). Children's Book Press.

Denise, A. A. (2019). *Planting stories: The life of librarian and storyteller Pura Belpré* (P. Escobar, Illus.). HarperCollins.

Engle, M. (2015). *The lightning dreamer: Cuba's greatest abolitionist*. Houghton Mifflin Harcourt.

Fink, N. (2015–present). Colección antihéroes (Anti-hero series) (P. Saá, Illus.). Sudestada/Chirimbote.

Fink, N. (2015–present). Colección antiprincesas (Anti-princess series) (P. Saá, Illus.). Sudestada/Chirimbote.

Geeslin, C. (2004). *Elena's serenade* (A. Juan, Illus.). Atheneum Books for Young Readers.

Guerrero, D. (2018). *My family divided: One girl's journey of home, loss, and hope* (E. Moroz, Illus.). Henry Holt and Company.

Herrera, J. F. (2001). *A movie in my pillow/Una película en mi almohada* (E. Gómez, Illus.) (English–Spanish ed.). Children's Book Press.

Hood, S. (2016). *Ada's violin: The story of the recycled orchestra of Paraguay* (S. W. Comport, Illus.). Simon & Schuster Books for Young Readers.

Iturralde, E. (2014). *Conoce a Simón Bolívar/Get to know Simón Bolívar* (Y. C. Álvarez, Illus.) (Spanish–English ed.). Personajes del mundo hispánico series. Alfaguara/Santillana.

Lázaro, G. (2006). *Julia de Burgos* (P. Marichal, Illus.). Cuando los grandes eran pequeños series. Lectorum.

Lázaro, G. (2007a). *José Martí* (M. Sánchez, Illus.). Cuando los grandes eran pequeños series. Lectorum.

Lázaro, G. (2007b). *Juana Inés* (B. González, Illus.). Cuando los grandes eran pequeños series. Lectorum.

Lázaro, G. (2008). *Pablo Neruda* (M. Donoso, Illus.). Cuando los grandes eran pequeños series. Lectorum.

Lázaro, G. (2009). *Jorge Luis Borges* (G. Genovés, Illus.). Cuando los grandes eran pequeños series. Lectorum.

Lázaro, G. (2014). *Gabriel García Márquez: Gabito* (R. Yockteng, Illus.). Cuando los grandes eran pequeños series. Lectorum.

Lázaro, G. (2017). *Rubén Darío* (L. Ruiz, Illus.). Cuando los grandes eran pequeños series. Lectorum.

Lázaro León, G. (2012). *Conoce a Gabriela Mistral/Get to know Gabriela Mistral* (S. H. Palacios, Illus.) (Spanish–English ed.). Personajes del mundo hispánico series. Alfaguara/Santillana.

Lázaro León, G. (2014). *Conoce a Pablo Neruda/Get to know Pablo Neruda* (V. Cis, Illus.) (Spanish–English ed.). Personajes del mundo hispánico series. Alfaguara/Santillana.

Mahin, M. J. (2018). *When angels sing: The story of Carlos Santana* (J. Ramírez, Illus.). Atheneum Books for Young Readers.

Martínez, C. G. (2019). *Not a bean* (L. González, Illus.). Charlesbridge.

Mora, P. (2007). *Yum! ¡Mmmm! ¡Qué rico! Americas' sproutings* (R. López, Illus.). (English–Spanish ed.). Lee & Low Books.

Morales, Y. (2018). *Dreamers* (Y. Morales, Illus.). Holiday House.

Osborne, L. B. (2016). *This land is our land: A history of American immigration*. Abrams Books for Young Readers.

Rodríguez, A. O. (2016). *Conoce a José Martí/Get to know José Martí* (P. De Bella, Illus.) (Spanish–English ed.). Personajes del mundo hispánico series. Alfaguara/Santillana.

Roth, S. L., & Trumbore, C. (2013). *Parrots over Puerto Rico* (S. L. Roth, Collages). Lee & Low Books.

Scott, E. (2012). *Buried alive! How 33 miners survived 69 days deep under the Chilean Desert*. Clarion Books.

Tonatiuh, D. (2014). *Separate is never equal: Sylvia Mendez and her family's fight for desegregation* (D. Tonatiuh, Illus.). Abrams Books for Young Readers.

Weaver, L. Q. (2010). *Darkroom: A memoir in black and white* (L. Q. Weaver, Illus.). University of Alabama Press.

Wheeler, J. C. (2013) *Yuyi Morales*. ABDO Publishing.

Wood, S. (2016a). *Esquivel! Space-age sound artist* (D. Tonatiuh, Illus.). Charlesbridge.

Wood, S. (2016b). *¡Esquivel! Un artista del sonido de la era espacial* (D. Tonatiuh, Illus.; C. E. Calvo, Trans.) (Spanish ed.). Charlesbridge.

References

Adichie, C. N. (2009, July). *The danger of a single story* [Video]. TED Conferences. https://www.ted.com/talks/chimamanda_adichie_the_danger_of_a_single_story.html

Barrera, R. B., & Garza de Cortes, O. (1997). Mexican American children's literature in the 1990s: Toward authenticity. In V. J. Harris (Ed.), *Using multiethnic children's literature in grades K–8* (pp. 129–154). Christopher-Gordon.

Brooks, W. M. (2012). Navigating difficult conversations. *Journal of Children's Literature, 38*(2), 97–98.

Campos, D. (2016). *Learning from Latino role models! Inspiring students through biographies, instructional activities, and creative learning.* Rowman & Littlefield.

Clark, E. R., Flores, B. B., Smith, H. L., & Gonzalez, D. A. (2016). *Multicultural literature for Latino bilingual children: Their words, their worlds.* Rowman & Littlefield.

Cooperative Children's Book Center. (2019, October 8). *Children's books by and/or about Black, Indigenous and people of color received by the CCBC 2018–.* CCBC diversity statistics. https://ccbc.education.wisc.edu/literature-resources/ccbc-diversity-statistics/books-by-and-or-about-poc-2018

Cummins, S., & Quiroa, R. E. (2012). Teaching for writing expository responses to narrative texts. *The Reading Teacher, 65*(6), 381–386. https://doi.org/10.1002/TRTR.01057

Duyvis, C. (2015). *#Ownvoices.* Corinne Duyvis. http://www.corinneduyvis.net/ownvoices

Gangi, J. M. (2004). *Encountering children's literature: An arts approach.* Pearson.

Martínez-Roldán, C. M. (2005). The inquiry acts of bilingual children in literate discussion. *Language Arts, 83*(1), 22–32.

Naidoo, J. C. (2011). *Celebrating cuentos: Promoting Latino children's literature and literacy in classrooms and libraries.* Libraries Unlimited.

Nilsson, N. L. (2005). How does Hispanic portrayal in children's books measure up after 40 years? The answer is "it depends." *The Reading Teacher, 58*(6), 534–548. https://doi.org/10.1598/RT.58.6.4

Pew Research Center. (2019, September 16). *Key facts about U.S. Hispanics and their diverse heritage.* Pew Research. https://www.pewresearch.org/fact-tank/2019/09/16/key-facts-about-u-s-hispanics

Quiroa, R. E. (2013). Promising portals and safe passages: A review of pre-K–12 Latino/a-themed literature. In J. C. Naidoo & S. P. Dahlen (Eds.), *Diversity in youth literature: Opening doors through reading* (pp. 45–62). American Library Association.

Quiroa, R. E. (2017). Curating a diverse and anti-biased collection: Building capacity to identify and use diverse youth literature in the classroom. *Literacy Today*, *34*(6), 22–24.

United States Census Bureau. (2019, August 20). *Hispanic Heritage Month 2019*. Author. https://www.census.gov/newsroom/facts-for-features/2019/hispanic-heritage-month.html

Indigenous Nations in Nonfiction

DEBBIE REESE, *Author of* American Indians in Children's Literature *blog*
BETSY MCENTARFFER, *Lincoln Public Schools*

The people shall continue.

—SIMON J. ORTIZ, *The People Shall Continue*

Each year, more books by Native writers who write about their own tribal nations are published. Their books make clear that they are citizens of distinct sovereign nations. Their success depends on educators being able to recognize and teach students to see American Indians not as people of cultural groups but as citizens of sovereign nations that have distinct cultures and a political status that other ethnic or racial groups in the United States do not have. This chapter is an overview of long-standing problematic content in nonfiction about Native peoples, and introduces a framework designed to offer educators and their students strategies with which to look critically at how Native peoples are depicted in nonfiction.

Chapter Guiding Questions

- Why and how have Indigenous people's identities and status as sovereign nations been historically, socially, and politically misrepresented in children's nonfiction?

- What types of youth nonfiction featuring Indigenous people are likely to get published, and what types are not likely to get published? Why does this matter?

- How can educators use An Indigenous Peoples' Framework for Evaluating Nonfiction to evaluate, select, and share nonfiction books with Native content?

- What elements of the Indigenous Peoples' Framework for Evaluating Nonfiction are most helpful to you? Why?

In 1829, William Apess published his autobiography, *A Son of the Forest*. In the opening chapter, he refers to the Pequot Tribe as his nation. Later, he recounts being placed with a white family during his childhood. One day, while picking berries with that family, they came upon a group of dark-skinned girls. He thought they were Indians. Terrified, he ran home. His childhood fear of Indians, he wrote, was:

> occasioned by the many stories I had heard of their cruelty toward the whites— how they were in the habit of killing and scalping men, women, and children. But the whites did not tell me that they were in a great majority of instances the aggressors—that they had imbrued their hands in the lifeblood of my brethren, driven them from their once peaceful and happy homes. (Apess, pp. 22–23)

We share this account of the impact of stories on a Native child two hundred years ago to demonstrate that Native people have been writing about that hurt for a long time. Parents of Native children talk about how stories hurt their children today. Apess's words "if the whites had told me" foreshadow what would develop into the critical questions we apply to analysis of children's literature today. They include: "What is this text trying to tell me?," "Who is marginalized or privileged by this text?," "Whose voice is missing or silenced?," "Who has the power in this text?," and "Who has written or illustrated this text?" When we pose those questions about books with Native characters or content, we adapt them by asking, for example, "What is this text trying to tell me about Native peoples, their sovereign nations, and their unique tribal culture(s)?"

Contemporary Context

During Donald Trump's 2016 presidential campaign, people on Native social media networks remembered his 1993 testimony in Congress that the Native people of a tribal nation in Connecticut "don't look Indian to me" (quoted in Lightman, 1993). Trump's statement reflects the power that stereotypical imagery has to influence expectations of what a Native person should look like. Children's books and contemporary culture in the United States are rife with biased, erroneous, and stereotypical images of Native peoples. This is especially visible in the fall when schoolchildren are taught about Christopher Columbus and Thanksgiving. In recent years, we have seen a growing awareness of the bias embodied in those two subjects. Social justice activism is driving a change, for example, in the observance of Columbus Day. On October 11, 2019, *Indian Country Today* published a map that showed eleven states and 129 cities that recognize Indigenous Peoples' Day instead of Columbus Day (Chavez, 2019). This shift demonstrates the possibilities before us all, as educators, if we are willing to speak up about the misrepresentations we see and promote the accurate representations all children need so that, as Simon Ortiz (1977/2017) so eloquently stated, "the people shall continue."

The Impetus of a Framework

Simon J. Ortiz's (1977) (Acoma Pueblo) *The People Shall Continue* is a picturebook history illustrated by Sharol Graves (Absentee Shawnee) of the continent currently known as North America. We use "currently known as" with intention: names used today are based on who is in power at this moment in time. History demonstrates that names and geographic boundaries change with the passage of time and the shifting of power over those places.

Ortiz is widely regarded as a leading figure in Indigenous literatures. Lee & Low Books (through its Children's Book Press imprint) brought his book back into print in 2017 to mark its fortieth anniversary. We believe that *The People Shall Continue* has much to offer as a work of nonfiction for children, and we also think it can be used to create an Indigenous Peoples' Framework for Evaluating Nonfiction. The words and topics Ortiz chose are important. He was, in essence, making an intervention in a centuries-long cycle of misrepresentation of Indigenous peoples.

Before turning to Ortiz's book and the framework we are introducing, we first provide a look at stereotypes, a brief history of significant depictions of Indigenous people, and a look at biographies and series books. Then we introduce and explain our framework, demonstrating how educators can use it to evaluate books they may want to include in their classrooms.

The Landscape of Indigenous Peoples in Nonfiction

Indigenous peoples have been stereotyped in children's fiction and nonfiction for hundreds of years. Regardless of genre, they are often shown as savage, bloodthirsty, or devil-worshipping creatures that attack courageous American pioneers, or as noble figures who lament the tragic end of their way of life. Images of savage Indians can invoke fear and suggest to young children that all

Indians are bad; the noble images can instill a superficial embrace of things like mascots or a sadness that Indigenous peoples have "vanished." Native characters are often depicted in feathered headdresses and fringed clothing as they ride their ponies and use bow and arrows or tomahawks to hunt buffalo, dance wildly around fires, sit on the ground "Indian style" (with legs crossed), or raise one hand and say "how" as a greeting. English words like *brave* or *chief* are used to refer to Native men, while Algonquin words like *squaw* and *papoose* are erroneously used for all Native women and infants, regardless of their nations or positions within the community. Today, some Native words—like *squaw*—are regarded as derogatory because they are used to characterize Native women as beasts of burden or as sexually promiscuous (Lambert & Lambert, 2014; Molin, 1999). These images occur in books that are specifically about Native peoples, but they also occur incidentally in books about other topics.

In 1657, Johann Amos Comenius wrote *Orbis Pictus* (*World in Pictures*). Today, it is regarded as the first encyclopedic picturebook for children and is of such import that the National Council of Teachers of English (NCTE) named its nonfiction award the Orbis Pictus Award. In style, Comenius's book is much like today's picturebook encyclopedias—but it is also a text that denigrates those who are not Christian. In the section on religions, Comenius depicted an Indian outdoors, worshipping the devil (Comenius & Bardeen, 1659/1968). Hendrik van Loon's (1921) *The Story of Mankind* was the first book to receive the Newbery Medal. In it, van Loon wrote that the Spaniards had tried to use Indians as laborers in mines, but, when taken away from a life in the open, the Indians "had laid down and died" (p. 422). With a knowledge base of Native peoples that is shaped by stereotypical images of hostile Indians, most readers do not have the skills to question harmful or inaccurate passages in these books.

Alongside those books are ones that celebrate moments in history that were devastating to Native peoples. In 2014, Brian Floca's (2013) *Locomotive* won the Caldecott Medal. Set in 1859, the book is about a white family on their way from Omaha to Sacramento on the new transcontinental railroad. *Locomotive* says nothing about the impact of the railroads on Native peoples, or what was happening to Native peoples in California as more and more Americans moved into their homelands. None of these award-winning books is categorized as being about Indigenous peoples, but, because the books are award winning, the biased and stereotypical depictions of Native peoples in them are tacitly endorsed. Because award-winning nonfiction works are taught in classrooms, many children are positioned to acquire problematic understandings of Indigenous peoples.

What Gets Published: Series and Biographies

Our combined decades of work in children's literature told us nonfiction about Indigenous peoples often falls into two categories: series books and biographies. We ran a search in WorldCat using *Native Americans* as the search term in the keyword field and limited the search to juvenile/nonfiction/books published across multiple years. Removing errant records (duplicates and ones that were scooped up in a search because they share a series title), we arrived at a sample of twenty-six books. Nineteen of them are published in a series (six of those are by Valerie Bodden for Creative Education's First Peoples series). This verifies our observation that most books about Indigenous peoples are books in a series.

We had also read that there are more books about Native people who were "Helpers" of white settlers than there are about Native leaders who were "Resisters" who fought to protect their nations from white settlers. In our sample, the books in the Helpers category are as follows: 73 about Sacagawea (the Lemhi Shoshone guide and interpreter to Lewis and Clark), 57 about Pocahontas (the Powhatan child widely depicted as having saved John Smith's life), and 19 about Squanto (the Patuxet man who is commonly known for helping the Pilgrims because he could speak English). Some Native people do not hold Helpers in high regard. Novelist Debra Magpie Earling (a member of the Confederated Salish and Kootenai Tribes of the Flathead Reservation), for example, wrote that Sacagawea was a traitor "who launched the parade of settlers who would come to claim our land" (2006, p. 45). In her essay in *Tribal College Journal*, Sherrole Benton (1995) (Oneida Nation) recalls reading positive information about Pocahontas and Squanto in her junior year of high school and thinking they were traitors. As an adult, she looked at the textbook her son was using to see what it said. Not much had changed, she wrote, and she wondered if Pocahontas "was a sell out or whether she was a neglected and angry daughter with few choices to make" (para. 31). Either way, Benton writes, "she fulfills the American imagination and their wish for an Indian princess who loves and accepts them all" (para. 31).

In the Resisters group, we counted 189 books about Indigenous leaders: 54 about Sitting Bull (Hunkpapa Lakota), 31 each about Chief Joseph (Nez Perce) and Crazy Horse (Oglala Lakota), 27 about Geronimo (Chiricahua Apache), 25 about Tecumseh (Shawnee), and 21 about Osceola (Seminole). These leaders resisted invasions of their homelands. This resistance is why their respective nations are sovereign nations today, but our experience of reading these books is that biographers depict their resistance as doomed or tragic.

Beyond Helpers and Resisters, we were glad to see 14 biographies of Wilma Mankiller, principal chief of the Cherokee Nation who was a recipient of the Presidential Medal of Freedom in 1998, and 30 about Sequoyah, the Cherokee man who developed a written alphabet of the Cherokee language. Also of note are the 49 biographies of entertainers and athletes like Jim Thorpe (Sauk), Will Rogers (Cherokee), and Maria Tallchief (Osage). Though most of the biographies in our sample are written by non-Native authors, a few are by Native authors. They include 5 by Charles Eastman (Dakota), 3 by S. D. Nelson (Lakota), 1 by Liselotte Erdrich (Ojibwe), and 1 by Joseph Medicine Crow, a Crow leader who received the Presidential Medal of Freedom from President Obama in 2009.

Moving beyond numerical analysis of what gets published, we also offer some qualitative observations. One area that has improved over time is the use of the word *regalia* (tribally specific clothing worn for ceremonial or similar events) instead of *costume* (something anybody can put on for a party or a play). That said, our analysis of series books also showed us that many continue to have problematic content, such as oversimplified and biased presentations of theories as fact (e.g., the Bering Land Bridge); lack of information (e.g., about Native diplomacy and trade before and after European arrival); lack of context (e.g., illustrations that depict Native people attacking white settlers); inaccuracy in visual representations (e.g., use of sepia-toned photographs taken by photographers who composed photographs to reflect a vision of authenticity according to the photographer's idea of that concept); use of incorrect or outdated names; the avoidance or inaccurate depictions of conflicts; a tendency to depict Native peoples' survival as dependent on the benevolence of white people; and an overuse of past tense verbs and an overemphasis on the past.

Among the criteria librarians use to cull their libraries is year of publication. The assumption is that older books are more likely to have outdated information when compared to newer ones. However, a recent copyright year does not necessarily indicate accuracy in the book's content. A notable example is *Pueblo* (Lajiness, 2017) in ABDO Publishing's Native Americans (Big Buddy Books) series. It uses outdated words like *Anasazi* and has glaring errors like the use of past tense words in captions of present-day Pueblo people in regalia. The content of some older series, especially those where Native people were involved in the creation of the content, is far more accurate. While older books may be out of print, we highly recommend that schools acquire used copies of those books rather than purchasing newer books with errors. For example, we recommend the A First Americans Book series by Virginia Driving Hawk Sneve (Lakota) published in the 1990s by Holiday House, in which each book provides factually accurate information about a specific Native Nation, past and present (e.g., Sneve, 1993, 1994a, 1994b, 1995, 1996).

After reviewing several different recently published series books, we found the American Indian Life—The Past and Present series by Capstone Press to be more accurate than books in other series. Each book starts with a double-page spread of contemporary people of the tribal nation the book is about. On those initial pages, Indigenous cultural and ceremonial practices are depicted in a positive way. That is followed by historical information that details the struggles and prejudices the people of that nation experienced. A comparably equal number of pages are then devoted to the nation's communities and people today. We especially appreciate photographs of Native people in everyday clothing as well as in regalia.

In our analysis of books, we noted a small but important increase in concept books by Indigenous writers and illustrators. Cree–Métis writer and illustrator Julie Flett has created exquisite bilingual concept books about the alphabet, colors, and numbers. These include *We All Count: A Book of Cree Numbers* (2014) and *Black Bear, Red Fox: Colours in Cree* (2017). In the US, Salina Press publishes bilingual concept books in Hopi or Navajo languages. In 2014, the Chickasaw Nation's imprint White Dog Press published Wiley Barnes and Aaron K. Long's *C is for Chickasaw*, a bilingual Chickasaw alphabet book. In 2019, Sealaska Heritage published the Haayk Foundation's *Wilgyigyet: Learn the Colors in Sm'algyax* in its bilingual Baby Raven Reads series.

We would like to see more publishers incorporating Indigenous languages and tribally specific information into the numerous books published about plants and animals each year. An example of such a book is *A Children's Guide to Arctic Birds* (Pelletier, 2014) published by Inhabit Media, which includes Inuktitut words for the birds shown throughout the book. As concerns and activism about climate change and its impact on all forms of life on the planet increase, we hope to see publication of more books about Indigenous activism. In 2018, we saw one example: *Young Water Protectors: A Story about Standing Rock* by Aslan Tudor and Kelly Tudor (Apache). Published by EagleSpeaker, a small publishing house in Canada, it is an account of a young child who was at Standing Rock to protest the Dakota Access Pipeline.

An Indigenous Peoples' Framework for Evaluating Nonfiction

In developing An Indigenous Peoples' Framework for Evaluating Nonfiction, we draw heavily from Ortiz's (1977/2017) *The People Shall Continue*. Our framework has several distinct points that educators can use to evaluate a nonfiction book. It is not a checklist. Instead, it is a guide to help educators look closely at content. Some of our points may seem obvious, but, once educators start evaluating books, we believe they will notice the glaring problems that our framework addresses. A holistic use of the framework can help an educator decide to use a book as one that provides substantive information about Native peoples.

In the title and throughout the book, Ortiz (1977/2017) uses *People* instead of words like *Indians, Native Americans,* or *American Indians*. That is a powerful choice because it humanizes Indigenous peoples in ways that more generic terms do not. *Our first point, then, is that Native Americans are people.* We want educators to begin their evaluations with the word *people* foremost in their minds, and we recommend they look for the author's use of *people* versus *Indians, Native Americans,* or *American Indians.*

Ortiz (1977/2017) uses the word *nation* thirteen times. He does not use the word *tribe* once. There is a significance difference in those two words. If you do an image search on the internet, top hits for "nation" are ones of flags while the top hits for "tribe" are primarily photographs of people of color wearing traditional clothing. A nation's flag is a symbol of its status as a government that determines who its citizens are and how it will govern them. Photographs of people in traditional clothing do not communicate their status as citizens of nations. *Our second point is that Indigenous peoples are citizens of sovereign nations.* In their evaluations of books, we urge educators to look for the word *nation*. When they see *tribe* instead, we recommend they engage students in a discussion of the two words. We also recommend that educators teach students how to use the internet to locate websites of specific tribal nations. For example, educators can visit the online Tribal Directory prepared by the National Congress of American Indians (http://www.ncai.org/tribal-directory). There are several websites that purport to have comprehensive language or story collections, but close study of some of their pages point to flaws. Therefore, we strongly recommend using websites of specific nations that include reference to their status as federally recognized nations.

Our third principle includes an extension of #OwnVoices. Specifically, to emphasize the significance of tribal nations, *our third point is that the identity of the individuals who create a given text matters.* We recommend educators look for a note about the author's and the illustrator's tribal nations. *The People Shall Continue* (Ortiz, 1977/2017) includes biographical information for the author and illustrator that names their respective nations and provides readers with substantive information about their work and ancestry. The information assures readers that the book's creators have the knowledge and insights to craft the content of this book.

Ortiz's (1977/2017) book is an epic history of Indigenous peoples. It is not specific to a single tribal nation. Using an #OwnVoices tag for a work of nonfiction that is broad in scope has merit. The extension of #OwnVoices we introduce in this chapter is the use of a specific nation. A work of nonfiction by an Ojibwe writer would have a #OjibweVoice hashtag. When books are traditional stories (which are classified as nonfiction) that detail a ceremony or draw heavily from a specific nation's religious stories, we ask educators to verify that the writer is telling a story from their own tribal nation. We do this because we assume that a writer affiliated with the nation represented knows what can and cannot be shared with outsiders.

Thus, we are introducing the idea of using a tribally specific hashtag and including author identity as a point of evaluation. Whether a writer or illustrator is Native or not, biographical material about them should provide information that indicates they have the expertise to create accurate content and knowledge about what can and cannot be shared with outsiders to their tribal nation. If they are not Native, educators can look for notes that indicate that someone with the necessary expertise was consulted.

Ortiz (1977/2017) opens *The People Shall Continue* with brief references to creation stories told by distinct nations. He references different geographical areas, indicating that Indigenous peoples tell creation stories specific to where they believe they came into being. Those are religious stories and ought to be treated with the same respect afforded to creation stories from other religions. They are not folktales like "Little Red Riding Hood," but they are often categorized that way in library systems. Compare the subject lines in your local library for *Noah's Ark* (Spier, 1977) and *Beaver Steals Fire* (Confederated Salish and Kootenai Tribes, 2008). Both are creation stories. Both are sacred to the people who tell them. Creation stories like *Noah's Ark*, however, are categorized as Bible stories, while Native creation stories are categorized as folklore, myths, or legends, thereby putting them in the same realm as stories like "Little Red Riding Hood." *Our fourth point, therefore, is that there should be evenhanded treatment of creation stories across religions.* When evaluating a book that is a creation story, examine the title and story for words like *folktale* that, in essence, denigrate the status of a peoples' religious stories.

Ortiz (1977/2017) did not go into detail about creation stories. In the book, he did not provide details about religious or spiritual ceremonies. He chose not to include that information. Reference or encyclopedic books with outsiders' accounts of Native ceremonies and their "retellings" of creation stories generally misrepresent the ceremony and the significance of the story (Reese, 2007). These misrepresentations have had significant consequences for Native peoples. They have been used to create government policies that prohibited Native peoples from practicing their religions. The historical record is replete with accounts of the wanton destruction of sites that are sacred to Native peoples and persecution of Native individuals who are found conducting ceremonies (Native American Rights Fund, 1994, p. 1). Across the continent, Native peoples protect their ceremonies by keeping them hidden from outsiders and by closing roadways to ceremonial grounds when religious activities are taking place. In policy and in practice, Native people have, in essence, drawn the window curtains to protect themselves (Reese, 2018). In An Indigenous Peoples' Framework for Evaluating Nonfiction, we add the idea of a curtain to Rudine Sims Bishop's "mirrors, windows, and sliding glass doors" metaphor (see the editors' introduction to this book).

In our experience, Native writers do not divulge details about traditional stories or ceremonies. *Our fifth point is that educators must think carefully about details of ceremony and story that are provided in a book created by a non-Native writer, or someone who is writing outside of their own tribal nation.* We realize that, for most people, it will be very difficult to apply this point. One way to determine if the story or ceremony is one that a tribal nation is comfortable sharing is to go to that nation's website. We view a tribal nation's website as a primary source. On many, you will find historical documents, such as treaties. If you find the story or ceremony there, compare it with what you see in the book. Generally speaking, until the publishing industry reflects an understanding of this point, we recommend educators not use traditional stories written by outsiders of the tribal nation being depicted and that they be aware of misuse of these stories in other genres. Rebecca Roanhorse, for example, is not Diné and received considerable backlash from esteemed Diné writers and scholars for her misuse of Diné spirituality (Diné Writers' Collective, 2018).

Throughout *The People Shall Continue*, Ortiz (1977/2017) uses common English words like *woman* or *man* to humanize Native people, eliminating the dehumanizing gap that historically misused Indigenous words can create. For example, words like *squaw* and *papoose* are Native words but are specific to a particular nation (Algonquin) and should not be used as if every nation uses those same words. Ortiz also uses *healers* rather than *shaman*, a Sami word that is often erroneously used as if all tribal nations use that word for their healers. *Our sixth point is that educators need to look critically at word choices for people, their occupations, their actions, and the context in which those words are used.* This point should not be interpreted as saying that Native languages in nonfiction are not acceptable. We think they should be used, but in appropriate ways. If Ortiz's book was about his family and it included a sentence where he spoke of a healer, he could use that word (*healer*) or the Keres (the language his tribal nation speaks) word for healer.

In *The People Shall Continue*, Ortiz (1977/2017) names leaders and their nations. Sharol Graves's illustrations accurately depict those nations and their material culture (clothing, housing, etc.). *Our seventh point is that accuracy in illustrations must be addressed.* Accuracy in depiction of the distinct attributes of Native peoples of various nations disrupts the stereotypical image that suggests all Native peoples wear feathered headdresses and fringed buckskin, live in tipis, and hunt buffalo. Being able to discern accuracy requires expertise. We recommend that educators develop that expertise on a specific nation that was, or is, geographically near their school. They can begin that process by reading that nation's website, fiction and nonfiction books, and articles written by people of that nation. With that expertise, they will be able to guide students to see stereotypical, biased, and incorrect images in nonfiction books they read, especially in respect of nearby nations.

Our eighth point is that authors' use of invented dialogue should be questioned. Ortiz (1977/2017) did not invent dialogue for the named historical individuals (Tecumseh, Black Hawk, etc.) in his book. Unless there are documents that support the speech of a real person, using invented dialogue is not acceptable (Horning, 2010). We see it as particularly problematic when a writer invents dialogue or innermost thoughts for Native people who lived in historical periods far removed from today and for whom English was not their mother tongue.

Ortiz's picturebook includes episodes in history about which most Americans are not aware, including the fact that Europeans and Americans enslaved Native peoples, and later, implemented government policies and programs (like boarding schools). He also includes the destructive termination and relocation programs of the 1950s. *Our ninth point is that educators must read closely to see what writers include—and what they avoid.* To gain a better grasp of history, we recommend educators read Roxanne Dunbar-Ortiz's (2014) *An Indigenous Peoples' History of the United States* and consider bringing Dunbar-Ortiz et al.'s (2019) adaptation of it, *An Indigenous Peoples History of the United States for Young People*, into the classroom as a resource for students. These two books provide an accurate and comprehensive understanding of the scope and breadth of this history.

Our tenth point is that educators need to attend to verb tense. In his book, Ortiz (1977/2017) makes the point that Native people are part of the present day. Books about Native peoples must provide children with the basic fact that Native peoples are still here. Even if a book is about a historical person or moment, it can include information about that person's nation or how that nation views that moment today. Past tense can be used, of course, but not to the exclusion of present tense verbs or information about that nation in the present day.

Last, Ortiz speaks to the need to work together, to reach out and collaborate with others, so all the people can continue to live and thrive on the earth. *The eleventh point is our recommendation that educators reach out to others to expand their knowledge.* We acknowledge reaching out can be uncomfortable. It requires that educators admit what they thought they knew is not accurate. In the field of librarianship, the Association for Library Services to Children suggests librarians read content area blogs like *American Indians in Children's Literature* to gain insights into areas they may know little about.

Applying the Framework

As noted earlier, we do not intend our framework to be used as a checklist. Instead, it is meant as a guide that educators can use to evaluate a book. To demonstrate how educators can apply our framework, we use it with *The Pueblo* (Cunningham & Benoit, 2011), a forty-eight-page book for elementary-grade students in the A True Book series from Scholastic.

Published in 2011, Cunningham and Benoit's *The Pueblo* uses the word *tribe* or *group* instead of *nation*, but it has several pages that push against the primitive connotation of "tribe." For example, the authors go into detail about trade, irrigation, and architecture of the Pueblo peoples in the past and, importantly, into the present day. When referring to people, the text uses words like *farmers*, *medicine men*, *leaders*, *mothers*, *children*, and *men*. A page titled "What's in a Name?" tells readers that the term *Anasazi* is an antiquated and insulting term that has been replaced by *Ancient Puebloans*. One page depicts the Pueblo peoples' encounters with the Spanish, who tried to force them to become Catholic, with sentences like "The Spanish tortured Pueblos for resisting change" (p. 15). Another provides details that led to the Pueblo Revolt of 1680 when the Pueblo people drove the Spanish out of New Mexico for twelve years. The pages on religion are accurate and do not disclose ceremonial information, but we do note an overuse of past tense verbs on those pages. The book has only a few pages at the end about present-day Pueblo peoples—a problem across almost all the series we analyzed.

Using our framework to evaluate *The Pueblo*, we determined that we would use the book with students and call attention to the inappropriate predominance of past tense verbs. If the book is part of educators' personal libraries, we would encourage them to modify the past tense verbs. They could use permanent markers to change "Every Pueblo people had its own beliefs about kachinas" to "Every Pueblo has its own beliefs about kachinas." Educators who write in personal copies of books communicate that some information in books is inaccurate. The act of writing in a book demonstrates that texts are not hallowed artifacts. They are created by people who can—and do—make errors. We also suggest students do writing activities like submitting reviews (through their educator's account) of that book to online sites such as Amazon and Goodreads and write to the publisher requesting the change.

Conclusion

Problems that continue to predominate nonfiction about Native peoples are similar to those commonly seen in fiction. Too many books are set in the past and do not reflect the fact that Native peoples are part of today's society; the content is biased in ways that depict non-Native peoples as superior in lifestyle, values, and intellect; stereotypical and non-tribally-specific depictions predominate.

In recent years, the American Library Association revised its Competencies documents and its award committee guidelines. In both, the organization is asking people to become aware of their lack of expertise with respect to knowledge about Native peoples. The Competencies and award committee guidelines recommend that educators and committee members reach out to people who have the expertise they do not. When Betsy (the white person of this chapter's author duo) was first beginning to address her cultural competency, she attended a conference session led by Lisa Mitten (personal communication, July 17, 2017), Mohawk and former president of the American Indian Library Association. What she said made all the difference in Betsy's journey:

> We are all products of the same educational system in this country, which didn't tell us much of anything accurate about Native peoples. Even Indians have to unlearn a lot of the stuff educators told us about ourselves. You've spent a lifetime learning the wrong things. Don't expect to get it right overnight. Be patient with yourselves and give yourselves a break, but don't quit learning and don't give up.

In the final pages of his book, Ortiz (1977/2017) talks about the importance of working together across different peoples as we all strive to be citizens in a world with limited resources. In this period of a growing awareness of the ways that everyone is ignorant of, or complicit with, the denigration of populations that have been marginalized by mainstream society, we think it is necessary that educators be conscious of ourselves and how we came to view the world and books as we do, and how our views can change over time. We—the authors of this chapter—are two women. Debbie Reese is tribally enrolled and was raised traditionally at Nambé Pueblo, a sovereign Native Nation that has been on its homelands for thousands of years. She recognized problems in how Nambé was depicted, but it wasn't until graduate school in the 1990s that she began to fully grasp the range, depth, and harmful impact of misrepresentations of Indigenous peoples. Betsy McEntarffer is white, midwestern, middle class, and raised on the premise that her ancestors, pioneers homesteading on "free government land," were heroes to be admired. Enamored with Wilder's Little House books, she gradually began to recognize that the misinformation imparted to her made it possible to enjoy a life of white privilege that was harmful to Indigenous and all children.

Our journey of understanding continues to this day, and we hope that An Indigenous Peoples' Framework for Evaluating Nonfiction helps you on your journey of cultural competence so that all the people can continue.

Practical Strategies

- Provide each group with a copy of *The People Shall Continue* and copies of An Indigenous Peoples' Framework for Evaluating Nonfiction. Ask them to read the book aloud in their group and then discuss.

- Distribute nonfiction picturebooks from the school library to the small groups. Ask students to analyze the books using the framework and present their findings to the class.

- Ask students to create a visual display of their findings and place their displays in the school hallways and library.

- Provide each group with a copy of books that have been selected to receive the American Indian Youth Literature Awards. Ask each group to visit the online catalog for the school and local public library and see if the books are available.

- Provide each group with a copy of *An Indigenous Peoples' History of the United States for Young People* (Dunbar-Ortiz et al., 2019). Using your district's history textbook, compare the way a particular event is described in the textbook with how it is described in *An Indigenous Peoples' History*.

Ten Additional Nonfiction Books about Indigenous People

1 Charleyboy, L., & Leatherdale, M. B. (Eds.) (2017). *#NotYourPrincess: Voices of Native American women*. Annick Press.

2. Coulson, A. (2018). *Unstoppable: How Jim Thorpe and the Carlisle Indian School football team defeated the Army* (N. Hardcastle, Illus.). Capstone Press.

3. Denetdale, J. (2008). *The long walk: The forced Navajo exile.* Chelsea House.

4. Herrington, J. B. (2016). *Mission to space.* White Dog Press.

5. Jordan-Fenton, C., & Pokiak-Fenton, M. (2010). *Fatty legs: A true story* (L. Amini-Holmes, Illus.). Annick.

6. Loew, P. (2015). *Native people of Wisconsin.* Wisconsin Historical Society Press.

7. Rendon, M. (2013). *Powwow summer: A family celebrates the circle of life* (C. W. Bellville, Photog.). Minnesota Historical Society Press.

8. Robertson, S. (2014). *Rock and roll highway: The Robbie Robertson story* (A. Gustavson, Illus.). Henry Holt and Company.

9. Robertson, J. (2019). *Nibi emosaawdang/The water walker* (J. Robertson, Illus.; S. Williams & I. Toulouse, Trans.) (Ojibwa–English ed.). Second Story Press.

10. Sorell, T. (2018). *We are grateful: Otsaliheliga* (F. Lessac, Illus.). Charlesbridge.

Five Online Resources

1. American Indian Library Association. (2018). *Information resources for communities serving Native peoples.* https://ailanet.org#serving

2. First Nations Development Institute. (2018, March). *Native American children's literature: Recommended reading list.* https://www.firstnations.org/wp-content/uploads/2018/11/Revised_Book_Insert_Web_Version_March_2018.pdf

3. IBBY Canada. (2018). *From sea to sea to sea: Celebrating indigenous picture books.* https://www.ibby-canada.org/wp-content/uploads/2018/11/FromSeaToSeaToSea_Ibby_Catalogue_Final_Digital.pdf

4. National Congress of American Indians. (2020, February). *Tribal nations and the United States: An introduction* (2020 ed.). http://www.ncai.org/about-tribes

5. Smith, C. L. (2020, April). *Home and classroom teaching: Native American children's and teens' books & resources.* https://cynthialeitichsmith.com/2020/04/home-classroom-teaching-native-american-childrens-teens-books-resources

Book Awards

- American Indian Youth Literature Award—see https://ailanet.org/activities/american-indian-youth-literature-award

Children's Books Cited

Barnes, W. (2014). *C is for Chickasaw* (A. K. Long, Illus.). White Dog Press.

Comenius, J. A., & Bardeen, C. W. (Ed.) (1968). *The Orbis Pictus of John Amos Comenius* (English–Latin ed.) (1887 reprint). Singing Tree Press. (Original English ed. published 1659)

Confederated Salish and Kootenai Tribes. (2008). *Beaver steals fire: A Salish coyote story.* University of Nebraska Press.

Cunningham, K., & Benoit, P. (2011). *The Pueblo* (P. Benoit, Illus.). Scholastic.

Dunbar-Ortiz, R. (2014). *An Indigenous Peoples' history of the United States.* Beacon Press.

Dunbar-Ortiz, R., Mendoza, J., & Reese, D. (2019). *An Indigenous Peoples' history of the United States for young people.* Beacon Press.

Flett, J. (2014). *We all count: A book of Cree numbers* (J. Flett, Illus.). Native Northwest.

Flett, J. (2017). *Black bear, red fox: Colours in Cree* (J. Flett, Illus.). Native Explore.

Floca, B. (2013). *Locomotive* (B. Floca, Illus.). Atheneum Books for Young Readers.

Haayk Foundation. (2019). *Wilgyigyet: Learn the colors in Sm'algyax* (H. Y. D. Lang, Illus.) (English–Tsimshian ed.). Sealaska Heritage.

Lajiness, K. (2017). *Pueblo.* ABDO Publishing.

Ortiz, S. J. (2017). *The people shall continue* (S. Graves, Illus.) (40th anniv. ed.). Children's Book Press. (Original work published 1977)

Pelletier, M. (2014). *A children's guide to Arctic birds* (D. Christopher, Illus.). Inhabit Media.

Sneve, V. D. H. (1993). *The Sioux* (R. Himler, Illus.). A First Americans Book series. Holiday House.

Sneve, V. D. H. (1994a). *The Nez Perce* (R. Himler, Illus.). A First Americans Book series. Holiday House.

Sneve, V. D. H. (1994b). *The Seminoles* (R. Himler, Illus.). A First Americans Book series. Holiday House.

Sneve, V. D. H. (1995). *The Hopis* (R. Himler, Illus.). A First Americans Book series. Holiday House.

Sneve, V. D. H. (1996). *Cherokees* (R. Himler, Illus.). A First Americans Book series. Holiday House.

Spier, P. (1977). *Noah's ark* (P. Spier, Illus.). Doubleday.

Tudor, A., & Tudor, K. (2018). *Young water protectors: A story about Standing Rock*. Eagle-Speaker Publishing.

van Loon, H. (1921). *The story of mankind*. Boni & Liveright.

References

Apess, W. (1829). *A son of the forest: The experience of William Apess, a Native of the forest. Comprising a notice of the Pequod tribe of Indians*. Author. https://archive.org/details/sonofforestexper00inapes

Benton, S. (1995, February 15). Pocahontas as a traitor: For one child, the story of Pocahontas inspired pride—and anger. *Tribal College: Journal of American Indian Higher Education*, *6*(4). https://tribalcollegejournal.org/pocahontas-traitor-child-story-pocahontas-inspired-pride-anger

Chavez, A. (2019, October 11). Map: Making Indigenous Peoples Day official across the country. *Indian Country Today*. https://indiancountrytoday.com/news/map-making-indigenous-peoples-day-official-across-the-country

Diné Writers' Collective. (2018, November 5). Trail of Lightning is an appropriation of Diné cultural beliefs. *Indian Country Today*. https://indiancountrytoday.com/opinion/trail-of-lightning-is-an-appropriation-of-din%C3%A9-cultural-beliefs-4tvSMvEfNE-i7AE10W7nQg

Earling, D. M. (2006). What we see. In A. M. Josephy Jr. (Ed.), *Lewis and Clark through Indian eyes* (pp. 25–48). Vintage.

Horning, K. T. (2010). *From cover to cover: Evaluating and reviewing children's books*. HarperCollins.

Lambert, V., & Lambert, M. (2014). Teach our children well: On addressing negative stereotypes in schools. *American Indian Quarterly*, *38*(4), 524–540. https://doi.org/10.5250/amerindiquar.38.4.0524

Lightman, D. (1993). Trump criticizes Pequots, casino. *Hartford Courant*. https://www.courant.com/news/connecticut/hc-xpm-1993-10-06-0000003863-story.html

Molin, P. F. (1999). Eliminating the s word. In A. B. Hirschfelder, P. Fairbanks Molin, & Y. Wakim (Eds.), *American Indian stereotypes in the world of children* (pp. 33–40). Scarecrow.

Native American Rights Fund. (1994, Winter). "We also have a religion": The American Indian Religious Freedom Act and the Religious Freedom Project of the Native American Rights Fund. *Announcements*, *5*(1), 1–3. https://www.narf.org/nill/documents/nlr/nlr5-1.pdf

Reese, D. (2007). Proceed with caution: Using Native American folktales in the classroom. *Language Arts*, *84*(3), 245–256.

Reese, D. (2018). Critical Indigenous literacies: Selecting and using children's books about Indigenous peoples. *Language Arts*, 95(6), 389–393.

4 Beyond the Model Minority and Forever Foreigner: Asian American Children's Nonfiction

NOREEN NASEEM RODRÍGUEZ, *University of Colorado Boulder*
ESTHER JUNE KIM, *William & Mary*

"We all work in canneries, restaurants, or as house cleaners or servants. If you have brown skin, you can't get any other kind of job." He told Larry that he and others from his town in the Philippines put together what little money they had to buy food and rent a small apartment. Larry felt like he was punched in the gut. He thought, "This is life in America?"

—DAWN B. MABALON AND GAYLE ROMASANTA,
Journey for Justice: The Life of Larry Itliong

This chapter explores how four recently published Asian American picturebook biographies resist popular stereotypes of Asian Americans such as the model minority. Paired with primary sources, these books offer educators and students important opportunities to learn about Asian American histories and contemporary issues that are often omitted in schools.

Chapter Guiding Questions

- What popular cultural stereotypes of Asian Americans should be avoided in children's nonfiction?

- When/where are Asian Americans present in the school curriculum? How can they be included in meaningful, nonstereotypical ways through children's nonfiction?

- How are cultural and linguistic practices depicted in children's nonfiction featuring Asian Americans? How can you tell if those depictions are authentic and accurate?

- Why should educators consider how racism and discrimination are explained and depicted in children's nonfiction featuring Asian Americans?

The racial category of Asian American typically refers to individuals of East Asian, Southeast Asian, or South Asian descent (Lee, 2015) and encompasses a tremendous diversity of cultures, languages, religions, histories, and more. In the cultural mainstream, however, Asian Americans are often conflated with East Asians (Lee & Ramakrishnan, 2020). Such perspectives reflect an antiquated understanding of Asian American immigration, limited to primarily Chinese, Japanese, and Filipino Americans in the first half of the twentieth century. Since the passage of the 1965 Immigration and Nationality Act, Asians from every country on the continent have arrived in the United States. Asian Americans are the fastest-growing racial group in the United States (Taylor, 2013), constituting nearly 6 percent of the national population (Hoeffel et al., 2012), and are projected to make up 12 percent of the US population by 2060 (Colby & Ortman, 2015).

Although *Asian American* is widely understood as a racial category, the term first emerged in 1968, when Chinese American, Japanese American, and Filipino American students at the University of California Berkeley came together to create the Asian American Political Alliance (Maeda, 2012). It was a political organization designed to unite multiethnic Asians from a variety of immigrant and socioeconomic backgrounds, and it also affirmed the right of communities of color to self-determination. Similar efforts have been made in the world of children's literature. In this chapter, we explore the ways four Asian Americans are depicted in recently published picturebook biographies, and discuss how educators can teach about Asian Americans as more than just a racial category by exploring their shared yet distinct histories of racism and resilience.

Overview of Asian American Children's Literature

Despite their increase in the US population, Asian Americans remain largely invisible in school curricula (Hartlep & Scott, 2016), particularly at the elementary level (Rodríguez & Ip, 2018). Historically, in the field of children's literature, Asian characters have been portrayed stereotypically (Aoki, 1981; Council on Interracial Books for Children, 1976) and were most likely to be featured via folktales (Cai, 1994), such as in the classic texts *The Five Chinese Brothers* (Bishop, 1938) and *Tikki Tikki Tembo* (Mosel, 1968). These two books contain deeply stereotypical portrayals (e.g., bright yellow skin, slanted eyes) and are culturally inaccurate (Aoki, 1981; Cai, 1994; Rodríguez, 2018; Schwartz, 1977; Yokota, 2009). Yet these books remain in print and continue to be used widely with children. Like many other inauthentic texts about Asians and Asian Americans, these two books were written by cultural outsiders (Harada, 1995).

In recent decades, studies of Asian American children's literature have noted an increase in positive, nonstereotypical portrayals, historically accurate information, and representations of contemporary Asian American life (de Manuel & Davis, 2006; Harada, 1995; Rodríguez & Kim, 2018). However, these studies also suggest an ongoing need for improvement and a deeper understanding of the master narratives that exemplify Asian Americans both to Asian Americans themselves and within the popular American imagination (Ching & Pataray-Ching, 2003). We detail three of these areas below, with additional historical context provided for each.

Our exploration of issues in Asian American children's nonfiction attends to the histories of Asian Americans in the United States and their unique racial positioning in a country that initially viewed them as an insidious "yellow peril" and now often portrays them as a "model minority." This view of the Asian American experience draws heavily from Asian American studies and Asian American critical race theory, a framework we detail extensively in Rodríguez and Kim (2018) that draws from the scholarship of Chang (1993) and Iftikar and Museus (2018).

Major Issues in Asian American Children's Literature

Who Is Asian American?

First, Asian American children's literature, including both fiction and nonfiction, often contributes to the conflation of Asian Americans with East Asians, as most publications focus on Chinese American, Japanese American, and Korean American experiences (Yi, 2014; Yokota, 2009). Half a century ago, the emphasis on Chinese Americans and Japanese Americans aligned with the significant representation of these two groups in the US population. In the 2010 Census, the six largest Asian American subgroups were Chinese (23.2 percent of total Asian American population), Filipino (19.7 percent), Indian (18.4 percent), Vietnamese (10.0 percent), Korean (9.9 percent), and Japanese (7.5 percent) (Taylor, 2013). Thus, the overrepresentation of East Asian American stories excludes Southeast and South Asian Americans (Rodríguez, 2020; Shankar & Srikanth, 1998).

Moreover, Asians and Asian Americans are often conflated in demographic data collection in the United States. This lack of disaggregation contributes to perceptions of Asian Americans as forever foreigners (Tuan, 1998) who are all recent immigrants, thus erasing Asian Americans who have lived in the United States for generations. Many contemporary picturebooks still link the Asian American experience with recent immigration, through the main characters or

extended family, further perpetuating the forever foreigner stereotype (Rodríguez & Kim, 2018). Additionally, particularly in books written by cultural outsiders, Asians are frequently exoticized. When books center on intergenerational
cultural clashes or foods that are portrayed as weird and un-American, stories
ultimately focus more on Asianness than the hybridity of Asian America (Chattarji, 2010; Rodríguez & Kim, 2018).

Upholding the Model Minority Myth

Second, the model minority stereotype persists in Asian American nonfiction
(Council on Interracial Books for Children, 1976; Rodríguez & Kim, 2018). In
popular culture, Asian American students are considered to have innate abilities
in math and science, and many Asian immigrants and Asian Americans work in
medical, engineering, and technology fields. However, the overrepresentation
of Asian Americans in these areas is neither random nor genetic. Rather, the
model minority myth stems from a complex, racist history that is rarely taught in
schools. Most students have a cursory understanding of the Chinese Exclusion
Act of 1882, but the depth of anti-Asian vitriol is seldom explored in K–8 curricula. As mentioned in Chapter 1 of this volume, American capitalists recruited
Chinese laborers to work on the transcontinental railroad in the most dangerous
jobs and conditions and paid them far less than white workers. White unions
refused to allow Chinese membership and lobbied for immigration reforms and
policies targeted at their Chinese counterparts, resulting in laws designed to
inhibit economic competition and minimize immigration from China. Eventually, labor activists gained their greatest success through the Chinese Exclusion
Act. By 1917, exclusion applied to *most* Asian countries (Hsu, 2015).

Exceptions to Chinese exclusion were often made on the basis of economic
utility and class status. Merchants, diplomats, and students were exempt from
exclusion, provided they had the necessary paperwork, sponsorship, and sometimes the physical trappings of wealth. Chinese boys and men often circumvent-
ed exclusion by taking on the identities of established merchants and merchants'
sons, changing their names to match those on record. These sons were called *zi
jai*, or paper sons. Exclusion was renewed and enforced for over sixty years, and
was not repealed until 1943, when a political alliance with China was necessary
during World War II.

Such economic priorities dominate immigration laws into the present day
through immigration acts in 1965 and 1990, which gave preference to Asian
immigrants of particular classes and educational backgrounds. The H1-B visa,
issued predominantly to Asian workers (US Citizenship and Immigration Services, 2017), allows employers to sponsor workers with specialized skills. Thus,

one of the easiest pathways of Asian immigration to the United States was and remains through education and skills in science, technology, and engineering (Hsu, 2015).

In addition to selective immigration, Cold War concerns related to international relations, as well as the increasing civil rights gains and racial unrest at home during the 1950s and 1960s, contributed to the positioning of Asian Americans as a model minority. The perceived financial and academic success of Asian Americans has been used as a disciplining tool against African American and Latinx communities, while anti-Asian racism is erased and Asian American success is upheld as proof that racism is not a barrier to overcoming inequities (Kim, 1999). The continued representation of Asian Americans as the model minority may seem benign or even complimentary, but clearly perpetuates a system of white supremacy that inflicts violence through the erasure and negation of racism.

Avoidance of Anti-Asian Racism

Asian American communities continue to face racism and discrimination. Children's literature, including nonfiction, often limits any explicit mention of racism to the peritext (such as author's notes or other back matter) and utilizes a passive voice that shifts blame onto victims and away from perpetrators (Rodríguez & Kim, 2018). Illustrations may also temper racialized contexts. For example, children's literature and historical photographs about incarceration during World War II regularly omit the armed guards who ensured Japanese Americans stayed within the barbed wire fences. We purposefully use the term *incarceration* rather than *internment* to describe what happened to the 120,000 Japanese and Japanese Americans who were forced to leave their homes for isolated prison camps as a result of Executive Order 9066 following the bombing of Pearl Harbor. Historians such as Daniels (2005) and many Asian American scholars argue that, legally, internment can only be applied to foreign nationals. As two-thirds of the Japanese Americans who were forced to live in camps were US citizens, internment is a euphemism that denies domestic civil rights violations during World War II. Without the racialized historical context clearly established by both word and image, the experiences and (hi)stories of Asian American communities can easily be misconstrued.

In children's literature, racism is sometimes presented not as a pervasive and structural issue but as a problem that can be solved with mental strength. Rodríguez and Kim's (2018) study revealed that the racialized context of historical fiction and biographies was often understated if mentioned at all. For example, in picturebook biographies about the Chinese American pilot Maggie Gee and the Japanese American baseball player Kenichi Zenimura, the protagonists transcended racism by feeling free in their own minds (Rodríguez & Kim, 2018). Racism, by implication, was not structural, but relegated to the minds of those who experience discriminatory words, actions, and laws. Challenging white supremacy as Asian Americans then requires nothing from those perpetuating racism, but simply that we "get over it."

Book Selection

As Asian American teacher educators and scholars—specifically, Pakistani–Filipina (Noreen) and Korean American (Esther)—who study Asian American children's literature through a social studies lens, we are especially sensitive to the conflation of Asians and Asian Americans. Searches through traditional databases yielded results that did not distinguish books set in Asia from books set in the United States with characters of Asian descent. Our initial search for Asian American biographies began by perusing winners and honorees of the Orbis Pictus, Carter G. Woodson, and Robert F. Sibert awards, which recognize exemplary children's nonfiction literature.

We also searched for the above award- and honor-winning books on Amazon.com and perused the book recommendations generated by Amazon's algorithms. We also utilized recommended lists such as the Asian American book collection at Teaching for Change's Social Justice Books website, which includes books that disrupt common stereotypes. As we had recently conducted a study of Asian American children's literature published between 2007 and 2017 (Rodríguez & Kim, 2018), for this analysis, we selected four picturebook biographies published after the conclusion of our previous study: *It Began with a Page: How Gyo Fujikawa Drew the Way* (Maclear, 2019), *Journey for Justice: The Life of Larry Itliong* (Mabalon & Romasanta, 2018), *Maya Lin: Artist–Architect of Light and Lines* (Harvey, 2017), and *Paper Son: The Inspiring Story of Tyrus Wong, Immigrant and Artist* (Leung, 2019).

These books feature four historical and contemporary Asian Americans (Japanese American, Filipino American, and Chinese Americans, respectively) whose lives spanned a range of decades and illustrate the diversity of the Asian American experience. They are of particular interest to us as they do not spotlight individuals known for their innovations in science or sports; rather, this collection of biographies includes a labor activist, visual artists, and an architect—careers not commonly associated with Asian Americans. Additionally, these texts directly address the previously mentioned issues found in Asian American children's nonfiction.

Nonfiction Biographies

It Began with a Page: How Gyo Fujikawa Drew the Way

Gyo Fujikawa's love of art began at an early age, but, at school, Gyo's talents went unnoticed and she often felt isolated from her white peers. She went to college in the 1920s and became a professional artist, eventually writing and illustrating *Babies* (Fujikawa, 1963), one of the earliest children's books to feature multiracial characters. *It Began with a Page* (Maclear, 2019) pushes back powerfully against perceptions of Asian Americans as the model minority, as the first scene of the book shows Gyo's mother writing a poem and her father working in a field. The Fujikawas were a working-class family that supported Gyo's interest in art.

As author Maclear (2019) details Fujikawa's budding design career in New York, she also describes how life for Japanese Americans on the West Coast changed dramatically after the bombing of Pearl Harbor. While Fujikawa continued working on the East Coast, her family in California was forced to leave their possessions and home for a prison camp in Arkansas. *It Began with a Page* is a rare instance in children's nonfiction when Japanese American incarceration is depicted from the perspective of a Japanese American *not* living on the West Coast and who does not experience firsthand forced removal and imprisonment. One powerful scene portrays Gyo's mother burning the family's possessions rather than selling them for pennies before leaving for the prison camp. While Japanese Americans being able to take only what they could carry is addressed in many children's books about this topic, rarely do such books attend to the insulting and exploitative nature of this requirement, as white Americans experienced tremendous material and economic gains from Japanese American losses. Moreover, children's nonfiction seldom attends to how Japanese Americans resisted unjust conditions during World War II.

The next illustration in the text shows the prison camp from another rarely seen perspective. Unlike the famous camp images captured by photographers Ansel Adams and Dorothea Lange (see Table 4.1 for primary source sets), Julie Morstad's drawings in *It Began with a Page* detail an armed guard. When Adams and Lange were permitted by the US government to document camp life, they were prohibited from photographing the barbed wire and guard towers that surrounded the prisoners. Morstad's inclusion of a gun on the soldier's shoulder is a subtle but powerful acknowledgment of the unlawful and prejudicial incarceration of Japanese Americans.

Although Gyo's location on the East Coast spared her from imprisonment, Maclear (2019) makes clear that she did not escape discrimination from "angry strangers [who] saw her as the enemy" (p. 31). While the perception of Japanese Americans as "the enemy" is a common theme in Japanese American incarceration literature, less common is the difficulty faced by Japanese Americans in the aftermath. Maclear describes how the Fujikawas had no house or savings upon their release. *It Began with a Page* shows a remarkably nuanced account of Japanese American incarceration, revealing traumatic aspects of the experience that are often omitted in popular children's nonfiction about the event.

TABLE 4.1. Recommended Primary Sources by Book

It Began with a Page: How Gyo Fujikawa Drew the Way (Maclear, 2019)	• Ansel Adams's photographs of Japanese American Internment at Manzanar, Library of Congress collection—see https://www.loc.gov/collections/ansel-adams-manzanar/about-this-collection • Japanese American Internment, Library of Congress primary source set—see https://www.loc.gov/classroom-materials/japanese-american-internment • Densho Digital Repository, the Japanese American Legacy Project's digital collection—see http://ddr.densho.org • Japanese American Citizens League, curriculum guides and resources—see https://jacl.org/resources
Journey for Justice: The Life of Larry Itliong (Mabalon & Romasanta, 2018)	• *The Delano Manongs* (Aroy, 2014)—see https://www.delanomanongs.com • *Viva La Causa* (Brummel et al., 2008), Teaching Tolerance film kit—see https://www.learningforjustice.org/classroom-resources/film-kits/viva-la-causa • "America's Forgotten Farmworkers: If You Know Cesar Chavez, You Should Know Larry Itliong" (Timeline, 2018)—https://timeline.com/americas-forgotten-filipino-farmworkers-if-you-know-cesar-chavez-you-should-know-larry-itliong-ff90a4c08e2 • *Journey for Justice: Teachers' Guide* (Pagtakhan et al., 2001)—see https://www.bridgedelta.com/teachersguide • Walter P. Reuther Library's labor archives, Wayne State University—see http://reuther.wayne.edu
Maya Lin: Artist Artist–Architect of Light and Lines (Harvey, 2017)	**Source A:** "Becoming American: The Chinese Experience" interview with Maya Lin (Moyers, 2003) MAYA LIN: I didn't realize what it was. I was so miserable by the time I got to high school, and so I had pretty much retreated into my own world. BILL MOYERS: Miserable because? MAYA LIN: . . . I really did not feel like I fit in. But again, I never would have figured out it's—oh, it's because your parents are [Chinese]. (p. 4)
	Source B1: *Maya Lin: A Strong Clear Vision* (Mock, 1994)—see https://caamedia.org/films/maya-lin-a-strong-clear-vision MAYA LIN: It took me months to realize that obviously a lot of people are going to be extremely offended that the creator of the American Vietnam Veterans Memorial is not only not a veteran, but she is a she. She is an Asian. And I did ask the veterans' group I was working with, "Did mail come in? Did criticism come in?" And, sure, there was obviously letters saying, "How can you let a gook design the memorial?" (19:51)
	Source B2: "Lest We Forget" (Wallace et al., 1982) SCRUGGS [head of Vietnam Memorial Fund]: I think, with the same design, if it were designed by an Anglo-Saxon male, I think the difficulties we had would have been considerably less. (p. 9)

Continued on next page

TABLE 4.1. Continued

	Source B3: "Maya Lin" interview on *The Charlie Rose Show* (Mock, 1995) MAYA LIN: [Teaching] just sort of helped erase a lot of the, the sort of ugly, sort of racist backstabbing. I mean, it got very very ugly, and I think I happily forgot it....I think it was a very emotionally painful time. (8:32)
	Source C: Public Affairs Television "Becoming American" interview, *New York Times* and *Washington Post* articles • MAYA LIN: I remember at the very first press conference some reporter said, "Don't you think it's ironic that the memorial is the Vietnam Memorial and you're of Asian descent? (Moyers, 2003, p. 5) • "Student Wins War Memorial Contest: Chinese Woman, 21, Gets $20,000 for War Monument Design" (1981) • "An Asian artist for an Asian war" (McCombs, 1982)
Paper Son: The Inspiring Story of Tyrus Wong, Immigrant and Artist (Leung, 2019)	**Source D:** *Island: Poetry and History of Chinese Immigrants on Angel Island, 1910–1940* (Lai et al., 1991)
	Source E: "Detained on Angel Island" (Lai, 2019; see also Lai, 1978)
	Source F: "Imagine an Immigration Interview" (Smithsonian Institution, 2011)
	Source G: "Tyrus" (Tom, 2017)

Journey for Justice: The Life of Larry Itliong

When students learn about farmworker activism and labor rights, they typically learn about César Chávez, and perhaps Dolores Huerta. However, missing from most children's books about these individuals is the substantial activism of Filipino American farmworkers and their vital role in the creation of the United Farm Workers (UFW) labor union. Larry Itliong was the assistant director of the UFW, and *Journey for Justice* (Mabalon & Romasanta, 2018) is the first book to tell his story and the first illustrated nonfiction Filipino American history book for children.

Acclaimed Filipina American historian Dawn Mabalon and author Gayle Romasanta collaborated to tell Itliong's story, which begins with his early life in the Philippines. Mabalon and Romasanta (2018) detail how the Philippines at that time was not an independent country but "a colony of the United States, and the US controlled the island nation's schools, government, military, and the economy" (p. 2). Such examination of US imperialism and its widespread impact upon colonized people is exceedingly rare in children's literature, yet it is an essential aspect of the Filipino and Filipino American experience.

As readers learn about Itliong's life, they discover how the promise of economic opportunity was unattainable for many immigrants, regardless of how hard or long they worked. Itliong's experiences with discrimination, dehumanizing working conditions, and migration are described in vibrant detail. The authors dedicate tremendous attention to Itliong's lifetime of activism, from his first union membership in the 1920s in Alaska to the creation of a retirement village for elderly, single Filipino laborers in the 1970s. However, the level of detail results in dense text—possibly a challenge for educators hoping to share Itliong's story in a single lesson.

Many of the illustrations in *Journey for Justice* (Mabalon & Romasanta, 2018) were inspired by primary sources. There is also a teaching guide for the book and several online resources related to Filipino farmworkers (see Table 4.1), in addition to the documentaries *The Delano Manongs* (Aroy, 2014) and *Viva La Causa* (Brummel et al., 2008), which offer students opportunities to hear from farmworkers firsthand. Prior to the creation of the UFW, Itliong and other Filipino farmworkers were members of the Agricultural Workers Organizing Committee, which later merged with the primarily Mexican American National Farm Workers Association to become the UFW. Primary sources for all three organizations can be found online via the Walter P. Reuther Library (see Table 4.1). Utilizing excerpts of *Journey for Justice* alongside primary sources allows students to understand the role of interracial solidarity in the fight for justice, as well as the struggles that arose when different ethnoracial groups came together.

Maya Lin: Artist–Architect of Light and Lines

When paired with excerpts from interviews with Maya Lin (see Table 4.1), Jean Walker Harvey's (2017) biography provides an opportunity to construct a compelling modern nonfiction narrative of Asian Americans. Focusing on her growth as an artist, Harvey highlights the influence of Maya Lin's family (her father was a sculptor and her mother was a poet), the creativity and curiosity she expressed as a child, and the challenges she faced as the designer of the Vietnam War Memorial. However, the story upholds the model minority stereotype by highlighting details of the Lin's success with neither any mention of or allusion to the anti-Asian racism she faced as a student and artist nor the anti-Asian immigration policies that only allowed educated or well-funded Chinese entry into the United States.

On a page outlining artistic media used by the Lin family, Harvey (2017) writes, "Maya graduated co-valedictorian of her high school class" (p. 7). This reference to her academic success seems out of place; in interviews, Lin herself describes her high school experience as painful, a time and place where she did not fit in due to her Chinese ancestry (see quote in Source A, Table 4.1). Further on in the book, the controversy around Lin's Vietnam Veterans Memorial is described with no reference to the racism of some critics and only includes objections related to the design, such as "her design looked like a bat, a boomerang, a black gash of shame" (p. 21). In contrast, multiple interviews with Lin, videos and documents from the time, as well as the writings by the veteran who led the building of the memorial reveal racism as a significant element in the conflict.

Instead, the book illustrates Lin standing tall and stoic as "their angry words stung Maya. . . . Some people wanted to change the design. Maya was young, but she was brave. She didn't back down" (Harvey, 2017, p. 21). An important question to ask students at this point would be, "Why did she have to be brave?" Although students may point out "angry words" and criticism of her artistry, using historical primary sources can add complexity to this question of bravery. No longer is Lin's bravery solely a response to critiques of her design or her youth, but to racism (see Source B, Table 4.1), and specifically to being positioned as a forever foreigner (see Source C, Table 4.1). Erasing race from Maya Lin's story centers the model minority stereotype. Without an understanding of selective immigration policies as well as the contemporary ways that Asian Americans are racialized, current and historical anti-Asian racism is obscured, creating a fictive post-racial society in which hard work and bravery alone lead to success. For this book in particular, primary sources create a more robust and honest narrative.

Paper Son: The Inspiring Story of Tyrus Wong, Immigrant and Artist

In *Paper Son: The Inspiring Story of Tyrus Wong, Immigrant and Artist*, Julie Leung (2019) follows Tyrus Wong from his childhood immigration to the US to his career as an animator with Disney. His early life is detailed within a broader historical context that succinctly but powerfully reveals the structural challenges Asian immigrants faced upon entering the US. Through these many struggles and triumphs, what comes through most clearly is Tyrus Wong's love of art.

Wong was a paper son originally named Wong Geng Yeo. Leung (2019) puts a name and face to the enactment of laws and social pressures shaped by white supremacy that culminated in the Chinese Exclusion Act of 1882. On the second page, she explains how Tyrus Wong's father "pretended to be a merchant named Look Git. Wong Geng Yeo became his son, Look Tai Yow." A reproduction of Wong's immigration card is provided at the end of the book, allowing an in-depth exploration of Asian immigration to the United States that considers why officials would note immigrants' unique physical marks (for surveillance and tracking). A final name change by his teachers in Sacramento marked the Americanization of Wong Geng Yeo, as his paper son name Tai Yow was changed to Tyrus, a common racist microaggression that students of color still experience in schools (Kohli & Solórzano, 2012).

The portrayal of Tyrus Wong's experience at Angel Island includes the separation of children from their parents, the long duration, and the poor condition of the barracks. As students are likely unfamiliar with the Angel Island Immigration Station, primary sources can enhance students' understandings of Wong's story, from the poetry scratched into the walls of the barracks by detainees (see Source D, Table 4.1) to images of barracks and the medical examinations that illustrate the perception of immigrants as undesirable and unclean (see Source E, Table 4.1). Similarly, introducing students to a list of interview questions (though educators should avoid simulations) may reveal the difficult process for those entering through Angel Island (see Source F, Table 4.1). In a documentary film about his life and work, Tyrus Wong himself recounts the misery and fear he felt while waiting to rejoin his father as he visited Angel Island (see Source G, Table 4.1).

Both structural and everyday anti-Asian racism is described in *Paper Son* (Leung, 2019). In addition to the Chinese Exclusion Act, Asian immigrants faced difficulties finding work. Leung presents this simply, writing that "to be a Chinese immigrant was to be a servant, a laundryman, a waiter" (p. 2). Subsequent indignities Tyrus endured as an illustrator at Disney are presented in light of this context; thus, without explicitly stating reasons, Leung is able to convey racism as a cause. This narrative structure also allows Leung ultimately to center Tyrus's work as an artist without negating challenges overcome, nor challenges that are still present, for Asian Americans.

Cautionary Notes about Selecting Asian American Children's Nonfiction

Educators should be mindful that online and database searches often conflate the terms *Asian* and *Asian American*. For example, several children's nonfiction books have been written about Malala Yousafzai, the youngest Nobel Prize laureate from Pakistan. While Malala's story of resilience and activism is unquestionably inspiring, she is not Asian American; she was born and raised in Pakistan and now resides in England. In order to ensure distinctions such as these, educators must take the time to learn about Asian American cultures and histories prior to making book selections. We do not recommend books like *A Kid's Guide to Asian American History: More Than 70 Activities* (Petrillo, 2007), which is outdated, contains an overemphasis on arts and crafts, and offers few significant details. Instead, we recommend nonfiction texts like Lee's (2015) *The Making of Asian America* and Takaki's (1998) *Strangers from a Different Shore* to provide educators with Asian American historical content knowledge.

Two recently self-published biographical collections are *We Are Inspiring: The Stories of 32 Inspirational Asian American Women* (Trazo, 2019) and *Asian-Americans Who Inspire Us* (Wolf & Franco, 2019); these books offer young readers a brief introduction to a range of Asian Americans and are also written and illustrated by Asian Americans. However, as is typical of Asian American children's literature more generally, they mostly feature East and Southeast Asian Americans; South Asian Americans are underrepresented in both of these books. Although it includes both South Asian and South Asian American individuals, *Stories for South Asian Super Girls* (Khaira, 2019) profiles both well-known and lesser-known South Asian girls and is an excellent addition to any classroom or library. Last, Lee & Low Books recently released The Story Of series, which adapts the stories of several famous Asian Americans and Pacific Islanders; these informational books also include primary sources, timelines, and more.

The Asian/Pacific American Librarians Association has annual awards for picturebooks, children's literature, and young adult literature; a number of the award-winning and honor books are nonfiction, feature Asian Americans, and are ideal for student engagement. However, some selections are not based in the United States, and, because of this, educators should take careful note of focal subject and characters' identities and the setting of the nonfiction text. We also recommend that educators deliberately choose multiple books within and across ethnicities and nationalities; for example, share biographies of various Chinese Americans in a range of careers and across different time periods (e.g., artist Tyrus Wong, architect Maya Lee, physicist Chien-Shiung Wu, pilot Hazel Ying Lee). As Asian American history is typically not taught in any substantive way prior to high school (which tends to solely include Chinese people in the 1800s and Japanese American incarceration during World War II), peritext can be a vital tool in supporting readers' contextualization of events in the books listed above, as well as historical Asian American children's literature more broadly. Often, these elements include timelines, author's notes, primary sources, and bibliographies—each of the books in this chapter includes at least one of these components. It is important that educators consult these supporting materials *before* reading the book with students, particularly since Asian American history is often unfamiliar and thus historical context must be established prior to reading the primary text (see also Table 4.2).

De Manuel and Davis (2006) argue that Asian American children's literature "is working in its own way to replace the stereotypical depictions of the Asians and Asian Americans that children know best" (p. viii), from *The Five Chinese Brothers* and *Tikki Tikki Tembo* to Apu on *The Simpsons* and *Mulan*. Essential to this work are educators who actively disrupt portrayals of Asian Americans as Asian monoliths, recent immigrants, and model minorities. When presented to

TABLE 4.2. Additional Resources about Asian American History

	General Asian American History and the Model Minority Myth	Angel Island and Chinese Immigration in the 1800s	Japanese American Incarceration	Filipino Farmworkers
Further reading	*Strangers from a Different Shore* by Ronald Takaki (1998)	*Angel Island* by Erika Lee and Judy Yung (2010)	"Personal Justice Denied," a report of the US Commission on Wartime Relocation and Internment of Civilians (1983)	*America Is in the Heart* by Carlos Bulosan (1946)
	The Making of Asian America by Erika Lee (2016)	*The Good Immigrants: How the Yellow Peril Became the Model Minority* by Madeline Hsu (2017)	*Un-American: The Incarceration of Japanese Americans during World War II* by Richard Cahan et al. (2016)	*Little Manila Is in the Heart* by Dawn Mabalon (2013)
Online source	*Adam Ruins Everything: How America Created the Model Minority Myth* (TruTV, 2019)	"Breaking Ground," Episode 1 (Season 1) of *Asian Americans* (Chiang et al., 2020)	*A Lesson in American History: The Japanese American Experience* by Janet Hayakawa (2015) and the Japanese American Citizens League	*Grapes of Wrath: The Forgotten Filipinos Who Led a Farmworker Revolution* [Radio broadcast] (Morehouse, 2015)
	Why Do We Call Asian Americans the Model Minority? [Video] (AJ+, 2017)	Angel Island Immigration Station Foundation—see https://www.aiisf.org	Japanese American National Museum—see https://www.janm.org	"Why It Is Important to Know the Story of Filipino-American Larry Itliong" (Romasanta, 2019)
	Asian Americans [TV series] (Tajima-Peña, 2020)	Gold Mountain: Chinese Californian Stories—see https://www.californiamuseum.org/gold-mountain	Korematsu Institute Curriculum Toolkit—see http://www.korematsuinstitute.org/curriculum-kit-materials	"A Leader of Farmworkers, and Filipinos' Place in American History" (Cowan, 2019)
			Manzanar National Historic Site—see https://www.nps.gov/places/manzanar-national-historic-site.htm	"Remembering the Manongs and the Story of the Filipino Farm Worker Movement" (Arguelles, 2017)

young readers, nuanced Asian American nonfiction literature can be an important tool in antiracist and equity-centered education.

Practical Strategies

- Have students examine the literature resources available in your classroom or school library and locate as many nonfiction titles as they can about Asian Americans. Ask them to consider whose experiences are represented and whose are missing in these books.

- If your classroom or school uses a history textbook, have students research the accuracy and breadth of Asian American history addressed. Gather nonfiction and primary sources to supplement and counter any limitations in the textbook.

- Gather nonfiction texts and primary sources that represent diverse perspectives from a particular time period. Have students create a timeline of events, working to ensure that as many perspectives and identities as possible are represented. Engage students in a discussion that highlights the richness added through the inclusion of such multifaceted viewpoints.

- Using primary sources and children's nonfiction, have students research individuals or families who were impacted by the US incarceration of Japanese and Japanese Americans during World War II.

- Gather multiple nonfiction sources and have students examine them to identify which stereotypes of Asians and Asian Americans are reinforced or disrupted. Discuss connections that might be made between their findings and what they see regarding Asians and Asian Americans in social media and popular culture.

Ten Additional Nonfiction Books about Asian Americans

1. Atkins, L., & Yogi, S. (2017). *Fred Korematsu speaks up* (Y. Houlette, Illus.). Heyday.

2. Cha, D. (1996). *Dia's story cloth: The Hmong people's journey of freedom* (C. Thao Cha & N. Thao Cha, Illus.). Lee & Low Books.

3. Freedman, R. (2013). *Angel Island: Gateway to gold mountain*. Clarion Books.

4. Grady, C. (2017). *Write to me: Letters from Japanese American children to the librarian they left behind* (A. Hirao, Illus.). Charlesbridge.

5. Grimes, N. (2020). *Kamala Harris: Rooted in justice* (L. Freeman, Illus.). Atheneum Books for Young Readers.

6. Robeson, T. (2019). *Queen of physics: How Wu Chien Shiung helped unlock the secrets of the atom* (R. Huang, Illus.). Sterling.

7. Singh, S. J. (2020). *Fauja Singh keeps going: The true story of the oldest person to ever run a marathon* (B. Kaur, Illus.). Kokila.

8. Takai, G., Eisinger, J., & Scott, S. (2019). *They called us enemy* (H. Becker, Illus.). Top Shelf Productions.

9. Yoo, P. (2020). *The story of Olympic diver Sammy Lee* (D. Lee, Illus.). Lee & Low Books.

10. Yoo, P. (2021). *From a whisper to a rallying cry: The killing of Vincent Chin and the trial that galvanized the Asian American movement.* Norton Young Readers.

Five Online Resources

1. Asian/Pacific American Libraries Association. (2007, April 19). *About APALA.* http://www.ala.org/aboutala/affiliates/affiliates/apala

2. Bieber, J., Gong, S., & Young, D. (Executive Producers). (n.d.). *Asian Americans* [Film series]. WETA Washington, DC, and the Center for Asian American Media; PBS. https://www.pbs.org/show/asian-americans

3. Kitaab World. (n.d.). *Exploring South Asia through children's literature.* https://kitaabworld.com

4. Social Justice Books. (n.d.). *Asian Americans booklist.* https://socialjustice books.org/booklists/asian-americans

5. Zinn Education Project. (n.d.). *Asian Americans and moments in people's history.* https://www.zinnedproject.org/materials/asian-americans-and-moments-in-peoples-history

Book Awards

• Asian/Pacific American Award for Literature—see https://www.apala web.org/awards/literature-awards

• South Asia Book Award for Children's and Young Adult Literature—see https://southasiabookaward.wisc.edu/award-books

Children's Books Cited

Bishop, C. H. (1938). *Five Chinese brothers* (K. Wiese, Illus.). Coward-McCann.

Fujikawa, G. (1963). *Babies* (G. Fujikawa, Illus.). Grosset and Dunlap.

Grimes, N. (2020). *Kamala Harris: Rooted in justice* (L. Freeman, Illus.). Atheneum Books for Young Readers.

Harvey, J. W. (2017). *Maya Lin: Artist–architect of light and lines* (D. Phumiruk, Illus.). Henry Holt and Company.

Khaira, R. K. (2019). *Stories for South Asian super girls.* Kashi House.

Leung, J. (2019). *Paper son: The inspiring story of Tyrus Wong, immigrant and artist* (C. Sasaki, Illus.). Schwartz & Wade Books.

Mabalon, D. B., & Romasanta, G. (2018). *Journey for justice: The life of Larry Itliong* (A. Sibayan, Illus.). Bridge & Delta Publishing.

Maclear, K. (2019). *It began with a page: How Gyo Fujikawa drew the way* (J. Morstad, Illus.). HarperCollins.

Mosel, A. (1968). *Tikki tikki tembo* (B. Lent, Illus.). Henry Holt and Company.

Petrillo, V. (2007). *A kid's guide to Asian American history: More than 70 activities.* Chicago Review Press.

Trazo, A. (2019). *We are inspiring: The stories of 32 inspirational Asian American women* (A. Trazo, Illus.). BookBaby.

Wolf, A. Q., & Franco, M. (2019). *Asian-Americans who inspire us* (T. Siiriainen, Illus.). Wishful Wolf Press.

References

AJ+. (2017, October 8). *Why do we call Asian Americans the model minority?* [Video]. YouTube. https://www.youtube.com/watch?v=PrDbvSSbxk8

Aoki, E. M. (1981). Are you Chinese? Are you Japanese? Or are you just a mixed-up kid? Using Asian American children's literature. *The Reading Teacher, 34*(4), 382–385.

Arguelles, D. (2017, May 25). *Remembering the Manongs and the story of the Filipino farm worker movement.* National Parks Conservation Association. https://www.npca.org/articles/1555-remembering-the-manongs-and-story-of-the-filipino-farm-worker-movement

Aroy, M. (Director). (2014). *The Delano Manongs: Forgotten heroes of the United Farm Workers* [Film]. Media Factory.

Brummel, B. (Producer), Brummel, B., & Mayo, A. (Directors). (2008). *Viva la causa* [Film]. Bill Brummel Productions.

Bulosan, C. (1946). *America is in the heart.* University of Washington Press.

Cahan, R., Williams, M., Lange, D., & Adams, A. (2016). *Un-American: The incarceration of Japanese Americans during World War II.* CityFiles Press.

Cai, M. (1994). Images of Chinese and Chinese Americans mirrored in picture books. *Children's Literature in Education, 25*(3), 169–191.

Chang, R. S. (1993). Toward an Asian American legal scholarship: Critical race theory, post-structuralism, and narrative space. *California Law Review, 81*(5), 1241–1323.

Chattarji, S. (2010). The new Americans: The creation of a typology of Vietnamese American identity in children's literature. *Journal of American Studies, 44*(2), 409–428. https://doi.org/S0021875809991411

Chiang, S. L., Gandbhir, G., & Lee, G. (Producers). (2020, May 11). Breaking ground (Season 1, Episode 1) [TV series episode]. In Renee Tajima-Peña (Series Producer), *Asian Americans*. WETA Washington, DC, and the Center for Asian American Media; PBS. https://www.pbs.org/weta/asian-americans/episode-guide/episode-1-breaking-ground

Ching, S. H. D., & Pataray-Ching, J. (2003). Toward a socio-political framework for Asian American children's literature. *New Advocate, 16*(2), 123–128.

Colby, S. L., & Ortman, J. M. (2015, March 3). *Projections of the size and composition of the U.S. population: 2014 to 2060* (P25-1143). United States Census Bureau. https://www.census.gov/content/dam/Census/library/publications/2015/demo/p25-1143.pdf

Commission on Wartime Relocation and Internment of Civilians. (1983). *Personal justice denied: Report of the Commission on Wartime Relocation and Internment of Civilians*. United States Government Publishing Office.

Council on Interracial Books for Children. (1976). Asian Americans in children's books. *Interracial Books for Children Bulletin, 7*, 2–3.

Cowan, J. (2019, October 23). A leader of farmworkers, and Filipinos' place in American history. *The New York Times*. https://www.nytimes.com/2019/10/21/us/larry-itliong-farmworkers.html

Daniels, R. (2005). Words do matter: A note on inappropriate terminology and the incarceration of the Japanese Americans. In L. Fiset & G. M. Nomura (Eds.), *Nikkei in the Pacific Northwest: Japanese Americans and Japanese Canadians in the twentieth century* (pp. 183–207). University of Washington Press.

de Manuel, D., & Davis, R. G. (2006). Editors' introduction: Critical perspectives on Asian American children's literature. *The Lion and the Unicorn, 30*(2), v–xv.

Harada, V. H. (1995). Issues of ethnicity, authenticity, and quality in Asian-American picture books, 1983–93. *Journal of Youth Services in Libraries, 8*(2), 135–149.

Hartlep, N. D., & Scott, D. P. (2016). *Asian-American curricular epistemicide: From being excluded to becoming a model minority*. Springer.

Hayakawa, J. (2015). *A lesson in American history: The Japanese American experience*. Japanese American Citizens League. https://resourceguide.densho.org/A%20Lesson%20in%20American%20History:%20The%20Japanese%20American%20Experience,%20Curriculum%20and%20Resource%20Guide,%205th%20Edition%20(curricula)

Hoeffel, E. M., Rastogi, S., Kim, M. O., & Shahid, H. (2012, March). *The Asian population: 2010*. United States Census Bureau. https://www.census.gov/prod/cen2010/briefs/c2010br-11.pdf

Hsu, M. Y. (2015). *The good immigrants: How the yellow peril became the model minority.* Princeton University Press.

Iftikar, J. S., & Museus, S. D. (2018). On the utility of Asian critical (AsianCrit) theory in the field of education. *International Journal of Qualitative Studies in Education, 31*(10), 935–949. https://doi.org/10.1080/09518398.2018.1522008

Kim, C. J. (1999). The racial triangulation of Asian Americans. *Politics & Society, 27*(1), 105–138.

Kohli, R., & Solórzano, D. G. (2012). Teachers, please learn our names! Racial microaggressions and the K–12 classroom. *Race Ethnicity and Education, 15*(4), 441–462. https://doi.org/10/1080/13613324.2012.674026

Lai, H. M. (1978). Island of immortals: Chinese immigrants and the Angel Island immigration station. *California History, 57*(1), 88–103. https://doi.org/10.2307/25157818

Lai, H. M. (2019, 26 November). *Detained on Angel Island: Historical essay.* https://www.foundsf.org/index.php?title=Detained_on_Angel_Island

Lai, H. M., Lim, G., & Yung, J. (Eds.) (1991). *Island: Poetry and history of Chinese immigrants on Angel Island, 1910–1940.* University of Washington.

Lee, E. (2015). *The making of Asian America: A history.* Simon & Schuster.

Lee, E., & Yung, J. (2010). *Angel island: Immigrant gateway to America.* Oxford University Press.

Lee, J., & Ramakrishnan, K. (2020). Who counts as Asian? *Ethnic and Racial Studies, 43*(10), 1733–1756.

Mabalon, D. (2013). *Little Manila is in the heart: The making of the Filipina/o American community in Stockton, California.* Duke University Press.

Maeda, D. (2012). *Rethinking the Asian American movement.* Routledge.

McCombs, P. (1982, January 3). Maya Lin and the great call of China. *Washington Post.* https://www.washingtonpost.com/archive/lifestyle/1982/01/03/maya-lin-and-the-great-call-of-china/544d8f2b-43b4-45ec-989b-72b2f2865eb4

Mock, F. L. (Director). (1994). *Maya Lin: A strong clear vision* [Film]. American Film Foundation.

Mock, F. L. (1995, 26 December). Maya Lin [Radio broadcast]. *Charlie Rose.* https://charlierose.com/videos/20375

Morehouse, L. (2015, September 19). *Grapes of wrath: The Forgotten Filipinos who led a farmworker revolution* [Radio broadcast]. NPR. https://www.npr.org/sections/thesalt/2015/09/16/440861458/grapes-of-wrath-the-forgotten-filipinos-who-led-a-farmworker-revolution?t=1616675991626

Moyers, B. (Host). (2003). *Public Affairs Television "Becoming American" interview with Maya Lin* [Broadcast transcript]. PBS. https://www.pbs.org/becomingamerican/ap_pjourneys_transcript5.html

Pagtakhan, A., Lopez, D., Sabac, A., Tintiangco-Cubales, A., & Mabalon, D. B. (2001). *Journey for justice: The life of Larry Itliong—Teachers' Guide.* Bridge + Delta. https://www.bridgedelta.com/teachersguide

Rodríguez, N. N. (2018). Avoiding the single story: The need to critically examine children's literature and Asian and Asian American stereotypes. *Literacy Today*, 32–33.

Rodríguez, N. N. (2020). "This is why nobody knows who you are": (Counter)stories of Southeast Asian Americans in the Midwest. *Review of Education, Pedagogy, and Cultural Studies, 42*(2), 157–174. https://doi.org/10.1080/10714413.2020.1757377

Rodríguez, N. N., & Ip, R. (2018). Hidden in history: (Re)constructing Asian American history in elementary social studies classrooms. In S. B. Shear, C. Tschida, E. Bellows, L. Brown Buchanan, & E. E. Saylor (Eds.), *(Re)imagining elementary social studies: A controversial issues reader* (pp. 319–339). Information Age Publishing.

Rodríguez, N. N., & Kim, E. J. (2018). In search of mirrors: An Asian critical race theory content analysis of Asian American picturebooks from 2007 to 2017. *Journal of Children's Literature, 44*(2), 17–30.

Romasanta, G. (2019, July 24). Why it is important to know the story of Filipino-American Larry Itliong. Smithsonian. https://www.smithsonianmag.com/smithsonian-institution/why-it-is-important-know-story-filipino-american-larry-itliong-180972696

Schwartz, A. V. (1977). The five Chinese brothers: Time to retire. *Interracial Books for Children Bulletin, 8*(3), 3–7.

Shankar, L. D., & Srikanth, R. (Eds.). (1998). *A part yet apart: South Asians in Asian America.* Temple University Press.

Smithsonian Institution. (2011). *Imagine an immigration interview.* OurStory: Coming to America. https://amhistory.si.edu/ourstory/pdf/immigration/immigration_interview.pdf

Student wins war memorial contest: Chinese woman, 21, gets $20,000 for War Monument Design" (1981, May 7). *The New York Times.* https://www.nytimes.com/1981/05/07/us/student-wins-war-memorial-contest.html

Tajima-Peña, R. (Series Producer). (2020). *Asian Americans* [TV series]. WETA Washington, DC, and the Center for Asian American Media; PBS. https://www.pbs.org/weta/asian-americans

Takaki, R. T. (1998). *Strangers from a different shore: A history of Asian Americans.* Little, Brown and Company.

Taylor, P. (2013, April 4). *The rise of Asian Americans.* Pew Research Center. www.pewsocialtrends.org/wp-content/uploads/sites/3/2013/04/Asian-Americans-new-full-report-04-2013.pdf

Timeline. (2018, June 5). *America's forgotten Filipino farmworkers: If you know Cesar Chavez, you should know Larry Itliong.* https://timeline.com/americas-forgotten-filipino-farmworkers-if-you-know-cesar-chavez-you-should-know-larry-itliong-ff90a4c08e2

Tom, P. (Director). (2017, September 8). Tyrus (Season 31, Episode 7) [TV series episode]. In M. Kantor (Executive Producer), *American Masters.* WNET. https://www.pbs.org/wnet/americanmasters/tyrus-about-the-film/8917

TruTV. (2019, January 18). *Adam ruins everything: How America created the model minority myth* [Video]. YouTube. https://www.youtube.com/watch?v=Pg1X1KkVxN4

Tuan, M. (1998). *Forever foreigners or honorary whites?: The Asian ethnic experience today*. Rutgers University Press.

US Citizenship and Immigration Services. (2017). *Characteristics of H1-B Specialty Occupation Workers*. US Department of Homeland Security. www.uscis.gov/sites/default/files/files/nativedocuments/Characteristics_of_H-1B_Specialty_Occupation_Workers_FY17.pdf

Yi, J. (2014). My heart beats in two places: Immigration stories in Korean American picture books. *Children's Literature in Education, 45*(2), 129–144. https://doi.org/10.1007/s10583-013-9209-4

Yokota, J. (2009). Asian Americans in literature for children and young adults. *Teacher Librarian, 36*(3), 15–19.

Wallace, M., Safter, M., Reasoner, H. & Bradley, E. (Hosts). (1982, October 10). Lest we forget [TV series episode]. In T. Bettag (Producer), *60 minutes*. CBS Television Network. https://digital.lib.lehigh.edu/trial/vietnam/files/round4/60minutes.pdf

Diverse African American Nonfiction for Children: The Challenge of Race, History, and Genre

EBONY ELIZABETH THOMAS, *University of Pennsylvania*

Tell all the children our story.

—TONYA BOLDEN, *Tell All the Children Our Story: Memories and Mementos of Being Young and Black in America*

In children's nonfiction, the story of Black America is often presented as singular. While much of Black children's nonfiction is grounded in the painful histories of slavery, Jim Crow, the Civil Rights Movement, and post–Civil Rights urban America, new kinds of nonfiction are emerging. This chapter introduces readers to the unique challenges of race, history, and genre. At a time when Black Americans are both revered and maligned in the nation and around the world, Black children's nonfiction should be read, taught, and enjoyed as an essential cipher for decoding the story of the United States.

Chapter Guiding Questions

- How can children's nonfiction do more than simply transmit information about experiences (both past and present) of Black Americans?

- In what ways might nonfiction and primary source material uplift, give hope, and promote healing when so much of the story of Black America is grounded in violence and tragedy?

- How might critically analyzing African American nonfiction literature in preschool, elementary, and middle grades better prepare students for the demands of informational literacies in high school and beyond?

- What questions should be asked when educators examine books to see how Black focal subjects and characters, readers, and audiences are being positioned by children's nonfiction texts?

The enduring challenge of finding excellent children's nonfiction featuring Black children, teens, and families for classroom use is an age-old one. In *The Souls of Black Folk*, W. E. B. DuBois (1994) notes the presence of Blackness as always already being a problem, in both reality and imagination:

> Between me and the other world, there is ever an unasked question: unasked by some through feelings of delicacy; by others through the difficulty of rightly framing it. All, nevertheless, flutter round it.... To the real question, How does it feel to be a problem? I answer seldom a word. (p. 1)

The question that DuBois asked more than a century ago still stands sentinel over the presence of Black America in our national letters, culture, and life. That question haunts our nation, including the lives of Black children and families: "How does it feel to be a problem?"

As an African American woman and a scholar of children's literature, I recognize that children's books, including nonfiction, are not exempt from this chilling yet inescapable question. Children's nonfiction has long been considered the literature of fact, a kind of text that invites inquiry and questioning. Thus, when selecting and evaluating nonfiction, there are many questions educators must consider. For example, who will be reading the book? Have the book's creators imagined young readers as being white, middle class, heterosexual, nondisabled students born in the United States, or are child readers from all backgrounds considered? What makes the story difficult? For whom? Does the nature of that difficulty differ depending upon the demographic makeup of a classroom, school, or community? Finally, what are the implications of this text for how children learn about the history of race in the United States, as well as race relations today?

Before considering Black nonfiction for children, it must be noted that it is more common to find Black children in certain kinds of children's literature. For example, realistic genres like contemporary and historical fiction are well represented (Bishop, 1997; Harris, 1997; Nel, 2017). Most African American children's nonfiction focuses on accounts of historical periods (e.g., slavery, the Civil War, or the Civil Rights Movement of the 1960s) or biographies of notable figures (e.g., Harriet Tubman, Frederick Douglass, Rosa Parks, and the Rev. Dr. Martin Luther King Jr.). While there have been notable attempts to fill in the gaps, there is still a great need for Black children to see themselves in the imaginative genres such as science fiction, fantasy, and comics and in nonfiction beyond historical and contemporary settings. Nonfiction texts written by Black authors are an even smaller subset of the larger category.

When African American nonfiction is present in our classrooms and libraries, it often requires readers to confront difficult events in our national past. Many topics frequently found in Black nonfiction for young people—antebellum slavery, de jure segregation in the Jim Crow South, and abiding racial oppression today—contradict scripts. For example, concepts such as the "American Dream," "a nation of immigrants," and "melting pot" perpetuate myths of a benign country. This is not surprising. As Bradford (2007) notes, one of the key functions of children's literature is to "explain and interpret national histories—histories that involve invasion, conquest, and assimilation" (p. 97). However, interpreting these events can prove difficult. Accounts of past events written for elementary and middle school audiences are often framed within a meta-narrative or master story of progress, triumph, and optimism (Thomas, 2012). Although students are learning some valuable information about the past, ultimately, they are learning only a single story (Adichie, 2009)—that of the unassailable American Dream.

Because children's nonfiction is a primary means for the transmission of national histories, it is perhaps unsurprising that myths about the United States pervade historical children's nonfiction (see Forest et al., 2015; Schwebel, 2011). Specifically, African American historical children's nonfiction is often packaged, contextualized, and retold in ways that reinforce the message that principles of liberty and equality always prevailed over slavery, Jim Crow, and racism (Thomas, 2012).

The doctrine of American exceptionalism collides with a mandate common in children's literature that "no matter how realistically it is presented . . . books should end on a note of optimism, or at least hope" (Reynolds, 2007, p. 89). While exceptions abound, such as Connecticut poet laureate Marilyn Nelson's (2005) heartrending *A Wreath for Emmett Till*, African American children's historical nonfiction must do more than transmit information about the past. It has a reparative function—it must humanize and liberate. It must provide true stories that uplift, give hope, and heal.

Unfortunately, the lived realities of many of today's students clash with the master narratives found in some African American nonfiction. Although not strictly nonfiction, *Fortune's Bones: The Manumission Requiem* (Nelson, 2004) contains reproductions and references to primary sources throughout the text, as well as additional notes and lists of source material at the end of the book. In one poem, Nelson (2004) masterfully uses Buddhist monk Thích Nhất Hạnh's Vietnam War–era teachings to memorialize an enslaved man whose skeleton was publicly displayed for over two centuries:

You can own someone's body,
but the soul runs free.
It roams the night sky's
mute geometry.
You can murder hope, you can pound faith flat,
but like weeds and wildflowers, they grow right back.
For you are not your body,
you are not your body. (p. 25)

These are moving words indeed. However, many young readers' lived experiences may differ from those they read about in nonfiction and this may make them feel disconnected. And yet, in the age of Trayvon Martin, Michael Brown, Tamir Rice, stop-and-frisk policies, and "the new Jim Crow" (Alexander, 2012), many students of color might say, "Yes, they are indeed their bodies," in response to Nelson's lyrical poem.

This is not to discredit the growing number of children's nonfiction books that wrestle with traumatic events in history in nuanced ways. However, we also need "new and better stories, new concepts, and new vocabularies and grammar based on not the past but on the dangerous, exciting, and unexplored present" (Johnson, 2008, p. 42). In other words, to improve student motivation and engagement with nonfiction literature and history, we would do well to invite students to critically analyze what they are reading so it is also relevant to their lives today. African American children's nonfiction provides a potential space for both liberating and humanizing Black people—and it has been doing so for a long time.

Histories and Trends in Depicting African Americans in Children's Nonfiction

Although it is often noted that Larrick's (1965) *Saturday Review* article, "The All-White World of Children's Books," was the first major examination of the depiction of African Americans in children's literature (see Forest et al., 2015; Pescosolido et al., 1997), this vital work of humanizing Black children in literature goes back much further in the past (Bishop, 2007; Sims, 1982). African American parents, educators, and clergy were noting and writing about problematic representations of Black people in children's books as early as the mid-nineteenth century (Bishop, 2007; Connolly, 2013). To address the pervasive erasure and caricaturizing of Black children, church publications such as the African Methodist Episcopal Church's *Christian Recorder* and *The Repository* contained material for children and youth. These early publications were often didactic and evangelical in tone, intended to convey Victorian-era morals to their young audience.

With the first breath of the Harlem Renaissance, however, came the National Association for the Advancement of Colored People's periodical magazine *The Brownies' Book*, where luminaries such as Langston Hughes first were published. Hughes, along with contemporaries Arna Bontemps and Countee Cullen, were among the first to produce children's literature and poetry specifically featuring Black children. Meanwhile, Charlamae Hill Rollins at the Chicago Public Library (starting in 1927) and Augusta Braxton Baker at the New York Public Library (starting in 1937) did much to influence the development of the field (Yokota, 1993), as did the rise of Dr. Carter G. Woodson's Negro History Week, which later evolved into Black History Month.

During and after the Harlem Renaissance, writers began to position African Americans as active agents fighting for their own physical, social, and economic liberation from stifling oppression. As Capshaw Smith (2006) observed, "the major writers of the time were deeply invested in the enterprise of building a Black national identity through literary constructions of childhood" (p. xiii). Thus, much of the impetus of mid-century African American children's literature, including nonfiction, during the Civil Rights era and Black Arts Movement was reparative, telling celebratory tales about the victories and the achievements of African Americans in spite of collective trauma and monumental odds. These books promoted a bourgeois ideology of racial uplift and encouraged young people to lead the race politically and socially toward American ideals of progress and individual achievement.

However, despite the flowering of Black children's books in the mid- and late twentieth century, recent reports from the Cooperative Children's Book Center (2020) at the University of Wisconsin reveal the persistence of a diversity gap, including books by and about African American people. While there have been many rationales posited for the persistence of the diversity gap in children's literature, because of celebrations like Black History Month and the national holiday commemorating the Rev. Dr. Martin Luther King Jr., many of the small number of titles published annually are historical in nature.

Trauma and Healing in Subgenres of African American Children's Nonfiction

While many African American children's nonfiction titles reflect an emphasis on history by focusing on past events or figures, others are more contemporary in nature. This section foregrounds exemplary titles found across a number of the most common subgenres of nonfiction featuring Black focal subjects. Many of the featured titles do provide information confirming that the story of Black America is grounded in violence and tragedy, but all of the books also provide opportunities to uplift, give hope, and promote healing.

Biography

Biographies written for children convey information about a person's life and experiences. Often, these nonfiction books focus on people who have made significant contributions to society or who have achieved greatness in spite of tremendous hardships (Duke & Tower, 2004). Vashti Harrison has written three collective biographies for young readers; *Little Leaders: Bold Women in Black History* (Harrison, 2017) and *Little Legends: Exceptional Men in Black History* (Harrison, 2019) are picturebooks that describe the lives of notable African American women and men. The books include source material and features such as recommended further reading. *Dream Big, Little One* (Harrison, 2018) is a board book adaptation of *Little Leaders: Bold Women in Black History* and provides a way for educators and caregivers to begin talking about these important individuals with the youngest of children.

In addition to collective biographies, there are also numerous examples of single-subject biographies of African American individuals written for young readers. *My Story, My Dance: Robert Battle's Journey to Alvin Ailey* (Cline-Ransome, 2015) focuses on the life of Robert Battle, the current artistic director of the Alvin Ailey American Dance Theater. When he was young, Battle faced many hardships and wore painful leg braces that limited his movement. Through the support of educators and his family, including the cousin who raised him, Battle learned martial arts before developing a passion for ballet that led him to the Juilliard School and a successful career in dance. James Ransome's pastel illustrations are accompanied by actual photographs of Battle and quickly establish the warm tone of the book, capturing the essence of the focal subject's difficulties and triumphs. The book includes a foreword by Battle himself, as well as lists of references, sources for further reading, and an author's note. *Little Melba and Her Big Trombone* (Russell-Brown, 2014) tells the story of Melba Doretta Liston, who, throughout her life, loved music. Born in Kansas City in 1926, Liston would overcome racial and gender-based barriers to play jazz trombone. She became famous as a trombonist accompanying many well-known jazz age musicians like Duke Ellington, Quincy Jones, and Billie Holiday. The book includes an afterword, selected discography, and detailed author's sources (including books and articles, interviews and radio broadcasts, and websites).

Narrative Nonfiction

Narrative nonfiction "uses all of the best techniques of fiction writing: plot, character development, voice, and theme . . . without making anything up" (Partridge, 2011, p. 70). One such fascinating text is Michael Cottman's (2017) *Shackles from the Deep: Tracing the Path of a Sunken Slave Ship, a Bitter Past, and a Rich Legacy*. The book, an adaptation of an adult text titled *The Wreck of the Henrietta Marie: An African American's Spiritual Journey to Uncover a Sunken Slave Ship's Past* (Cottman, 1999), highlights information related to Cottman's historical investigations into the slave trade, specifically surrounding the loss of the slave ship the *Henrietta Marie* and, more important, the people on board that ship. The narrative nonfiction format of the text allows readers to share in Cottman's own feelings of connection to his African ancestors when he writes about holding a set of shackles that were once worn by those on board the *Henrietta Marie*. The book also highlights Cottman's own journey, including his travels in order to conduct research and what he subsequently learns about the slave trade, weaponry of the time, and much more. Elements common to nonfiction include a timeline, maps, recommendations for further reading, a list of resources, photos of artifacts, and an index.

Tonya Bolden's (2002) *Tell All the Children Our Story: Memories and Mementos of Being Young and Black in America* is formatted as a scrapbook and, through both visuals and narrative, highlights Black children across American history. Although some of the stories may be familiar to readers, Bolden works to highlight the lives of lesser-known individuals and events, such as the birth of the first child of African descent born in Jamestown. Divided into three sections, the book uniquely documents the stories of African Americans, from those who first arrived as enslaved people through the major events and time periods that followed in the United States, including the Revolutionary and Civil Wars through Reconstruction, the Civil Rights Movement, and through the present day. Intriguingly presented, the book combines unusual and varied art, including period photographs, paintings and drawings, cartoons, and reproductions of letters, journals, and other primary sources.

Memoir

Memoir brings together characteristics of biography and narrative nonfiction, telling the story of a person's life, usually written by that individual, with a greater focus on broader events that happened during the author's lifetime. It differs from autobiography in that it is not a strict retelling of facts, but also includes the more narrative elements of establishing emotional connections without the expectation of complete accuracy. Not surprisingly, perhaps, many memoirs by and about African American people focus on the stories of individuals who lived through and were involved with the Civil Rights Movement. Several of these books share perspectives of previously unheard voices, while others are structured in interesting and innovative ways.

Lynda Blackmon Lowery (2015) describes her role as the youngest marcher from Selma to Montgomery in *Turning 15 on the Road to Freedom: My Story of the 1965 Selma Voting Rights March*. Traditionally, readers learn about this march through stories of its leaders, including Congressman John Lewis or Amelia Boynton. This makes a memoir told from the perspective of someone who was a child at the time especially unique and potentially powerful for young readers who may be around the same age themselves. Lowery's voice is particularly unique in that she was willing to fight for what she believed in, even if it meant being jailed eleven times before she turned fifteen. At the same time, and despite severe violence being inflicted upon her, she maintained a nonviolent stance, standing beside the Rev. Dr. Martin Luther King Jr. for the rights of African American people. Accompanied by stark black-and-white illustrations by P. J. Loughran and period-specific photographs, the book is both straightforward and inspiring. In addition to acknowledgments, the book includes photo credits, author and illustrator notes, and an interview with the author covering topics like segregation, children's involvement in the making of history, and voting rights.

A relatively new genre, the graphic memoir is a form of both graphic novel and nonfiction text, both a history book and a memoir that is easily identified by its paneled (comic) illustration format as a primary means of conveying information. Perhaps the most famous example of a graphic memoir is the award-winning *March* trilogy by Congressman John Lewis, author Andrew Aydin, and illustrator Nate Powell. Told across three volumes, *March* is Lewis's recounting of his own life, as well as the broader events of the Civil Rights Movement in the United States.

Largely told through Lewis's flashback memories on the morning of President Obama's inauguration, *March: Book One* (Lewis & Aydin, 2013) covers Lewis's childhood and early years in the Civil Rights Movement. This volume includes information about *Brown v. Board of Education*, Emmett Till, Lewis's interactions with Civil Rights leaders like Rosa Parks and the Rev. Dr. Martin Luther King Jr., and his involvement as a college student in sit-ins at lunch counters in Nashville, Tennessee. The second volume, *March: Book Two* (Lewis & Aydin, 2015), begins by showing Lewis's attempts to build on the success of lunch counter integration by also working to integrate Nashville movie theaters. It then portrays Lewis's journey as a Freedom Rider and his eventual election, at age twenty-three, as chairman of the Student Nonviolent Coordinating Committee. In this volume, Lewis enters the national stage of the Civil Rights Movement at the March on Washington. *March: Book Three* (Lewis & Aydin, 2016) begins where *Book Two* left off, with the bombings of several churches, and focuses primarily on the right to vote and efforts to increase access to voter registration in the South. The third volume culminates with the march from Selma to Montgomery, followed not long thereafter by the signing into law of the 1965 Voting Rights Act. On its release, the *March* trilogy had a deep impact on children's publishing, not only because of its first-person account but also due to the visual impact of Powell's black-and-white illustrations of both Lewis's life and the events through which he lived.

By no means do these three broad categories constitute an exhaustive list. Many other types of African American nonfiction and informational books are available for young readers, including concept books such as *What Is Light?* (Sheppard, 2018), fictionalized biographies like *We Are the Ship: The Story of Negro League Baseball* (Nelson, 2008), biographical poetry such as *Carver: A Life in Poems* (Nelson, 2001), or informational text like *Making Our Way Home: The Great Migration and the Black American Dream* (Imani, 2020). These books can provide additional perspectives and voices; they go beyond merely transmitting information about experiences (both past and present) of Black Americans.

Challenges and Possibilities of Teaching with African American Children's Nonfiction

While there have been a fair number of key studies of African American children's books in education (see Harris, 1990; Sims, 1982; Tyson, 2002), examinations of the literature have focused on literary and didactic features of texts. Perhaps the most comprehensive recent review of African American children's literature was Brooks and McNair's (2009) report for *Review of Educational Research*. They divided existing research into three categories: African American children's literature as contested terrain, African American children's literature as cultural artifact, and African American children's literature as literary art. In comparison, research specific to African American nonfiction children's books has been limited.

Reading nonfiction has always created opportunities for students to extend their understanding of history in ways that challenge or complicate positive representations of traumatic events. All narratives—whether factual or fictional—are always contested representations of truth, embedded in language, culture, institutions, and politics. While the challenges of teaching history through literature have been taken up more generally in various content area studies (see Baker, 1984; Boerman-Cornell, 2011; Cole, 2007; Kharem, 2006; Loewen, 1996; Nodelman, 1990; Oglesby, 2007), criticism and research on African American children's nonfiction have been taken up less often. This is unfortunate. As we provide nonfiction texts and facilitate reading and discussion in our classrooms and other spaces, educators have to consider the history and voices presented by the texts (Edinger, 1998, 2000; Martin, 2004).

Using children's literature—even nonfiction—to teach history can be problematic. This is, at least in part, because the English language arts curriculum is much more than learning how to read and write. It is about students learning to read and write in sanctioned, socially acceptable ways. Luke (2004) has suggested we characterize the ultimate purpose of English language arts education as "political interventions, struggles over the formation of ideologies and beliefs, identities and capital" (p. 86). These interventions and struggles happen in libraries and classrooms all over the nation through direct and indirect instruction in language, literature, and history.

In previous work, I have described four prevalent metanarratives about the African American presence in the United States as found in primary source documents and textbooks—(1) secular triumph, (2) spiritual pilgrimage, (3) sociological reaction, and (4) cultural and/or biological deficit (Thomas, 2012). The *triumph* metanarrative is reparative, resulting from the celebratory tales told about the victories and the achievements of African Americans in spite of collective trauma and monumental odds. The metanarrative of *pilgrimage* presents Black suffering within the context of a collective metaphysical journey. On the other side of the coin, the *reaction* metanarrative views a distinctive African American identity as a phenomenon that evolved during slavery and segregation, and states that Black cultural markers are the cause of continued racism; it is an extension of the "melting pot" master story about the United States of America. Finally, and most maliciously, the *deficit* metanarrative positions people of African descent as inherently deficient. Although there are many other stories about the Black presence in the United States, these four broad explanatory tales can be found in every aspect of American culture—including in its literature for young people. Often, narratives of triumph prevail in African American children's nonfiction, perhaps to ameliorate the deficit, reaction, and pilgrimage metanarratives that prevailed before the Harlem Renaissance.

If our master stories about African American literature (including nonfiction), culture, and history are not informed by literary theory, politics, and cultural criticism (as well as the lived experiences of African Americans across a variety of spectra), we run the risk of perpetuating myths that have little basis in fact—or, perhaps worse, that present only a portion of the entire story.

The Challenges of Representation and Guidelines for Evaluating African American Children's Nonfiction

Writing of Holocaust literature, Dutro (2008) argues powerfully for centering collective trauma in our teaching of literature, especially in light of the challenging life experiences many of our students bring with them into the classroom. She writes of Holocaust literature:

> Teachers ask students—require them, actually—to be witnesses to testimony when Holocaust literature is included in courses. It is possible to predict that the tenor of such a collective reading experience would be somber, empathetic, and difficult, and that the talk around such texts ought to raise deep, immensely challenging feelings and questions surrounding life, death, and human capacity for evil and resilience. (Dutro, 2008, p. 427)

The same can be said of African American nonfiction children's literature, as well.

The social and emotional dimensions of students' literary responses must be considered when teaching about traumatic events too. As Africana Studies scholar Byerman (2006) notes, "If the African American story is one of extended Holocaust, then the national history cannot be understood as primarily the story of individual achievement and democratic progress" (p. 3). One of the tacit resolutions of the Civil Rights Movement was a national decision to begin the journey beyond slavery and the early period of race relations—and included the evasion of lingering questions, repression of unpleasant or embarrassing histories, and a desire not to see. However, if history is indeed a palimpsest, with lingering traces upon which each successive generation recasts details, characters, and events in order to respond to foregrounded concerns of the present, then it is useful to examine the place of African American nonfiction children's books as a space of artistic and critical resistance. At the same time, it is also useful to interrogate the ways in which we narrate a past that is purportedly much more violent toward Black bodies and personhood than the present time. Through nonfiction, educators can guide students as they wrestle with the cultural metanarratives of triumph and unfettered progress that are too frequently unquestioned and passed on through curricular materials and literature.

In her comprehensive volume *Free within Ourselves: The Development of African American Children's Literature*, influential African American children's literature scholar Rudine Sims Bishop (2007) provides a five-point summary of the literary tradition created about (and around) African American children and youth. These points also provide succinct guidelines for educators tasked with selecting excellent nonfiction. Authentic African American children's literature:

1. celebrates the strengths of the Black family as a cultural institution and vehicle for survival

2. bears witness to Black people's determined struggle for freedom, equality, and dignity

3. nurtures the souls of Black children by reflecting back to them, both visually and verbally, the beauty and competencies that we as adults see in them

4. situates itself through its language and its content, within African American literary and cultural contexts; and

5. honors the tradition of story as a way of teaching and as a way of knowing. (p. 273)

Conclusion

Given the above criteria, I offer in closing the following questions educators can ask regarding how Black focal subjects and characters, readers, and audiences are being positioned by a children's nonfiction text:

- What kind of story is being told? What kinds of metanarratives, or master stories, does this story tell about Black history, culture, and life?
- Who is telling the story? Is the narrator omniscient or a character within the story? Is the story told from a Black person's perspective or is someone else telling their story for them?
- What are the roles of Black people in the text? Is race or ethnicity the primary focus, or is it relegated to the sidelines? If a particular time period is being presented, is race represented accurately for that era?
- How are Black people represented? Are Black people positioned as human beings with agency, or do they simply exist to prove a point? How are Black bodies positioned or represented in the text and illustrations?

These considerations are critical at a moment in education in which increased emphasis is being placed on informational literacies. For example, following the Common Core State Standards, by the time students reach grade 9, they are required to analyze primary documents of historical and literary significance (e.g., Washington's Farewell Address, the Gettysburg Address, Roosevelt's Four Freedoms speech, King's "Letter from Birmingham Jail"). Educators therefore have a responsibility to prepare students for the demands of informational literacies in high school and beyond. It is critically important, then, for students to have the opportunity to engage with high-quality African American nonfiction that they can then compare with information they are gaining from other sources. Along with considerations of accuracy, educators must also select and share exemplary nonfiction that not only foregrounds the collective trauma experienced by Black people throughout American history, but that also offers opportunities for healing.

Practical Strategies

- Distribute copies of single-subject biographies of African American people. Ask students to identify whose stories are being told, and whose stories are being left out. Is there more to this historical figure than is being portrayed? Why do they think the book creators chose to represent the focal subject in this way?

- Provide students with several nonfiction books about the same historical event told from multiple different perspectives. Ask them to compare and contrast the various retellings and identify whose voices and experiences are included in specific texts and whose are not.

- Locate and use primary sources, such as diaries, letters, and photographs, that show sides to historical African American figures that are not shown in social studies textbooks. After examining these sources alongside the textbook, ask students to consider why certain stories about these historical figures are taught while others are not.

- Have your students do author or illustrator studies focused on various African American nonfiction book creators. Investigate their qualifications and/or their reasons for doing this work. Do they speak to their research and artistic processes? Have students identify ways one can go about checking them for accuracy (and then have them do so). Have them discuss their findings.

- Provide students with copies (or adaptations) of the criteria and questions included near the end of this chapter. Use those materials to analyze recent nonfiction winners of the Carter G. Woodson Book Award that depict African American people.

Ten Additional Nonfiction Books about African American People

1. Barton, C. (2018). *What do you do with a voice like that?: The story of extraordinary Congresswoman Barbara Jordan* (E. Holmes, Illus.). Beach Lane Books.

2. Bloomberg, R. (2006). *York's adventures with Lewis & Clark: An African American's part in the great expedition.* Collins.

3. Bolden, T. (2016). *How to build a museum: Smithsonian's National Museum of African American History and Culture.* Viking Books for Young Readers.

4. Bolden, T. (2018). *Facing Frederick: The life of Frederick Douglass, a monumental man.* Abram Books for Young Readers.

5. Bryan, A. (2016). *Freedom over me: Eleven slaves, their lives and dreams brought to life by Ashley Bryan* (A. Bryan, Illus.). Simon & Schuster.

6. Cline-Ransome, L. (2018). *Game changers: The story of Venus and Serena Williams* (J. E. Ransome, Illus.). Simon & Schuster.

7. Nelson, V. M. (2019). *Let 'er buck! George Fletcher, the people's champion* (G. C. James, Illus.). Carolrhoda Books.

8. Nelson, K., & Obama, B. (2009). *Change has come: An artist celebrates our American spirit* (K. Nelson, Illus.). Simon & Schuster.

9. Shetterly, M. L. (2018). *Hidden figures: The true story of four Black women and the space race* (L. Freeman, Illus.). HarperCollins.

10. Wallace, S. N. (2018). *Between the lines: How Ernie Barnes went from the football field to the art gallery* (B. Collier, Illus.). Simon & Schuster.

Five Online Resources

1. The Brown Bookshelf. (2021). *About the Brown Bookshelf.* https://thebrownbookshelf.com

2. Campbell, E. (2021). *CrazyQuiltEdi.* https://crazyquiltedi.blog

3. Dunn, J. L. (2021, February 3). *Our new name: Learning for justice.* https://www.learningforjustice.org/magazine/our-new-name-learning-for-justice

4. Just Us Books, Inc. Store. (n.d.). https://justusbooks.com

5. Teaching for Change. (n.d.). Social Justice Books: A Teaching for Change project. https://socialjusticebooks.org

Book Award

- Coretta Scott King Book Awards—see http://www.ala.org/rt/emiert/cskbookawards

Children's Books Cited

Bolden, T. (2002). *Tell all the children our story: Memories and mementos of being young and black in America.* Harry N. Abrams.

Cline-Ransome, L. (2015). *My story, my dance: Robert Battle's journey to Alvin Ailey* (J. E. Ransome, Illus.). Simon & Schuster.

Cottman, M. H. (2017). *Shackles from the deep: Tracing the path of a sunken slave ship, a bitter past, and a rich legacy.* National Geographic Children's Books.

Harrison, V. (2017). *Little leaders: Bold women in black history* (V. Harrison, Illus.). Little, Brown Books for Young Readers.

Harrison, V. (2018). *Dream big, little one* (V. Harrison, Illus.). Little, Brown Books for Young Readers.

Harrison, V. (2019). *Little legends: Exceptional men in black history* (V. Harrison, Illus.). Little, Brown Books for Young Readers.

Imani, B. (2020). *Making our way home: The great migration and the Black American dream* (R. Baker, Illus.). Ten Speed Press.

Lewis, J., & Aydin, A. (2013). *March: Book one* (N. Powell, Illus.). Top Shelf Productions.

Lewis, J., & Aydin, A. (2015). *March: Book two* (N. Powell, Illus.). Top Shelf Productions.

Lewis, J., & Aydin, A. (2016). *March: Book three* (N. Powell, Illus.). Top Shelf Productions.

Lowery, L. B. (2015). *Turning 15 on the road to freedom: My story of the 1965 Selma Voting Rights March* (P. J. Loughran, Illus.). Speak.

Nelson, M. (2001). *Carver: A life in poems.* Front Street Press.

Nelson, M. (2004). *Fortune's bones: The Manumission Requiem.* Front Street Press.

Nelson, M. (2005). *A wreath for Emmett Till* (P. Lardy, Illus.). Houghton Mifflin.

Nelson, K. (2008). *We are the ship: The story of Negro League baseball* (K. Nelson, Illus.). Little, Brown Books for Young Readers.

Russell-Brown, K. (2014). *Little Melba and her big trombone* (F. Morrison, Illus.). Lee & Low Books.

Sheppard, M. (2018). *What is light?* (C. A. Johnson, Illus.). Simon & Schuster Books for Young Readers.

References

Adichie, C. N. (2009, July). *The danger of a single story* [Video]. TED Conferences. https://www.ted.com/talks/chimamanda_adichie_the_danger_of_a_single_story.html

Alexander, M. (2012). *The new Jim Crow: Mass incarceration in the age of colorblindness*. New Press.

Baker, H. A. (1984). *Blues, ideology, and Afro-American literature: A vernacular theory*. University of Chicago Press.

Bishop, R. S. (1997). Selecting literature for a multicultural curriculum. In V. Harris (Ed.), *Using multiethnic literature in the K–8 classroom* (pp. 1–19). Christopher-Gordon.

Bishop, R. S. (2007). *Free within ourselves: The development of African American children's literature*. Greenwood Press.

Boerman-Cornell, W. (2011). *Learning to see history: A content analysis of the affordances of graphic novels for high school teaching* [Unpublished doctoral dissertation]. University of Illinois at Chicago.

Bradford, C. (2007). *Unsettling narratives: Postcolonial readings of children's literature*. Wilfrid Laurier University Press.

Brooks, W., & McNair, J. C. (2009). "But this story of mine is not unique": A review of research on African American children's literature. *Review of Educational Research*, *79*(1), 125–162. https://doi.org/10.3102/0034654308324653

Byerman, K. E. (2006). *Remembering the past in contemporary African American fiction*. University of North Carolina Press.

Capshaw Smith, K. (2006). *Children's literature of the Harlem Renaissance*. Indiana University Press.

Cole, E. A. (2007). Introduction: Reconciliation and history education. In E. A. Cole (Ed.), *Teaching the violent past: History education and reconciliation* (pp. 1–30). Rowman & Littlefield.

Connolly, P. T. (2013). *Slavery in American children's literature, 1790–2010*. University of Iowa Press.

Cooperative Children's Book Center. (2020, October 27). *Children's books by and/or about Black, Indigenous and people of color received by the CCBC, 2018–*. CCBC Diversity Statistics. https://ccbc.education.wisc.edu/literature-resources/ccbc-diversity-statistics/books-by-about-poc-fnn

Cottman, M. H. (1999). *The wreck of the Henrietta Marie: An African-American's spiritual journey to uncover a sunken slave ship's past*. Harmony Books.

DuBois, W. E. B. (1994). *The souls of Black folk*. Dover Publications.

Dutro, E. (2008). "That's why I was crying on this book": Trauma as testimony in responses to literature. *Changing English*, *15*(4), 423–434. https://doi.org/10.1080/13586840802493076

Edinger, M. (1998). *Far away and long ago: Young historians in the classroom*. Stenhouse.

Edinger, M. (2000). *Seeking history: Teaching with primary sources in grades 4–6*. Heinemann.

Forest, D. E., Garrison, K. L., & Kimmel, S. C. (2015). "The university for the poor": Portrayals of class in translated children's literature. *Teachers College Record, 117*(2), 1–40.

Harris, V. J. (1990). African American children's literature: The first one hundred years. *Journal of Negro Education, 59*(4), 540–555. https://doi.org/10.2307/2295311

Harris, V. (1997). Children's literature depicting blacks. In V. Harris (Ed.), *Using multiethnic literature in the K–8 classroom* (pp. 1–19). Christopher-Gordon.

Johnson, C. (2008). The end of the Black American narrative. *American Scholar, 77*(3), 32–42.

Kharem, H. (2006). *A curriculum of repression: A pedagogy of racial history in the United States*. Peter Lang.

Larrick, N. (1965). The all-white world of children's books. *Saturday Review, 11*(11), 63–65.

Loewen, J. W. (1996). *Lies my teacher told me: Everything your American history textbook got wrong*. Touchstone.

Luke, A. (2004). At last: The trouble with English. *Research in the Teaching of English, 39*(1), 85–95.

Martin, M. (2004). *Brown gold: Milestones of African American children's picture books, 1845–2002*. Routledge.

Nel, P. (2017). *Was the Cat in the Hat Black?: The hidden racism of children's literature and the need for diverse books*. Oxford University Press.

Nodelman, P. (1990). History as fiction: The story in Hendrik Willem van Loon's "Story of Mankind." *The Lion and the Unicorn, 14*(1), 70–86.

Oglesby, E. (2007). Historical memory and the limits of peace education: Examining Guatemala's memory of silence and the politics of curriculum design. In E. A. Cole (Ed.), *Teaching the violent past: History education and reconciliation* (pp. 175–204). Rowman & Littlefield.

Pescosolido, B. A., Grauerholz, E., & Milkie, M. A. (1997). Culture and conflict: The portrayal of Blacks in U.S. children's picture books through the mid- and late-twentieth century. *American Sociological Review, 62*(3), 443–464. https://doi.org/10.2307/2657315

Reynolds, K. (2007). *Radical children's literature: Future visions and aesthetic transformations in juvenile fiction*. Palgrave Macmillan.

Schwebel, S. (2011). *Child-sized history: Fictions of the past in U.S. classrooms*. Vanderbilt University Press.

Sims, R. (1982). *Shadow and substance: Afro-American experience in contemporary children's fiction*. National Council of Teachers of English.

Thomas, E. E. (2012). The next chapter of our story: Rethinking African American metanarratives in schooling and society. In E. E. Thomas & S. R. F. Brooks-Tatum (Eds.), *Reading African American experiences in the Obama era: Theory, advocacy, activism* (pp. 29–50). Peter Lang.

Tyson, C. A. (2002). "Get up offa that thing": African American middle school students respond to literature to develop a framework for understanding social action. *Theory & Research in Social Education, 30*(1), 42–65. https://doi.org/10.1080/00933104.2002.10473178

6

Cultural Dexterity through Multiracial Nonfiction

AMINA CHAUDHRI, *Northeastern Illinois University*

If I stop and watch
I see young and old
Indians, Negroes, Whites—
All mixed together.

—PATRICIA HRUBY POWELL, *Loving vs. Virginia*

Nonfiction literature about multiracial experiences is limited to books about diverse families and biographies. In this chapter, a small corpus of titles is analyzed using a lens of cultural dexterity to highlight the pedagogical possibilities embedded in quality nonfiction about multiraciality. While readers, book creators, and publishers may view the concept of mixed families with dissonance, the books both highlight and counter this with depictions of confident and loving multiracial families. Ultimately, this selection of titles can encourage readers to consider their own partial lenses, the ideologies they may have absorbed, and to consider the construct of racial identity in general, and multiracial identity in particular.

Chapter Guiding Questions

- How has the construct of multiracial identity been historically, socially, and politically shaped? How is it changing?
- In what ways are nonfiction accounts of multiracial experiences in children's literature useful for readers imagining different ways of thinking about identity?
- What are some important factors to consider when identifying potential multiracial nonfiction books for classrooms and libraries?

• How might teachers use multiracial nonfiction as a part of their culturally responsive pedagogy?

Contemporary Multiracial America

To speak about multiracial identity is to try to pin down a wriggling, shifting thing and give it shapes, edges, and features that it simultaneously embraces and rejects. It means assuming that there are discrete racial categories (e.g., white, Black) that can be combined to create others: mixed, multiracial, biracial, mestiza, hapa; quanta of full, half, quarter lineages; and impossible percentages that refer primarily to biology and occasionally to historical or cultural ancestry. It means collapsing centuries of human contact into language that casts a false sense of recentness to a phenomenon that defies temporality. Even the language evades definition; mixed, multiracial, biracial, hapa, and mestizo/mestiza, and mixed-blood have replaced mulatto, octoroon, half-blood, and other labels once common but now considered derogatory. Portmanteaus—blended words, such as *Blaxican*, *Amerasian*, *Eurasian*, and *Afroasian*—abound. Mildred Loving's fictionalized words in the epigraph quoted at the start of this chapter reflect labels she would have known in the early twentieth century. Identity labels can be confusing; they limit and define and are laced with subtext and assumptions. Yet labels provide the language with which to talk about the construction of identity. Labels are also contextually bound. I grew up in Pakistan, the child of a white, English mother and a Brown, Pakistani father in a postcolonial context so riddled with history that my being "mixed" was just another way of being. It was not until I immigrated to the US and found myself having to respond to the inevitable "What are you?" and "Where are you (really) from?" questions that I had to become biracial. It is a label that hovers around me, there when I need it, invisible when I don't.

Throughout American history, the strategic use of identity labels in public discourse is becoming more frequent as whiteness, formerly unnamed and invisible, is regularly implicated in police brutality of men of color, in white supremacist activism, and as progressive whites struggle to define themselves in opposition to those tropes. For multiracial Americans, the taxonomic language of a complex history of slavery, colonialism, civil rights, multiculturalism, assimilation, and immigration has resulted in identifications that are constantly shifting. In this chapter, for example, I use the terms *mixed-race*, *multiracial*, and *biracial* interchangeably to preclude linguistic monotony, but also to be inclusive of some of the ways people identify today and to draw attention to the mutability of language in this context.

Another way to clarify and define is to reach for landmark moments and statistical data. For instance, in 2000 the US Census permitted participants to select multiple racial categories from among the given choices, and, that year, 6.8 million people did so. A decade later, that number rose to more than nine million. This national recognition of multiracial identity served as a form of validation, for, as Maria P. P. Root (1992) reminds us, "in essence, to name oneself is to validate one's existence and declare visibility" (p. 7). In 2006, Kip Fulbeck's The Hapa Project, through a museum exhibition (2006a) and an accompanying book (2006b), drew attention to the various and fluid ways people identified racially. President Obama's election in 2008 caused some tumult as biracials and African Americans rushed to claim him as theirs. The mainstream media's penchant for du jour multiculturalism is also evidenced in their fascination with Meghan Markel, a member of Britain's royal family, who is of white and African American descent. Gradually, but firmly, multiracial identity has nudged its way into the corners of the national discourse about race and has the potential to influence the ways we think about racial identity construction.

Multiracial Children's Literature

The year 2017 marked the fiftieth anniversary of the 1967 unanimous Supreme Court decision to overturn the ban on interracial marriage. In the world of children's and young adult literature, two notable nonfiction books brought this decision to the forefront: *The Case for Loving: The Fight for Interracial Marriage* by Selina Alko (2015) and *Loving vs. Virginia: A Documentary Novel of the Landmark Civil Rights Case* by Patricia Hruby Powell (2017). According to reports from the *New York Times* (Saulny, 2017) and Pew Research Center (Morin, 2015), mixed-race youth are the fastest growing demographic, and one in seven infants in 2017 was multiracial. This increase in the number of multiracial school-age children should be of interest to educators and planners of curricula. However, data from the Cooperative Children's Book Center (2017) indicates that less than 10 percent of publications are by and about people of color. Further, studies in children's literature—fiction and nonfiction—point to a dearth of books with biracial content (Chaudhri & Teale, 2013; Yokota & Frost, 2003).

I provide this context in order to frame the discussion of the limits and possibilities of the nonfiction books analyzed here. As a theoretical framework, I draw on Sheryll Cashin's (2017) idea of *cultural dexterity*, a process of personal and social transformation that involves the recognition of racial differences as social assets and an examination of internalized biases that prevent us from welcoming difference into our lives. In this regard, cultural dexterity shares traits with cultural pluralism, wherein smaller populations of people maintain their unique cultural identities. It also provides a lens through which to examine nonfiction literature with multiracial content. First, I share examples of books for emergent and early elementary-grade readers, picturebooks that celebrate diversity in family units. Next, I demonstrate the potential ways Alko (2015) and Hruby Powell's (2017) books about the *Loving* case encourage elementary, middle, and high school readers to develop language and understandings about racial difference and race as constructs. The third section analyzes two biographies of Barack Obama, one for younger and the other for older readers. A feature common across all these books is that the authors integrate interracial and multiracial experiences explicitly through language and image, allowing educators to scaffold discussions about the complicated construct of race.

Availability and Accessibility of Nonfiction Books Depicting Biracial People

The scarcity of multiracial nonfiction books for children (my extensive searches resulted in just seventy-six titles) is troubling as it means that educators seeking quality literature for their classrooms have limited options. Further, the availability of books seems tied to historical context, which means that readers are subject to what the publishing industry deems profitable. Emerging on the heels of the Civil Rights Movement, groups like the Association of Multiethnic Americans, A Place for US, and Reclassify all Children Equally became vocal, in the late 1980s and early 1990s, about the ways schools and other institutions prescribed racial demographics. This was also around the time that several authors published resource books for caregivers and teens about "coping" with biracial identity (Nash, 1995; Rosenberg, 1986).

Educators searching for nonfiction about multiracial experiences are very likely to find biographies of notable people. Publication dates for the biographies of celebrities coincide with peaks in their careers. There was a surge in books about Tiger Woods, but several are now out of print, presumably a result of his fall from grace. In their study of biographies of Barack Obama, May et al. (2010) note that more than twenty books were published between 2006 and 2008, and that number continued to rise during his presidency. Perhaps in an effort to stay current with the Census change that permitted multiple racial identifications in 2000, Simon & Schuster launched a series of biographies titled Transcending Race in America: Biographies of Biracial Achievers. The series celebrates the accomplishments of contemporary notables such as Beyoncé, Prince, Salma Hayek, and Soledad O'Brien, and historical figures like Rosa Parks, Frederick Douglass, and W. E. B. DuBois. This suggests that, for better or for worse, recognition of biracial exceptionalism will continue to keep some individuals in the public eye.

In terms of genre, there is currently little variety within the realm of children's nonfiction literature on this topic. The predominance of biographies is perhaps not surprising. In fact, the celebratory tone of these biographies stands in contrast to the grim portrayal of some biracial characters in children's fiction. The titles I selected for analysis in this chapter are almost anomalies in their unique styles and formats. Most of the seventy-six titles I identified are informational texts with traditional expository narratives and features such as timelines, linear chronologies, and fact boxes. In the subsequent sections, I highlight the unique text features of the titles included here so that educators can appreciate the books for their pedagogical potential as well as for their multiracial content.

The diversity within today's multiracial population is not reflected in the literature. With the exception of a few books, almost all feature people of Black and white racial heritage. Two exceptions are *I Am Hapa*, by Crystal Smith (2016), with photographs from Michael Satoshi Garcia, and *Mixed: Portraits of Multiracial Kids*, by Kip Fulbeck (2010), which are both books of photographic portraits of children, accompanied by brief descriptive text about myriad components of identity, and include a variety of racial mixes. Departing from contemporary depictions, Andrea Davis Pinkney's (2012) acclaimed *Hand in Hand: Ten Black Men Who Changed America* (illustrated by Brian Pinkney) and artist–storyteller Morgan Monceaux's (1999) *My Heroes, My People: African American and Native Americans in the West* (written with Ruth Katcher) acknowledge white and Indigenous ancestry in noted African American historical figures.

Cultural Dexterity

Mixed-race nonfiction can develop readers' understanding of the complexity of racial identity construction in text as well as their lives. Cashin (2017) posits the concept of cultural dexterity as a way of dismantling the color line and its associated micro- and macroaggressions. It can be described as a process, an awakening that comes about as a result of new experiences that expand knowledge. Dexterity involves unlearning and relearning ways of being, confronting internalized prejudices, doing the difficult work of "seeing difference and smiling at it" (Cashin, 2017, p. 184). Interracial intimacy (romantic, platonic, familial), Cashin posits, begins the work of dexterity by removing the boundaries between differences and allowing them to exist symbiotically. In opposition to approaches that erase differences in favor of a shared humanity, cultural dexterity reframes difference as integral to our shared humanity and as necessary for social transformation.

Some books about mixed-race experiences provide an opportunity for adults to scaffold learning for young readers that enables them to start thinking actively about—and developing language to talk about—race. The nonfiction titles discussed here are explicit (to varying degrees) about multiracial identity and thus form a small collection of texts pertinent to the process of dexterity. Contact with books that explicitly discuss racial and multiracial identity can be considered part of the process of developing cultural dexterity in readers. Furthermore, the multiracial subjects themselves serve as examples of dexterous people whose lives have been intimately involved with matters of racial identity.

Teaching and Learning with Multiracial Nonfiction

Historically, biography has functioned as a form of conduct literature, intended to shape the child reader's developing self in socially desirable ways (Hintz & Tribunella, 2013). Early biographies for children demonstrated such desirable behaviors in real, upstanding, admired people who were potential role models. A lack of women and people of color in these books led to a push within the multicultural education movement for biographies that included people from marginalized communities, distinctive for their roles in social movements. Biographies of public figures can function to counter the abundant negative stereotypes that children frequently encounter. Furthermore, high-quality informational texts provide the intellectual and pedagogical enrichment that can make them invaluable in reading programs (Fleming et al., 2016, p. 109).

For pedagogical purposes, nonfiction books for children and teens that include mixed-race content offer many of the same text features found in nonfiction books more generally: picture captions, text boxes, sidebars, factoids, and the occasional chart or table. In terms of content, these biographies are often organized chronologically, starting with the subject's birth, which is where their multiracial identity is established through the naming or visual depiction of their phenotypically different parents. The rest of the content focuses on the journeys (childhood, accomplishments in the field, awards, election results, etc.) that resulted in the fame for which they are known, with scarce or no mention of racial identity or its role in those journeys. Essentially, the biographies celebrating the accomplishments of multiracials such as Halle Berry, Alicia Keys, Derek Jeter, Tiger Woods, and Barack Obama are reminiscent of Sims's "melting pot" books: books that appeal to a universal audience. The problem with such narratives, Sims (1982) points out, is that "they make a point of ignoring our differences" (p. 33). However, it is in the recognition that our differences and similarities are coexistent, rather than mutually exclusive, that transformative possibilities lie.

Educators' reasons for choosing nonfiction with multiracial content will vary, but it is likely that, as with other multicultural literature, biracial biographies may be used to teach about life experiences. Mindful educators will know not to take any life story as representative of anything more than it is, or to generalize that all multiracial life experiences are similar. Similarities lie not in people's lives, but in social perceptions of those lives that often manifest in obtrusive questions such as "What are you?" Historically, a misconception about interracial marriages is that they were unsuccessful; a misconception about multiracial people is that they were confused and unstable, unwilling or unable to belong to any group. These perceptions remain evident in a significant amount of children's fiction (Chaudhri, 2017). For example, several accounts in Kip Fulbeck's (2010) *Mixed: Portraits of Multiracial Kids* also testify to the public bewilderment that multiracial families frequently encounter when observers cannot make sense of the family's phenotypical composition. These portraits can be productively used in classroom discussions about why people might ask, "What are you?"

The titles discussed below offer educators opportunities to design teaching and learning experiences that explicitly involve the concept of difference: difference as a fact, as an asset, as an inevitable component of the human experience. These well-written and beautifully illustrated books integrate biracial identity in ways that can encourage readers to explore, analyze, and engage with language and ideas about race, racism, and racial identity.

Books about Families

There is currently an abundance of books that interrupt or preclude perceptions of heteronormative, two-parent, racially homogenous biological families. Today, young readers can see illustrations of and read about families comprising queer parents, single parents, adoptive parents, joint families, and more. Interracial families are often included in these books, rendering multiracial children no different from other children within the broad context of difference. The authors and illustrators of the books analyzed here rely on creative language, art, captions, photographs, memoir, personal experience, and myriad other forms to create realistic, fact-based worlds for their readers that aim to depict the reality of a particular social world.

Picturebooks often rely heavily on phenotype as a marker of racial identity, equating race primarily with skin color and sometimes with hair type and facial features. This simplistic rendering may be appropriate for the emergent readers for whom *A Family Is a Family Is a Family* (O'Leary, 2016) is intended. This book uses humor and originality to introduce readers to differences among and between families. The information readers acquire about multiracial identity is contained in a single two-page spread depicting a brown-skinned and brown-haired woman, a pale-skinned and red-haired man, and a child between them whose skin and hair are a blend of both parents. The text supports the image, stating, "Some people say I look like my dad and some people say I look like my mom. I think I look like myself" (p. 17). The subtext is that this child has been at the receiving end of the dissonance perceived by people trying to categorize her racially. A young reader may or may not pick up on the racial undertones of the depictions and focus instead on the larger-than-life self-portraits that the family is drawing. In the drawings, the apparently multiracial child has drawn herself with the colors that each of her parents has used to draw themselves—green, purple, and maroon—thus inviting consideration away from the actual and more racially recognizable skin tones of the people. In a supported reading of *A Family Is a Family Is a Family*, readers can be directed to share their understanding of the relationship between text and image, articulating and constructing their own meaning of the concept of difference as it pertains to the interracial family in particular, and to other kinds of difference in general. Within a secure environment, drawing on an affirming book such as this one, young readers can form positive associations with the concept of difference, which, if established over time, can preclude or at least diminish the formation of prejudice.

Similarly, *Who's in My Family? All about Our Families*, written by Robie H. Harris (2015) and illustrated by Nadine Bernard Westcott, celebrates all manner of differences (diet, clothing, hobbies, types of homes, and so on) and leaves it to the discerning eye to note that, in some family units, the parents are racially different from each other and the child or children are multiracial. Also by Harris (2016), *Who We Are: All about Being the Same and Being Different*, as the title announces, depicts a many-hued and styled cast of characters whose differences are affirmed. These books do not label differences in conventional language of race and ethnicity; rather, they lead readers to construct their own meaning using visual clues, prior knowledge, and inference. Educators who guide the reading of books like these allow readers to begin to understand the concept of difference with positive associations, planting the seeds of cultural dexterity.

Two books for older readers (early and intermediate elementary grades), both titled *Families*, also highlight differences in family units. The first, *Families* by Susan Kuklin (2010), is a photo documentary that pairs first-person narratives and family portraits. The book features a total of fifteen families, six that I identified as interracial, although only one describes itself as such. All the photographs convey the love and strength shared by family members, which is echoed in the narratives. The book attests to the participants' cultural dexterity in their willingness to welcome the differences within their families and to develop the language with which to articulate it. As a whole, the book provides readers with a textured rendering of family diversity on many levels. The vocabulary of difference is varied, but always positive and affirming. This book could be used as an introduction to a study of the ways people are different. It could also be deconstructed by a readership with a nuanced awareness of difference in order to consider why the children choose to describe their differences in the ways they do. Kuklin's (2010) *Families* could be used as a mentor text in an elementary or middle school writing or art class with students exploring, through text and image, the ways their own families experience difference.

The second book titled *Families*, by Shelley Rotner and Sheila M. Kelly (2016), is a similar tribute to difference without using identity-specific language. It is intended for a younger audience, as evidenced by its simple and spare text and reliance on visual communication. The book begins "There are all kinds of families" (p. 1) and proceeds to describe large, small, single parent, and joint families, lesbian and gay parents, and myriad other family units. Photographs depict a diverse array of people, not just racially, but in other ways too, so readers are left with no doubt as to the endless familial possibilities. Racial differences are apparent among pairs of parents, between parents and children, and in pictures of large family gatherings in which all sorts of skin tones are evident. Laughing faces and happily engaged people bear testimony to a cultural dexterity that, Cashin would agree, begins with familial intimacy and proximity.

Books about Loving v. Virginia

Selina Alko (2015) and Sean Qualls's beautiful narrative nonfiction picturebook *The Case for Loving: The Fight for Interracial Marriage* introduces Mildred and Richard Loving's story to a primary or early elementary-grade readership. Alko's language is both evocative and straightforward in laying out the injustice Richard and Mildred faced:

> The two were in love; they felt it should be their right to get married. Sadly, it was not. Not in Virginia or sixteen other states. In those places, marriage between people of different races was against the law! (p. 7)

The Case for Loving does not sugarcoat or evade the cruelty of racism. Alko trusts her readers to bear witness to the terror Mildred and Richard must have felt when the police burst into their bedroom, arresting them for "unlawful cohabitation" (pp. 12–13), and the pain they experienced having to leave their home and live in exile in Washington, DC. In the author's note, Alko connects her own interracial family (she is white and her husband, and the book's other illustrator, Sean Qualls, is African American) to the *Loving* case, pointing out their lives would not be possible without that victory. Alko's work is aligned with Cashin's (2017) belief that, "for the culturally dexterous, race is *more* salient, not less, and difference is a source of wonder, not fear" (p. 5, emphasis in original). Readers will come away with a bittersweet story of victory, the knowledge that laws can be unjust, and that there are places, like Central Point, Virginia, where people of different races lived and loved despite the racist contexts of the time.

Loving vs. Virginia: A Documentary Novel of the Landmark Civil Rights Case, written by Patricia Hruby Powell (2017) and illustrated by Shadra Strickland, is a stunning visual and literary retelling of the Lovings' romance and battle against racist Virginia laws. The book defies genre classification by using both free verse poems, imagined from Mildred and Richard Loving's perspectives, and primary source artifacts that scaffold readers' experience and add depth and context without interrupting the flow of the narrative. The artifacts include photographs (antischool integration rallies by white protesters, lunch counter sit-ins), quotations (Governor George Wallace defining segregation), and excerpts from legal documents (the Virginia law to preserve racial integrity, the Fourteenth Amendment for equal protection, sound bites from Bernard S. Cohen's Supreme Court testimony). An extensive bibliography, along with comments from the author and illustrator, lend transparency to the research and artistic processes involved in creating the text. These, combined with the lyricism and careful formatting of the narrative poems, provide layers of pedagogical possibility.

Both books about the Lovings invite readers to consider how the law used racial labels to define individuals and society, laying bare the deep racism as well as the resistance to such racism. Furthermore, while the *Loving* case is typically viewed as having bridged Black and white racial boundaries, Mildred is on the record (their marriage license) as identifying as American Indian, a detail that is sometimes overlooked or changed (Reese, 2015, paras. 12, 24, 25), and that has ramifications for how we choose to view the case and its consequences.

Biographies of Barack Obama

The abundance of biographies about Barack Obama that have been tagged by the Library of Congress as containing content about "racially mixed people" is further evidence of the arbitrariness of this identity label. Obama himself identifies as African American and, according to a *New York Times* report, he checked that box on the 2010 Census (Roberts & Baker, 2010). He is publicly hailed as the country's first African American president and only rarely as the country's first biracial president. Yet biographies of Barack Obama are the most numerous nonfiction books for children and young adults with multiracial content. In their study of Obama biographies, May et al. (2010) argue for the need for critical literacy practices that guide readers to understand the ways authorial selection or omission of events in Obama's life vary and are never neutral.

Children's biographies of Obama rely extensively on his memoir, *Dreams from My Father* (1995), and overlap considerably in terms of content. All forty-four books that I found for this research include text and/or photographs of Obama as a boy with his white mother from Kentucky, white grandparents in Hawaii, and Black Kenyan father, thus establishing Obama as the product of a culturally dexterous family. However, only the two books I analyze here sustain Obama's biracial heritage beyond that initial description. Both are written in a narrative style and read like stories, thus allowing readers to connect more directly than traditional expository nonfiction styles allow. Nikki Grimes's (2012) *Barack Obama: Son of Promise, Child of Hope* (illustrated by Bryan Collier) stands out from the other picturebook biographies because of its aesthetic beauty and engaging double narrative. *Son of Promise* opens with a child protagonist, David, providing a point of connection for readers. He is watching a man being celebrated by a crowd of people on television. He does not know who Barack Obama is, and his mother tells him. She begins with a description of Obama's family as stretching "from Kansas to Kenya, his mama white as whipped cream, his daddy black as ink. His mama's folks, Gramps and Toot, were part of the first family he ever knew. Love was the bridge that held them all together" (p. 4). The accompanying illustration depicts a young Obama in the foreground, with his parents and grandparents gathered behind him creating a sense of closeness that David wishes he had. The narrative proceeds to describe Obama's childhood in Hawaii with peers from all over the world. This plurality, Grimes asserts, imbued in young Barry an innate sense of cross-racial, cross-cultural harmony: "Never once did he ask if all those people could get along. They just did" (p. 6). David remarks that this sounds like his own classroom, thus drawing one of a series of parallels between himself and Obama. This double narrative—David's layered over Obama's—keeps the text in the present so readers can be encouraged to examine the (lack of) diversity within their own environments.

Grimes includes Obama's negotiation of his racial identity, depicting him as wondering who he is given that he looks like neither parent, and peers are pressuring him to choose his "own way" (p. 20). Having couched the racial subtext like this, Grimes precludes an opportunity for young readers to encounter the discourse of racial identity negotiation, but nevertheless invites them to recognize that even someone who rose to become the president of the United States had to contend with questions about his identity and belonging. This personal struggle becomes complicated on a different level when, later, we see Obama observing "the river of hurt and hate and history that separated blacks and whites. Being both, he could not take sides" (p. 22). This statement highlights Obama's biraciality in a political light and suggests complicated loyalties. Critical readers can be guided to share their understandings of his position as the "bridge for others" (p. 22) in light of his racial identity.

A biography intended for older readers, *Barack Obama: "We Are One People"* by Michael A. Schuman (2009), is part of the African-American Biography Library series for grades 6 and higher published by Enslow Publishers. This 160-page narrative has an easy, literary style that reads like a story, free of the aridity of some expository writing. For example, in his description of Obama's parents, Schuman succinctly compresses their vastly different backgrounds into a single paragraph that captures their essence and their resistance to conformity. The text indicates that they "shared the same views about religion. Although Barack, Sr.'s parents were Muslims, he had become an atheist. . . . Ann had grown up in a family with a Christian background, but found her fellow Christians tended to be narrow-minded" (p. 16).

In this way, Schuman's biography might serve, like Powell's (2017) *Loving vs. Virginia*, as a mentor text for research and biographical writing. In addition to *Dreams from My Father* (Obama, 1995), Schuman relies on a rich and varied set of resources for this biography. Extensive chapter endnotes provide readers with sources for facts, quotes, and opinions, and lay bare the craft of biographical research.

Throughout the narrative, Schuman returns to Obama's racial heritage as an important element in the future president's formation of his sense of self. Although Schuman does not use Cashin's (2017) language about cultural dexterity, it is exactly this concept to which he ascribes Obama's success in life and in politics.

Schuman's tone, use of language, and authorial choices clearly suggest an admiration of Barack Obama, and students can be taught to read the text critically to become aware of how these elements work together to communicate a desired effect. Obama is portrayed as a man of "unusual" beginnings. Although Schuman implies these unusual beginnings are favorable, how the word *unusual* is understood is a matter of context. Contemporary readers in multicultural environments, some of whom may be biracial themselves, might not consider an interracial family to be "unusual." Therefore, critical examination of language and terminology in this well-researched and appealing narrative reveals that Schuman's lens, like those of all authors of nonfiction, is not neutral and must be questioned.

Conclusion

The analyses offered here are by no means conclusive or comprehensive in the scope of what they offer in terms of content about multiracial identity in nonfictional contexts. Rather, I hope readers will be drawn to start noticing the subtle ways in which mixed-race families are included in books about diverse family structures, particularly those that seek to instill the idea that differences of all sorts are part of the texture of contemporary society and are to be appreciated rather than ignored or marginalized. Some of these books may contain illustrations eye-catching enough to motivate children to pick them up and engage with the images, thus enabling incidental literacy development. But the real transformative potential lies in the scaffolding that an adult provides in guiding, pointing out, and asking questions that lay the foundation for acceptance of diversity.

Cashin (2017) argues that the sheer number of people who are coming into contact with each other, either intimately or superficially, harkens the start of a different racial and cultural consciousness. Statistics indicate that an increasing number of people are, indeed, blurring racial lines through the people they choose as partners and how they identify and express their own identities. Acceptance of difference lies in those moments of contact. Whether that acceptance becomes *dexterity* is contingent on whether differences are maintained and integrated as assets or if they are assimilated and erased. Literature depicting mixed-race lives should reflect the present and project future realities, affirming the identities, family structures, and communities of schoolchildren and youth. As previously mentioned, the dearth and narrow focus of publications means that most multiracial children are not seeing themselves reflected in books. While the publishing world catches up to reality, educators and caregivers can use existing texts as springboards for coursework and conversations that break down prejudiced ideas about racial (and other) identity constructions.

Practical Strategies

- Mentor texts for writing—*Mixed* (Fulbeck, 2010), *Families* (Kuklin, 2010; Rotner & Kelly, 2016), and *Living in Two Worlds* (Rosenberg, 1986) can be used as models for autobiographical writing in writers workshop. Students can focus on voice and organization as they read these texts closely, and then shape their own unique stories. Include a mini-lesson on portrait photography and have students take photos to include.

- Double-entry journals—Using any of the books, teachers can teach the process of writing in response to reading by selecting quotes or sections for students to read closely and discuss, and then write their responses.

- Research projects—Younger students can use *The Case for Loving* (Alko, 2015) to explore other types of family structures that they know of, or can be taught about, that have had to struggle for recognition. Older students can do the same using *Loving vs. Virginia* (Powell, 2017). *My Heroes, My People* (Monceaux & Katcher, 1999) and *Hand in Hand* (Pinkney, 2012) can be used as mentor texts for writing short biographical pieces, then compiled into a class anthology.

- Rewrite the story—Examine Grimes's (2012) use of two subjects in *Barack Obama: Son of Promise, Child of Hope*. Invite students to replace David's story with their own or a friend's story showing how they too are similar to or different from Barack Obama.

- Multimedia celebration of family diversity—Create a slideshow, photo album, bulletin board, or other visual celebration of the families of members of a classroom. Encourage discussion of the various elements of a family beyond biology and residence.

Ten Nonfiction Books about Mixed-Race Experiences

1. Alko, S. (2015). *The case for loving: The fight for interracial marriage* (S. Qualls & S. Alko, Illus.). Arthur A. Levine.

2. Fulbeck, K. (2010). *Mixed: Portraits of multiracial kids*. Chronicle Books.

3. Grimes, N. (2012). *Barack Obama: Son of promise, child of hope* (B. Collier, Illus.). Simon & Schuster.

4. Harris, R. H. (2015). *Who's in my family? All about our families* (N. B. Westcott, Illus.). Walker.

5. Harris, R. H. (2016). *Who we are! All about being the same and being different* (N. B. Westcott, Illus.). Candlewick.

6. Monceaux, M., & Katcher, R. (1999). *My heroes, my people: African Americans and Native Americans in the west* (M. Monceaux, Illus.). Frances Foster.

7. Noah, T. (2019). *It's Trevor Noah: Born a crime, stories from a South African Childhood*. Delacorte Press.

8. O'Leary, S. (2016). *A family is a family is a family* (Q. Leng, Illus.). Groundwood.

9. Pinkney, A. D. (2012). *Hand in hand: Ten black men who changed America* (B. Pinkney, Illus.). Jump at the Sun.

10. Powell, P. H. (2017). *Loving vs. Virginia: A documentary novel of the landmark civil rights case* (S. Strickland, Illus.). Chronicle Books.

Five Online Resources

1. Chaudhri, A. (2013, January). *Classroom connections: Multiracial characters*. Booklist. https://www.booklistonline.com/Classroom-Connections-Multiracial-Characters/pid=5857944

2. Gernand, S. (2016, March 7; 2017, March 1). *70+ picturebooks about mixed race families* and *21 middle grade novels with multiracial characters*. Colours of Us. https://coloursofus.com/picture-books-about-mixed-race-families and https://coloursofus.com/21-middle-grade-novels-with-multiracial-characters

3. Goodreads. (n.d.). *Mixed-race readings*. Listopia. https://www.goodreads.com/list/show/3736.Mixed_Race_Readings

4. Miles, A. (2018, February 5). *Mixed-race YA fantasy heroines*. Book Riot. https://bookriot.com/mixed-race-ya-fantasy-heroines

5. Mixed.Up.Mamma. (2018, September 20). The ULTIMATE Guide to Diverse Children's Books with Multiracial Characters. *Mixed.Up.Mamma*. https://mixedracefamily.com/the-ultimate-guide-to-diverse-books-with-multiracial-characters

Children's Books Cited

Alko, S. (2015). *The case for loving: The fight for interracial marriage* (S. Qualls & S. Alko, Illus.). Arthur A. Levine.

Fulbeck, K. (2010). *Mixed: Portraits of multiracial kids*. Chronicle Books.

Grimes, N. (2012). *Barack Obama: Son of promise, child of hope* (B. Collier, Illus.). Simon & Schuster.

Harris, R. H. (2015). *Who's in my family? All about our families* (N. B. Westcott, Illus.). Walker.

Harris, R. H. (2016). *Who we are! All about being the same and being different* (N. B. Westcott, Illus.). Candlewick.

Kuklin, S. (2010). *Families* (S. Kuklin, Photog.). Hyperion Books for Children.

Monceaux, M., & Katcher, R. (1999). *My heroes, my people: African Americans and Native Americans in the west* (M. Monceaux, Illus.). Frances Foster.

O'Leary, S. (2016). *A family is a family is a family* (Q. Leng, Illus.). Groundwood.

Pinkney, A. D. (2012). *Hand in hand: Ten black men who changed America* (B. Pinkney, Illus.). Jump at the Sun.

Powell, P. H. (2017). *Loving vs. Virginia: A documentary novel of the landmark civil rights case* (S. Strickland, Illus.). Chronicle Books.

Rotner, S., & Kelly, S. M. (2016). *Families* (S. Rotner, Photog.). Holiday House.

Smith, C. (2016). *I am hapa* (M. S. Garcia, Photog.). East West Discovery Press.

References

Cashin, S. (2017). *Loving: Interracial intimacy in America and the threat to white supremacy.* Beacon.

Chaudhri, A. (2017). *Multiracial identity in children's literature.* Routledge.

Chaudhri, A., & Teale, W. H. (2013). Stories of multiracial experiences in literature for children, ages 9–14. *Children's Literature in Education, 44*(4), 359–376. https://doi.org/10.1007/s10583-013-9196-5

Cooperative Children's Book Center. (2017, July 30). *Children's books by and/or about Black, Indigenous and people of color received by the CCBC—U.S. publishers only, 2015–2017.* CCBC Diversity Statistics. https://ccbc.education.wisc.edu/literature-resources/ccbc-diversity-statistics/books-by-and-about-poc-2002-2017

Fleming, J., Catapano, S., Thompson, C. M., & Carillo, S. R. (2016). *More mirrors in the classroom: Using urban children's literature to increase literacy.* Rowman & Littlefield.

Fulbeck, K. (2006a). *Kip Fulbeck: Part Asian, 100% hapa* [Exhibition]. Japanese American National Museum, Los Angeles, CA, United States. https://www.janm.org/exhibits/kipfulbeck

Fulbeck, K. (2006b). *Part Asian, 100% hapa.* Chronicle Books.

Hintz, C., & Tribunella, E. L. (2013). *Reading children's literature: A critical introduction.* Bedford/St. Martin's.

May, L. A., Holbrook, T., & Meyers, L. E. (2010). (Re)storying Obama: An examination of recently published informational texts. *Children's Literature in Education, 41*(4), 273–290. https://doi.org/10.1007/s10583-010-9107-y

Morin, R. (2015, June 16). *Among multiracial adults, racial identity can be fluid*. Pew Research Center. https://www.pewresearch.org/fact-tank/2015/06/16/among-multiracial-adults-racial-identity-can-be-fluid

Nash, R. D. (1995). *Everything you need to know about being a biracial/biethnic teen*. Rosen.

Obama, B. (1995). *Dreams from my father: A story of race and inheritance*. Three Rivers.

Reese, D. (2015). Revisions to the case for Loving. *American Indians in Children's Literature*. https://americanindiansinchildrensliterature.blogspot.com/search?q=the+case+for+loving

Roberts, S., & Baker, P. (2010). Asked to declare his race, Obama checks "black." *The New York Times*.

Root, M. P. P. (1992). Within, between, and beyond race. In M. P. P. Root (Ed.), *Racially mixed people in America* (pp. 3–11). SAGE.

Rosenberg, M. B. (1986). *Living in two worlds* (G. Ancona, Photog.). Lothrop, Lee & Shepard Books.

Saulny, S. (2017). Black? White? Asian? More Americans choose all of the above. *The New York Times*.

Schuman, M. A. (2009). *Barack Obama: "We are one people."* Enslow Publishers.

Sims, R. (1982). *Shadow and substance: Afro-American experience in contemporary children's fiction*. National Council of Teachers of English.

Yokota, J., & Frost, S. (2003). Multiracial characters in children's literature. *Book Links*, *12*(3), 51–57.

Religious Holidays in Nonfiction Literature for Young Children

DENISE DÁVILA, *University of Texas at Austin*
SARAH ELOVICH, *Early Childhood Education Consultant*

When you trust something, you have faith in it. If you believe something to be true, you show your faith by being loyal to it. For millions of people across the globe, their faith is the kind of thing they trust, hold true, and are loyal to. They pray and worship, and read the words that help them to remain faithful.

—LAURA BULLER, *A Faith Like Mine*

This chapter provides a framework for understanding and critically examining the themes highlighted in children's nonfiction literature about the celebration of religious holidays. Focusing on a holiday book series for young readers, the authors share criteria for evaluating the treatment of different religions in children's nonfiction literature. In addition, they highlight professional resources to support educators in facilitating classroom discussions about religion.

Chapter Guiding Questions

- What are the implications of the separation of church and state, as outlined in the United States Bill of Rights, for teaching about religion using children's nonfiction?

- How can educators evaluate youth nonfiction texts for neutral treatment of religion?

- Why should educators use children's nonfiction texts about religions of the world?

- How can educators exercise neutrality in teaching students about world religions in ways that advance pluralistic thinking in the classroom?

The phrase "separation of church and state" may be as misunderstood as it is familiar. Separation of church and state is an idea linked to the Establishment Clause of the First Amendment to the United States Constitution, which states: "Congress shall make no law respecting an establishment of religion." It ensures that citizens are protected from being coerced into adopting a state-mandated religion. While the phrase "separation of church and state" does not appear verbatim in the Constitution, this philosophical "wall" has been referenced repeatedly by the US Supreme Court in cases involving religious activities in public schools. The Establishment Clause prevents students from being compelled to practice a particular religion during public school hours. It does not, however, prohibit public school educators from neutrally teaching children about the religions of the world.

As described by the First Amendment Center (FAC)—a branch of the Freedom Forum Institute that facilitates programs to help people better understand one another—the separation of church and state actually supports the study of religion in public schools:

> When applying the Establishment Clause to public schools, the [US Supreme] Court often emphasizes the importance of "neutrality" by school officials toward religion.... Neutrality means protecting the religious-liberty rights of all students while simultaneously rejecting school endorsement or promotion of religion.... Public schools uphold the First Amendment when they protect the religious-liberty rights of students of all faiths or none. Schools demonstrate fairness when they ensure that the curriculum includes study *about* religion as an important part of a complete education. (Freedom Forum Institute, 2020a, paras. 3, 5, 8, emphasis added)

In addition to advocating for inclusivity and neutrality in supporting the study of religion in public schools, the FAC recommends that elementary schools facilitate children's "early exposure" to the world's religions that will provide "a foundation for later, more complex discussions in secondary school literature and history courses" (Freedom Forum Institute, 2020b, para. 2).

In this chapter, we draw a distinction between religious tolerance and religious neutrality with respect to classroom teaching. One of the chapter's authors, Denise, is a teacher educator. She was raised in a family that practices both Catholicism and Central American folk religion. Her research examines the inclusion of religious content in books and discussions in schools, libraries, and community spaces. Sarah, the chapter's other author, is a writer and education consultant. She was raised in a family that practices Judaism. She has years of experience in early childhood education, girls' education, and museum- and community-based education for youth. Both of us are advocates of religious awareness and pluralism.

We see that the problem with merely promoting tolerance of religious neutrality or pluralism is that, in the words of the founder of the Pluralism Project at Harvard University, Diana Eck (2006), it "does nothing to remove our ignorance of one another, and leaves in place the stereotype" of religious persons who are not privileged in mainstream society ("What Is Pluralism?"). The stereotype is usually based on "fears that underlie old patterns of division and violence" (Eck, 2006, "What Is Pluralism?"). Eck's theory about tolerance aligns with the famous words of US politician Wendell Willkie, who, upon receiving the American Hebrew Medal in 1942 during World War II, proposed, "No man has the right in America to treat any other man 'tolerantly,' for 'tolerance' is the assumption of superiority" (quoted in Madison, 1992, p. 79).

Eck's and Willkie's warnings about religious (in)tolerance correspond with the historical acceptance of religious illiteracy across the US populace (i.e., the lack of knowledge about religions other than one's own; Prothero, 2007). Given that public schools might be one of the only places in which youth learn about world religions, it is important to examine how religious neutrality is reflected, if at all, in the materials educators select for instruction. Our objective in this chapter is to help educators evaluate children's nonfiction books for religious neutrality. Contained in nonfiction literature is the power to either perpetuate religious (in)tolerance, or to unlock youth's pluralistic thinking (Möller, 2014; Torres, 2016; Yenika-Agbaw & Napoli, 2011).

Any study of religion must include the study of culture, and any study of culture must include the study of religion (Beyers, 2017). Many states' social studies curricular standards for the primary grades foster children's cultural awareness through the exploration of family customs and traditions, holidays, and celebrations, each of which can be influenced by religion. This chapter is guided by the concept that studying about religions (as opposed to the study and practice of religion) is an important part of public schools' social studies curriculum standards, which emphasize the study of different cultures (National Council for the Social Studies, 2014). To support such an endeavor, the National Council for the Social Studies and twenty-one other educational, religious, and constitutional/free speech organizations collaborated in developing and publishing a road map for educators through the FAC called "A Teacher's Guide to Religion in the Public Schools" (Haynes & Thomas, 2007).

As described by the guidelines set forth by the FAC, as well as the American Academy of Religion (AAR), a religiously neutral public education should (a) advance students' awareness of different religions, but neither the acceptance nor practice of any particular religion; (b) promote students' exposure to different religious views, but not impose any particular perspective; and (c) support students' education about all religions, but neither privilege nor denigrate any religion (Moore, 2010). In concert with the FAC and AAR guidelines, in this chapter, we analyze the publisher Scholastic's Rookie Read-About Holidays nonfiction book series for young children. We applaud Scholastic's development of an early-reader series that recognizes several different religious holidays. Collectively, the books in the series demonstrate that, although cultural customs and traditions vary, many families engage in celebratory events and activities that include common experiences such as visiting sacred or special places, sharing special foods together, singing songs or reciting prayers, and spending time with friends and relatives. We acknowledge the fine qualities and vision of Scholastic's long-standing series.

Our analysis is guided by the following questions:

- How does each book position the perspectives and practices of the focal religious group relative to mainstream US culture?
- How, if at all, does each book advance the concepts of religious pluralism and neutrality?

We apply these questions in evaluating five of the series books: *Easter* (Marx, 2001/2009), *Diwali* (Trueit, 2007), *Holi* (Krishnaswami, 2003), *Ramadan* (Marx, 2002), and *Hanukkah* (Herrington, 2014). These books correspond with four of the major world religions: Christianity, Hinduism, Islam, and Judaism, respectively. Our evaluation is informed by the AAR's and FAC's guides to religion in public schools (Haynes & Thomas, 2007; Moore, 2010).

Analyzing for Neutrality: Scholastic's Rookie Read-About Holidays Series

Overview of the Series

A total of thirty-three religious and secular holidays currently feature in the Rookie Read-About Holidays series, with titles including *Independence Day*, *Martin Luther King Jr. Day*, and *Memorial Day*. Ten books focus on religious holidays: *Chanukah, Hanukkah, Christmas, Diwali, Easter, Holi, Passover, Purim, Ramadan*, and *Rosh Hashanah and Yom Kippur*. Of these ten titles, five are associated with Judaism, two with Christianity, two with Hinduism and Sikhism, and one with Islam. Buddhism is not represented in the series, despite the fact that it is the fifth largest religious group affiliation in the world (Hackett & McClendon, 2017). Nevertheless, we still appreciate that a major publisher has created and distributed a series that includes religious holidays from several religions practiced in the US. Library data from WorldCat.org describe the worldwide ubiquity and popularity of Scholastic books and suggest that the Rookie Read-About Holidays series is, arguably, a de facto standard in many library collections for children. A book about a commonly celebrated Buddhist festival, such as Vesak, would be an appropriate addition to the series to ensure neutrality across this internationally popular series.

Curriculum Standards

Scholastic's (2018) promotional materials for the Rookie Read-About Holidays series indicate that the books are suited for use in grades PreK to 1. The books feature "simple, engaging nonfiction text and vivid photographs [to] introduce young learners to important holidays from around the world." Moreover, "Young readers will learn about how these holidays began and how they are celebrated today." In alignment with many states' literacy and social studies curriculum standards, Scholastic's promotional materials also highlight that each book includes key features of informational texts such as a calendar, holiday-themed craft, "little-known facts about the subject," and photo glossary.

Given that the holiday focus of the books aligns with many states' social studies curricular standards for grades K–1, it is not surprising that the Rookie Read-About Holidays series is positioned as an aid to early elementary educators. The marketing language indicates that the books help to facilitate the teaching of curricular standards for both social studies and literacy instructional objectives. In other words, they provide one-stop shopping for librarians and early childhood educators who are accountable for meeting their states' requirements for public education. Hence, the series has maintained its appeal for many years.

Holiday Connections to Religious Traditions

None of the five Rookie Read-About Holidays books that we analyze in this chapter introduces or describes the core religious tenets of Islam, Judaism, Hinduism, Sikhism, or Christianity. However, each does connect its holiday theme to Muslim, Jewish, Hindu, Sikh, or Christian traditions. Highlighted in Table 7.1 are excerpts from the narratives of each book that recognize the religious context

TABLE 7.1. Connecting Holiday to Religious People

Book	Excerpt
Hanukkah (Herrington, 2014)	Every year Jewish people around the world celebrate Hanukkah (HAN-nuh-kuh). Special lights, food, gifts, and blessings are all part of this <u>religion's</u> holiday. (p. 5, first page of narrative)
Ramadan (Marx, 2002)	Do you celebrate Ramadan? (p. 3, first page of narrative). Ramadan is a holiday for Muslim (MUHZ-luhm) people. (p. 4, second page of narrative) They follow a <u>religion</u> called Islam (ISS-luhm). (p. 5, third page of narrative)
Diwali (Trueit, 2007)	People of the Hindu (HIN-doo) and Sikh (SEEK) <u>religions</u> celebrate the holiday of Diwali. (p. 4, second page of narrative)
Holi (Krishnaswami, 2003)	Holi is a Hindu (HIN-doo) holiday. The Hindu <u>religion</u> began in India. (p. 5, second page of narrative)
Easter (Marx, 2009)	Do you celebrate Easter? (p. 3, first page in narrative) People of the Christian <u>religion</u> celebrate Easter. (p. 7, third page of narrative)

of the holiday celebration. Note that all of the excerpts include the word *religion* in the introduction of the holiday.

Commendably, the excerpt from the book *Hanukkah* (Herrington, 2014) also includes a sentence that could be adapted for each of the books in this analysis: "Every year Jewish people around the world celebrate Hanukkah" (p. 5). It would also be true to say, "Every year, Muslim people around the world celebrate Ramadan." Nevertheless, only the book *Hanukkah* recognizes the focal religion, Judaism, as a major religion that is practiced worldwide. None of the other books includes such a statement. We find this inconsistency in the series to be curious, given the global demographics of major religious groups (Hackett & McClendon, 2017). Certainly, each of the religions introduced in the Rookie Read-About Holidays series could be similarly acknowledged as one of the major religions of the world.

Phonetic Aids

Another inconsistency across the five books in our analysis corresponds with the inclusion of phonetic aids in the texts. Five to seven in-text phonetic aids appear in each of the non-Christian religious holiday books. Across these books, these aids support the pronunciation of single-syllable and multi-syllable religious and secular words that could be unfamiliar or difficult to decode for young readers (e.g., *Sikh, temple, celebrate*).

In light of the liberal use of in-text phonetic aids in the books about non-Christian holidays, we expected to see an equal proliferation of aids in the books about Christian holidays. We anticipated that an in-text phonetic spelling for the two-syllable name "Jesus" would appear in the early pages of these books. The

English pronunciation of *Jesus* differs not only from the Spanish pronunciation of *Jesús*, but also from the English pronunciations of visually similar names and words like *Jesse* and *jester*.

Despite our expectations for consistency across the series, we were surprised to find that only one in-text phonetic aid appears in the book *Easter* (Marx, 2001/2009). It is for a secular word: "This holiday has a lot of symbols (SIM-bulls)" (p. 8). The inclusion of the phonetic spelling for the word *symbols* points to a presumption that young readers are prone to be unfamiliar with the pronunciation of *sym-* as "SIM-." To confirm that the absence of phonetic aids was not simply an anomaly for the book *Easter*, we checked the other Rookie Read-About Christian holiday title. We also found that in *Christmas* (Trueit, 2013), just one phonetic aid appears—at the bottom of page 10 as a sidebar to the main narrative text. It is for the one-syllable French word *crèche* (kresh) (p. 10), which accompanies a photo of a decorative nativity scene on page 11. No phonetic spellings are included for any words in the main text of this book.

A consistent use of phonetic aids would ensure not only the literacy development of young readers, but also the tacit implication that all religions are on equal ground in the US and none is to be understood as "foreign" or "other." The imbalance we highlight reflects a subtle disparity between the Christian and non-Christian holiday books, and a rebuff of the FAC's and the AAR's guidelines for religious neutrality.

Questions of the Reader

Associated with the concept of reader familiarity, this next section examines two books in the series that speak directly to the reader in the form of a second-person narrative. Both books, *Easter* (2001/2009) and *Ramadan* (2002), are written by the same author, David F. Marx, and employ sets of yes-or-no questions for readers. The other books in our analysis neither use questions nor speak directly to readers. We begin with the questions presented in *Easter*. The book starts with the query, "Do you celebrate Easter?" (p. 3). It is accompanied by a photo of a fair-skinned girl who is holding a basket of dyed Easter eggs. The second question appears several pages later, alongside a photo of a circular Easter bread containing dyed eggs. The text asks, "Does your family bake Easter bread?" (p. 18). The sequence of these questions reflects a logic of first assessing individuals' familiarity with a group (e.g., Christians) and then asking about a type of activity that is specific to a subset of group members (e.g., baking Easter bread). If the first line of inquiry determines that the respondents do not have any familiarity with the group or topic, then there is little value in initiating a second line of inquiry about specific group activities or elements of a topic. In this instance, we speculate that the author presumed that the majority of readers would respond positively to the opening query about celebrating Easter to validate the subsequent query about making Easter bread.

The set of yes-or-no questions in *Ramadan* (Marx, 2002) appears to follow a different logic in comparison to the questions in *Easter* (Marx, 2001/2009). The text for *Ramadan* starts with the same question structure: "Do you celebrate Ramadan (RAHM-i-dahn)?" (p. 3, phonetic aid in text). It assesses readers' familiarity with Muslim traditions. Similar to the opening image in *Easter*, this initial query is accompanied by a full-size photo of a young girl. She is wearing a cloth hijab, holding flowers, and standing in front of an adult in a dark gray jacket (p. 3). If *Ramadan* were to follow the same sequencing as *Easter*, the next question would ask, "Does your family fast during Ramadan?" However, the book does not inquire about the ways in which some Muslims observe Ramadan. Instead, the text reads, "Fasting all day is not easy. Do you think *you* could promise to fast?" (p. 25, emphasis added). This query prompts young readers to assess their personal capacities to avoid eating between dawn and dusk. If, on the other hand, the book *Easter* followed the logic of *Ramadan*, the book's second question would read, "Making Easter bread is not easy. Do you think you could promise to exercise the discipline needed to develop the skills of a baker?" This question, like the question about having the self-discipline to fast during Ramadan, presumes that readers have limited familiarity with the focal activity.

Moreover, unlike the descriptive image that accompanied the second question in *Easter* (Marx, 2001/2009), the image selected for *Ramadan* (Marx, 2002) does not show people fasting. The photo shows children eating cotton candy, a sugary sweet temptation that could be difficult to avoid, especially at a carnival or festival (p. 25). The book's focus on the challenge (rather than the significance) of promising to fast is suggestive of an underlying authorial/editorial presumption: the target reading audience for *Ramadan* is primarily non-Muslim children who have little or no familial experience with fasting as a form of religious observance. If this presumption were valid, then the majority of readers would be expected to answer "no" to the first question in the book (i.e., "Do you celebrate Ramadan?"). Correspondingly, the second question is geared toward non-Muslim readers.

In sum, the logic of the question sequence in the book *Easter* (Marx, 2001/2009) appears to be based on the premise that readers are members of Christian communities. The logic of the question set in *Ramadan* (Marx, 2002) also seems to be based on the premise that readers are members of Christian or other non-Muslim communities. The author's/publisher's presumption that readers would respond positively to the first query in *Easter* and negatively to the first query in *Ramadan* lacks neutrality. It alludes to an implicit perspective that Christianity is familiar and Islam is unfamiliar, if not exotic.

Prayer and Places of Worship

Each book we examined suggests that persons who celebrate the focal holiday are likely to pray and/or visit a place of worship as part of their celebrations (see Table 7.2). For example, in the celebration of Holi, some Hindus "visit the temple (TEM-pul)" (Krishnaswami, 2003, p. 24). During Ramadan, some Muslims say "prayers in a mosque (MOSK)" (Marx, 2002, p. 12). Although straightforward, some of the descriptions lack neutrality for a pluralistic reading audience. For example, inconsistent with the descriptions included in the books *Holi* and *Ramadan*, the description in *Diwali* (Trueit, 2007) states, "Some [families] also go to worship at a Hindu temple, or church" (p. 23). This sentence seems to propose that a Hindu temple is akin to a church, which is specific to Christian faiths. It is inappropriate to elevate the elements of one religion (e.g., Christianity) as the baseline or standard by which to compare the elements of other religions (e.g., Hinduism). Such comparisons are neither neutral nor included in the other books, even as churches are common in many communities. The author's description is problematic because it privileges Christianity in the discussion of another religion, which is contrary to the FAC and AAR guidelines for religious neutrality.

TABLE 7.2. Prayer and Places of Worship

Book	Excerpt
Hanukkah (Herrington, 2014)	During Hanukkah, candles in a special candleholder are lit each night at sundown. It is called a menorah (muh-NOR-uh). <u>Prayers</u> are said when the menorah is lit. (p. 18)
Ramadan (Marx, 2002)	Ramadan is a special time for Muslims. It is a time for <u>prayers</u>. (p. 8) These people are <u>saying prayers</u> in a mosque (MOSK). (p. 12) A mosque is a Muslim temple. (p. 13)
Diwali (Trueit, 2007)	Many families get up before sunrise. They may <u>pray</u> at an altar in their home. Some also go to worship at a Hindu temple, <u>or church</u>. The temple is called a mandir (mun-DEER). (p. 23)
Holi (Krishnaswami, 2003)	Some people visit the temple (TEM-pul) on Holi. (p. 24) They promise to be good friends and neighbors. (p. 25)
Easter (Marx, 2009)	Many Christians go to <u>church</u> on Easter morning. (p. 22)

The Authors and Readers

Although the books *Diwali* (Trueit, 2007) and *Ramadan* (Marx, 2002) appear to be intended for non-Muslim and non-Hindu audiences, the books *Hanukkah* (Herrington, 2014) and *Holi* (Krishnaswami, 2003) are inclusive of Jewish and Hindu religious groups, respectively. In fact, *Hanukkah* is the only book in our analysis that employed a religious consultant. Rabbi Fuchs's endorsement of *Hanukkah* suggests that the book's ideal audience includes Jewish people. The book *Holi* is more subtly inviting to Hindus. On the final page of the book, between the index and the photo credits, is an "About the Author" entry describing the writer, Uma Krishnaswami, who has published many recent books for young readers that feature Indian cultures and traditions. According to the entry, "Krishnaswami was born in New Delhi, India. She spent much of her childhood in the north and remembers celebrating Holi with neighbors and friends" (p. 32). This bio implies that, having celebrated Holi as a child in northern India, Krishnaswami is personally familiar with Hindu traditions and therefore a credible source of information. Moreover, in one line of narrative, Krishnaswami shifts from talking about Hindus, writing, "Today, Hindu people live in many countries of the world" (p. 4), and includes herself with Hindus in stating, "Holi is celebrated to remind us that good wins over evil" (p. 11). In other words, Krishnaswami signals that the audience for *Holi* includes readers who are also Hindu like she is. Thus, while some of the Rookie Read-About Holidays books position readers as outsiders to the focal religion, others are speaking to readers as insiders.

Glossaries and Text Features

At the end of each of the holiday books is a "Words You Know" glossary that reveals more information about the publishing teams' perceptions of the books' religious content and reading audiences. Each word in the "Words You Know" list is accompanied by an image from the body of the book. Table 7.3 describes each of the glossaries.

The words and images selected for the glossary of the book *Ramadan* (Marx, 2002) merit special attention. It is the only glossary to feature a person who follows Islam. Conversely, the glossaries for the books *Hanukkah* (Herrington, 2014), *Diwali* (Trueit, 2007), *Holi* (Krishnaswami, 2003), and *Easter* (Marx, 2001/2009) do not feature the words *Jew*, *Hindu*, *Sikh*, or *Christian*. As described earlier in this chapter, the positioning of Muslims differs from the positioning of Christians, Jews, Hindus, and Sikhs in the series. The book *Ramadan* features images of Muslim children and adults, although few are of boys and men in kufi hats. The glossary word *Muslim* is accompanied by a photo of a young girl in a hijab

TABLE 7.3. Glossaries of Words and Images

Book	"Words You Know"
Hanukkah (Herrington, 2014)	• painted wood dreidel/**dreidel** • golden "coins"/**glet** • menorah with clown motif/**menorah** • engraving of Maccabees temple/**temple**
Ramadan (Marx, 2002)	• carnival/**celebration** • youth eating candy/**fast** • 2 girls in hijabs/**friendship** • mosque exterior/**mosque** • 1 girl in a hijab/**Muslim** • 2 females praying/**prayer**
Diwali (Trueit, 2007)	• child and diyas/**diyas** • flower vendor/**flowers** • fireworks/**fireworks** • siblings and gift/**gifts** • Hindu temple/**mandir** • rangolis/**rangolis** • Rama image/**Rama** • Sita image/**sita** [*sic*]
Holi (Krishnaswami, 2003)	• blossoming tree/**blooming** • 2 men hugging/**friends** • bonfire/**bonfire** • colored powder/**gulal** • Indian sweets/**mithai** • water squirter/**pichkari** • red dot forehead/**tika**
Easter (Marx, 2009)	• basket/**Easter basket** • bonnet/**Easter bonnet** • bread/**Easter bread** • eggs/**Easter eggs** • Jesus Christ/**painting of Christ** • lilies/**Easter lilies** • parade/**parade spectators** • Symbol/**rabbit**

that covers all of her head and neck, most of her eyebrows, and the full circumference of her face. Viewed in the context of a series in which no other religious persons are defined in glossaries, the use of this photo lacks neutrality because it suggests that people who follow Islam are readily identified by their clothing. Conversely, the followers of other world religions are indistinguishable.

Conclusion

Religious pluralism, which supports an equitable society based on the understanding and appreciation of religious differences, is a value that we hope educators and children will adopt in teaching and learning about various religions.

Neutrality is the lens through which religion and culture should be presented in public school classrooms to support children's citizenship in a pluralistic society. Our hope is that this chapter has illustrated that, although readily accessible book series like Rookie Read-About Holidays promote young children's awareness about religious holiday traditions, they can also reinforce subtle biases that reflect a lack of neutrality on the part of the publisher. Perhaps the absence of neutrality reflects an editorial team's limited awareness of the national guidelines for talking about religion in public schools. Perhaps some of the inconsistencies between the Judeo-Christian and non-Judeo-Christian books in the analyzed series reflect an implicit form of (in)tolerance that privileges some religions over others. In the end, this chapter alludes to the need for more nonfiction books for young children that neutrally describe world religions in ways that promote pluralism and conform to national guidelines for talking about religion in public schools.

Although it would be irresponsible to use the books in isolation, teachers can still work with Scholastic's Rookie Read-About Holidays series in combination with other reliable texts and resources until there is a greater selection of nonfiction titles in the US marketplace. For example, *Ramadan* (Marx, 2002) could be paired with nonfiction biographies such as *Salaam: A Muslim American Boy's Story* (Brown, 2006) and *Coming to America: A Muslim Family's Story* (Wolf, 2003). As observed by Torres (2016), these two biographies disrupt stereotypes about Muslim women by featuring women who choose to wear head coverings only for visits to the mosque or on special occasions alongside women who choose to wear knee-length skirts and head coverings at all times.

When it comes to evaluating and pairing nonfiction books about world religions and religious holidays, the more perspectives educators have, the better informed their decisions will be. Journal articles and publications that critically examine children's books about religion could be helpful in identifying appropriate titles. Borrowing books from the library and critically examining them will be important in determining the quality of the text. In addition, some book awards can serve as good resources for identifying high-quality nonfiction children's literature featuring families' religious customs and traditions (see also Book Awards, below). For example, the Middle East Book Award highlights books about people of the Middle East, including followers of Islam. The Sydney Taylor Book Award honors books that offer authentic portrayals of Jewish life experiences. The South Asia Book Award recognizes children's literature that features South Asia and/or South Asians, including Hindus, Sikhs, and Muslims. Alternatively, Bala Kids, an imprint of Shambhala Publications, promotes books that feature Buddhism. Any of the aforementioned resources support educators in making informed choices about inclusive book selections.

Professional resources for educators can also be helpful when it comes to evaluating the neutrality of nonfiction youth literature about religion. We recommend "A Teacher's Guide to Religion in the Public Schools" (Haynes & Thomas, 2007), which has been referenced throughout this chapter and is accessible through the Freedom Forum Institute. This guide can be used for evaluating the language of nonfiction books about religion and for starting classroom conversations around different religious traditions. In addition to following the guide to check for neutrality, educators should look for information about the resources and the experts consulted by the writer to develop a particular book.

Finally, given the dearth of children's nonfiction books about varying religious groups and holidays, educators could seize the opportunity to invite students to document and curate stories about the religious traditions and customs of their home and school communities. The possibilities for learning about the religious perspectives of their friends and neighbors could help students realize the kind of societal religious pluralism that prioritizes the understanding of differences over the dangers of mere tolerance. In the end, there is no greater time than the present for publishers and educators to evaluate the ways in which the materials they produce and present to children either reinforce a caste system of religious (in)tolerance or promote pluralism for a global society. Complicity with the status quo is no longer acceptable when it comes to religious diversity and the future of US culture and society.

Practical Strategies

- Provide students with copies of several books from the Rookie Read-About Holidays series. Have students critically analyze the content of these books and discuss the assumptions made about religion and readership.

- Using high-quality children's nonfiction books, assign small groups of students a different major world religion to research. Have them present what they learn about how core values, traditions, and practices of that religion have been preserved and/or how they have evolved and changed over the years.

- Expand geography and social studies curricula by having students learn about various religious beliefs and practices within their communities. Ask them to interview religious leaders in their communities about religious holidays. Compare what they learn from these experiences to what is represented in children's nonfiction books about those same holidays.

- Using primary sources, introduce students to ties between religious traditions and architecture around the world. For example, you could share images of places of worship from varied geographic locations and from different faith traditions. Together, learn what these architectural representations reveal about faith, culture, and place.

Ten Additional Nonfiction Books about Religion and Religious Holidays

1. Buller, L. (2005). *A faith like mine*. DK Publishing.

2. Demi (2017). *Talking to God: Prayers for children from the world's religions*. Wisdom Tales.

3. Frith, A. (2017). *See inside world religions* (B. Ablett, Illus.). Usborne Publishing.

4. Glossop, J. (2003). *The kids book of world religions* (J. Mantha, Illus.). Kids Can Press.

5. Heiligman, D. (2006). *Celebrate Diwali: With sweets, lights, and fireworks*. National Geographic Kids. (Note: Additional books from the National Geographic Kids' Holidays Around the World series are cited in Chapter 8 of this book.)

6. Lumbard, A. Y. (2014). *Everyone prays: Celebrating faith around the world* (A. Sadeghian, Illus.). Wisdom Tales.

7. Meredith, S. (2005). *The Usborne book of world religions* (N. J. Hewetson, Illus.). Usborne Publishing.

8. Mooney, C. (2015). *Comparative religion: Investigate the world through religious tradition* (L. Chandhok, Illus.). Nomad Press.

9. Osborne, M. P. (1996). *One world, many religions: The ways we worship*. Knopf Books for Young Readers.

10. Star, F. (Ed.). (2016). *What do you believe?* DK Publishing.

Five Online Resources

1. American Academy of Religion. (n.d.). *Teaching about religion in K–12 public schools in the United States*. https://www.aarweb.org/AARMBR/Publica

tions-and-News-/Guides-and-Best-Practices-/Teaching-and-Learning-/
Teaching-about-Religion-in-K-12-Public-Schools.aspx

2. Freedom Forum Institute. (n.d.). *The Religious Freedom Center*. https://
www.religiousfreedomcenter.org

3. National Coalition Against Censorship. (2019, March 20). *The First Amendment in schools, resource guide: Religious expression in the public schools.*
https://ncac.org/resource/the-first-amendment-in-schools-resource-
guide-religious-expression-in-the-public-schools

4. Pew Research Center. (2019, October 3). *Religion in the public schools.*
https://www.pewforum.org/2019/10/03/religion-in-the-public-schools-
2019-update

5. Posnick-Goodwin, S. (2018, December 4). *Teaching about religion*. National
Education Association. https://www.nea.org/professional-excellence/
student-engagement/tools-tips/teaching-about-religion

Book Awards

- Middle East Book Award—see http://www.meoc.us/book-awards.html
- South Asia Book Award—see https://southasiabookaward.wisc.edu
- Sydney Taylor Book Award—see https://jewishlibraries.org/Sydney_
  Taylor_Book_Award

Children's Books Cited

Brown, T. (2006). *Salaam: A Muslim American boy's story* (K. Cardwell, Photog.). Henry
Holt and Company.

Herrington, L. M. (2014). *Hanukkah*. Rookie Read-About Holidays series. Scholastic.

Krishnaswami, U. (2003). *Holi*. Rookie Read-About Holidays series. Scholastic.

Marx, D. F. (2002). *Ramadan*. Rookie Read-About Holidays series. Scholastic.

Marx, D. F. (2009). *Easter*. Rookie Read-About Holidays series. Scholastic. (Original work
published 2001)

Trueit, T. (2007). *Diwali*. Rookie Read-About Holidays series. Scholastic.

Trueit, T. (2013). *Christmas*. Rookie Read-About Holidays series. Scholastic.

Wolf, B. (2003). *Coming to America: A Muslim family's story* (B. Wolf, Photog.). Lee & Low Books.

References

Beyers, J. (2017). Religion and culture: Revisiting a close relative. *HTS Teologiese Studies/ Theological Studies, 73*(1), 1–9. https://doi.org/10.4102/hts.v73i1.3864

Eck, D. L. (2006). *What is pluralism?* https://pluralism.org/about

Freedom Forum Institute. (2020a). *The First Amendment says that the government may not "establish" religion. What does that mean in a public school?* FAQ. https://www.freedom foruminstitute.org/about/faq/the-first-amendment-says-that-the-government-may-not-establish-religion-what-does-that-mean-in-a-public-school

Freedom Forum Institute. (2020b). *How should study about the Bible be handled in elementary education?* FAQ. https://www.freedomforuminstitute.org/about/faq/how-should-study-about-the-bible-be-handled-in-elementary-education

Hackett, C., & McClendon, D. (2017, April 5). *Christians remain world's largest religious group, but they are declining in Europe.* Pew Research Center. https://www.pew research.org/fact-tank/2017/04/05/christians-remain-worlds-largest-religious-group-but-they-are-declining-in-europe

Haynes, C. C., & Thomas, O. (2007). *A teacher's guide to religion in the public schools.* First Amendment Center. https://www.freedomforuminstitute.org/wp-content/up-loads/2016/10/FCGcomplete.pdf

Madison, J. (1992). *Wendell Willkie: Hoosier internationalist.* Indiana University Press.

Möller, K. (2014). Mirrors and windows through literature featuring Arabs, Arab Americans, and people of Islamic faith. *Journal of Children's Literature, 40*(2), 65–72.

Moore, D. L. (2010). *Guidelines for teaching about religion.* American Academy of Religion.

National Council for the Social Studies. (2014). *Position statement: Study about religions in the social studies curriculum.* https://www.socialstudies.org/positions/study_about_religions

Prothero, S. (2007). *Religious literacy: What every American needs to know but doesn't.* Harper-Collins.

Scholastic. (2018). Description, Rookie Read-About Holidays. http://scholasticlibrary .digital.scholastic.com/978-0-531-25224-6.html

Torres, H. (2016). On the margins: The depiction of Muslims in young children's picture-books. *Children's Literature in Education, 47*(3), 191–208. https://doi.org.ezproxy.lib .utexas.edu/10.1007/s10583-015-9268-9

Yenika-Agbaw, V., & Napoli, M. (2011). *African and African American children's and adolescent literature in the classroom: A critical guide.* Peter Lang.

Jewish American Children's Nonfiction

RACHEL KAMIN, *The Joseph and Mae Gray Cultural & Learning Center*
MICHELE WIDDES, *Sunset Ridge School*

In our world, there are many faiths. We celebrate our faiths in many ways. We pray. We chant and sing. We read our holy books. We listen to and learn from others.

—MAYA AJMERA, Magda Nakassis, and Cynthia Pon, *Faith*

This chapter addresses the need to explicitly incorporate books about the Jewish experience, religion, and people as part of American history and culture. To help in building a collection that moves beyond food, holidays, and the Holocaust, recommended nonfiction examples include picturebooks, informational text, memoirs, and biographies. In light of the resurgence of anti-Semitism in the United States and around the world, educators should be mindful when building a multicultural collection to include books about Jews and Judaism.

Chapter Guiding Questions

- Jewish children have been lucky to see themselves often mirrored in literature. But why might educators be hesitant to use these books as windows for non-Jewish readers?

- How can educators build an informational text collection that includes accurate and authentic content about religious diversity in America?

- What are the characteristics of accurate and authentic representations of the Jewish experience in youth literature?

- What are stereotypes, prejudices, and misconceptions about Jews, Judaism, and Jewish culture and history?

Anti-Semitism continues to be one of the oldest forms of hatred, and recent events in the United States indicate that misinformation, persecution, and violence targeting Jews expressly because of their religion continues. The Poway, California, synagogue shooting in 2019, the mass shooting at the Tree of Life synagogue in Pittsburgh, Pennsylvania, in 2018, and the white supremacist rally in Charlottesville, Virginia, in 2017 show that educators need to directly address this idea:

> Prejudice grows from ignorance, and ignorance is conquered by reading. Introducing Jewish literature to a wide audience is a crucial part of the fight against anti-Semitism in a dangerous world where hate is on the rise. (Rabinowitz, 2019, para. 3)

As Bari Weiss (2019) explains in *How to Fight Anti-Semitism*, most Americans "understand Judaism as a religion or as an ethnicity because these are the modern categories by which we understand much of the world." But, "Judaism is not merely a religion, and it is not merely an ethnicity. Judaism is a people . . . with a language, a culture, a literature, and a particular set of ideas, beliefs, texts, and legal practices" (p. 28). Depending on the parameters used for identification, Jews are a minority ranging from 2 to 3 percent of the total United States population (Liu, 2013). In *Insider/Outsider: American Jews and Multiculturalism*, David Biale, Michael Galchinsky, and Susannah Heschel (1998) illustrate that, "although the absorption process for marginalized European immigrants like Italians, Irish, and Jews was not always painless in America, these immigrants were not usually the Other around which the majority defined its identity and consolidated its power" (p. 2). Jews were seen as "white" in relation to Blacks or African Americans, Native Americans, and people of color, but they still faced persecution, prejudice, and stereotyping.

The Jewish experience has not been explicitly addressed in resolutions by organizations such as the Cooperative Children's Book Center and We Need Diverse Books, which focus on issues of diversity in children's literature. Anita Silvey's (1996) *Children's Books and Their Creators* reflects on the state of multicultural publishing and features contributions by and about Native American, African American, Latinx, and Asian American writers, but Jewish children's literature is absent as an ethnic or cultural category. Jewish literature is also not included in *Using Multiethnic Literature in the K–8 Classroom* (Harris, 1997), *Critical Multicultural Analysis of Children's Literature: Mirrors, Windows, and Doors* (Botelho & Rudman, 2009), or *Multicultural Children's Literature: A Critical Issues Approach* (Gopalakrishnan, 2011). But Jews in America occupy an "anomalous status: insiders who are outsiders and outsiders who are insiders" (Biale et al., 1998, p. 5). This unique position has perhaps been the reason why the Jewish experience has historically been absent from the discussions on multiculturalism and representation. As a synagogue librarian specializing in children's literature and a veteran middle school educator, and both of us identifying as Jewish, this position feels inherently familiar.

Religion in the Classroom

The idea of teaching about religion, or groups viewed as religious, without teaching adherence to religion can bump into First Amendment concerns, which may deter public school educators. The American Academy of Religion has a resource document for K–12 educators that provides an overview of how and why religion can and should be taught in schools. It is provided based on the following premises: "Illiteracy regarding religion (1) is widespread, (2) fuels prejudice and antagonism, and (3) can be diminished by teaching about religion in public schools using a non-devotional, academic perspective, called religious studies" (Moore, 2010, p. i). As Codell (2019) states, "Holes in collection diversity are holes in preparing students for encounters with the human diversity . . . so, if you have no Jewish kids in your school, you need Jewish children's books even more" (para. 4). In addition, books about sacred places, beliefs, and customs can introduce students to unfamiliar vocabulary and communities. This may make students more respectful and aware when navigating the real world. While this chapter focuses on Judaism, this same philosophy should apply when building a collection that represents a multitude of religions.

Comparative religious studies for younger students can be addressed through picturebooks; the following three picturebooks portray accurate and authentic representations of Judaism, as much as is possible within a brief survey text. The book *Faith* by Ajmera et al. (2009) explores in a photo essay format the many ways that faith is expressed around the world. Native American, Rastafarian, Christian, Buddhist, Jewish, Daoist, Muslim, Hindu, and Mennonite faiths are included with examples from over thirty countries. Judaism is represented with photographs of a bar mitzvah celebrant, yeshiva boys studying, a father and son lighting the menorah, an *upsherinish* hair-cutting ceremony, a girl braiding challah, a funeral in Israel, and the shaking of the *lulav* on the holiday of Sukkot. The book's photos depict children across the spectrum of individual religions and celebrate the diversity of the world's religions.

Similar in scope is *Sacred Places* by Philemon Sturges (2000), with exquisite paper cut illustrations by Giles Laroche, which shows various places sacred to different religions, including churches, mosques, synagogues, temples, and shrines. Judaism is represented by King Solomon's Temple and the Western Wall in Jerusalem and the Ha'ari Synagogue of the Sephardim in Tsefat, Israel, as well as by Temple Mickve Israel in Savannah, Georgia (one of the oldest synagogues in America), and Temple Solomon in Montreal, Canada. The approach is respectful and impartial, and the selection of sites is diverse, making this an accessible introduction to world faiths, as well as a spiritual introduction to architecture.

The title *What Is God?* (Boritzer, 2009) might make some public school educators nervous, but it is deceiving; the book really answers the question, "What is religion?" The focus is on a discussion of various religions—Christianity, Judaism, Hinduism, Islam, and Buddhism—and their commonalities. For example, "Most religions say that you should not lie, most religions say that you should not steal, most religions say that you should not hurt people. There are many ways all religions are the same" (Boritzer, 2009, p. 22). Other aspects of religion, such as holy books and prayer, are also included, and the text and pictures are appropriate and accessible for elementary students.

Beyond Food and Holidays

In discussing Jewish characters in children's literature, Cummins and Toder (2000) note that "if one were to take Jewish-themed picturebooks as representative of American Jewish experience, one would assume that Jews celebrate many holidays but do not do much else with their time" (p. 38). Frequently, educators approach multiculturalism through information about food and holidays. Because of its proximity on the calendar to Christmas, Hanukkah is sometimes the one and only Jewish holiday represented and integrated into classroom discussions. Hanukkah is in actuality a relatively minor, post-Biblical holiday, and much less important than Rosh Hashanah, Yom Kippur, or Passover. Limiting students' exposure to Judaism to one winter holiday and presenting it as the "Jewish Christmas" can unintentionally perpetuate stereotypes and ideas of "otherness."

The focus on food and holidays may also be a result of well-meaning educators unprepared to consider the complexities or potential implicit messages in holiday text selection, particularly in nonfiction. *Stories Matter: The Complexity of Cultural Authenticity in Children's Literature* (Fox & Short, 2003) includes a chapter by Fang et al. (2003) that focuses neither on nonfiction nor on Jews or Judaism, but the message and the reminder that educators need to be critical evaluators of how, when, and why they use particular texts are relevant to many populations. Fang and colleagues (2003) advise that "it is not possible for teachers to know everything about every culture" but that "teachers should cultivate a questioning and wondering stance" (p. 299).

For an overview of the Jewish holidays for very young children, consider

Here Is the World: A Year of Jewish Holidays (Newman, 2014). Each two-page spread pairs a rhyming couplet that briefly introduces a holiday with a beautiful full-bleed illustration depicting a contemporary family. For elementary students, *Dance, Sing, Remember: A Celebration of Jewish Holidays* (Kimmelman, 2000) includes a brief explanation of twelve Jewish holidays accompanied by a short story, game, or other activity. For older students, *Jewish Holidays All Year Round: A Family Treasury* (Cooper, 2002), published in association with the Jewish Museum in New York, pairs reproductions of objects from the museum's collection and colorful pen-and-ink drawings by Elivia Savadier with facts about each of the holidays, lore, crafts, and recipes. While most Jewish holiday offerings for children tend to focus on, and feature, families of eastern European descent, *Passover around the World* (Lehman-Wilzig, 2007) and *Hanukkah around the World* (Lehman-Wilzig, 2009) celebrate these holidays through the eyes of Jews in places such as Turkey, Uzbekistan, Italy, Australia, India, Iran, Morocco, and Tunisia, briefly showing their distinct cultures and holiday traditions. Deborah Heiligman's books in the Holidays around the World series (published by National Geographic) include *Celebrate Hanukkah* (2006), *Celebrate Passover* (2007a), and *Celebrate Rosh Hashanah & Yom Kippur* (2007b), and show striking photographs of diverse Jewish communities participating in holiday rituals from places such as China, Uganda, Yemen, and Zimbabwe.

The Holocaust: Not the Totality of the Jewish Experience

Other than books about Hanukkah, books about the Holocaust are often the only texts used in classrooms that explicitly depict Jewish identities. As Totten (2001) stresses in *Teaching Holocaust Literature*, books must be accurate, age appropriate, authentic, readable, thought provoking, discussable, nonsentimental, and capable of arousing empathy. Silver (2010) provides an astute analysis of the difficulties and challenges with books for children about the Holocaust:

> Children's books are expected to affirm life, to offer hope, and to end on, if not a happy note, then at least a positive one. The realities of war and the Holocaust defy these goals, so it is hard to achieve them without distortion. (p. 167)

Meltzer's (1976) *Never to Forget* was one of the first American children's books to explain the history of hatred that led to the Holocaust, the resultant process of destruction, and the courageous spirit of resistance. Following that publication, many excellent children's books about the Holocaust have been about rescuers, typically non-Jews who defied the Nazis by hiding their friends and neighbors, including more recent examples such as *My Survival: A Girl on Schindler's List* (Finder, 2019), *Courage and Defiance: Stories of Spies, Saboteurs, and Survivors in World War II Denmark* (Hopkinson, 2015), *A Light in the Darkness: Janusz Korczak, His Orphans, and the Holocaust* (Marrin, 2019), *Passage to Freedom: The Sugihara Story* (Mochizuki, 1997), *The Grand Mosque of Paris: A Story of How Muslims Rescued Jews during the Holocaust* (Ruelle & DeSaix, 2008), and the many books published recently about Irena Sendler. But, as Silver (2010) points out, "If there had been as many rescuers as it seems there were from children's books, then six million Jews would not have died, including a million and a half children" (p. 167). She continues, "The urge to show humans at their best distorts the fact that the Holocaust showed humans at their worst" (p.167). When building a library and accessing resources representing Jews throughout history, educators should be mindful not to limit their collections to books that only portray Jews as victims.

While the stories of resistance, rescue, courage, ingenuity, and survival are a beacon of light amid the dark horrors of the Holocaust, reality can be twisted when books about the Holocaust try to extract only a message of hope (Silver, 2010). This is evident simply by the number of books connected to Anne Frank. Grasping onto Anne's comment in her diary that "in spite of everything, I still believe that people are really good at heart," authors tend to gloss over the fact that Anne Frank and the occupants of the Secret Annex were arrested and murdered. Many of these texts focus on symbols, such as the tree outside Anne's window, and often simply state that Anne did not survive the war. While maintaining a gentle detachment makes the dramatic episode more palatable for younger readers (or, at least, for the adults in their lives), the terrible truth of the Holocaust and Hitler's "final solution" is diminished. In building a collection of resources, educators need to be mindful that this is a complex and mature subject, one that requires a varied approach and a carefully curated booklist.

With all accounts or stories based on history, accuracy is of primary importance. In the case of Holocaust literature, accuracy is very frightening. For this reason, many educators do not feel that children under the age of ten should be exposed to books about the Holocaust. The Step into Reading series, written at a K–2 reading level, offers a book about Anne Frank. While publishers may market books about the Holocaust to younger readers, educators will want to consider both their teaching contexts and their students when selecting and introducing books on this topic.

Educators will also want to be aware of the fact that many books about the Holocaust are "deceptively packaged to look like picturebooks: heavily illustrated and often short of text" (Silver, 2010, p. 167). Based on the serious, frightening, and complex subject matter, these picturebooks about the Holocaust can be used very effectively with older students. Excellent nonfiction examples include

The Brave Cyclist (Hoffman, 2019), *The Flag with Fifty-Six Stars* (Rubin, 2005), and *Memories of Survival* (Krinitz & Steinhardt, 2005). Primary source-based biographies such as the award-winning *Hana's Suitcase* (Levine, 2002), *To Hope and Back: The Journey of the St. Louis* (Kacer, 2011), and *The Journey That Saved Curious George: The True Wartime Escape of Margret and H. A. Rey* (Borden, 2005) are appropriate for middle grade and older readers and offer complex narrative structures and content that bely their initial picturebook appearance.

Only twelve states require Holocaust education as part of their secondary school curricula, while a recent Claims Conference "Holocaust Knowledge and Awareness Study" found significant gaps in knowledge of the Holocaust among Americans. Eleven percent of adults and 22 percent of millennials haven't heard of the Holocaust, while only 58 percent of American adults believe something like the Holocaust could happen again (Conference on Jewish Material Claims Against Germany & Schoen Consulting, 2018, p. 2). Therefore, it is imperative that high-quality, age-appropriate, accurate, and authentic books about the Holocaust be integrated into the curriculum and have a prominent place in classroom and library collections. However, as Marjorie Ingall (2019), a columnist for the online magazine *Tablet* and member of the Sydney Taylor Book Award Committee, stresses, "We need superlative Holocaust books. . . . No more books that offer ahistorical feel-good fantasy or that destroy hope, no more books that get history wrong . . . no more books that universalize entirely too much from our particular lived experience" (para. 5).

Jewish Contributions to American Culture

Books about the Holocaust should not be the only nonfiction books with Jewish content that children engage with in school, and books about Jewish history should not exclusively concentrate on the tragedies experienced by Jews. In "A Content Analysis of Orbis Pictus Award-Winning Nonfiction, 1990–2014," Crisp (2015) notes that a large majority of African Americans represented in the Orbis Pictus winners are framed within the context of slavery or the Civil Rights Movement. He writes, "Depicting African American focal subjects almost exclusively within these contexts is limiting and does not represent the totality of African American experiences" (p. 252). The same theory should be applied to Jewish focal subjects, who are typically framed within the context of the Holocaust or anti-Semitism. This is very limiting and does not represent the totality of Jewish experience or identity. As Ingall (2019) asserts, "Why, when we have a 6,000-year-long story, is there so much focus on one of the worst things that ever happened to us? The Holocaust isn't the sum total of who we are" (para. 1).

She maintains that, while it is vital to teach the Holocaust in an age-appropriate, responsible way, "books reflecting the diversity of the Jewish American experience" are also essential (para. 1).

Over more than four hundred years, Jewish immigrants and their descendants have made major contributions to America's growth and development. In *Forged in Freedom*, Finkelstein (2002) brings to life the key turning points in history that affected both the United States and American Jewry. From labor and justice, political coming of age, and the fight against bigotry to the growth of a rich and varied culture and the creation of uniquely American expressions of Judaism, Finkelstein highlights the ways that American Jews have both shaped, and been shaped by, the culture and ideals of the United States.

From the country's earliest days, Jews have helped contribute to the ideals of the nascent United States. An excellent primary source is a letter from George Washington in 1790 to the Hebrew Congregation of Newport in which he writes, "the Government of the United States, which gives to bigotry no sanction, to persecution no assistance, requires only that they who live under its protection should demean themselves as good citizens" (Founders Online, n.d., para. 3). This dialogue eventually helped form the First Amendment itself, and the definition of America as a secular country without an official state-sponsored religion. In *To Bigotry, No Sanction: The Story of the Oldest Synagogue in America*, Fisher (1998) uses the exchange between Washington and the Jewish community as a jumping-off point to discuss the history of Jews in America, beginning with the Jewish presence in Spain, the persecution and expulsion of the Jews in 1492, and the migration of Jews to the Americas. He then focuses on how, through erecting buildings like the Touro Synagogue in Newport (the oldest synagogue in the United States), Jews made a place for themselves in the New World. *Heeding the Call: Jewish Voices in America's Civil Rights Struggle*, also by Finkelstein (1997), focuses on Jewish figures who helped fight for equal rights in America, from the first settlers in 1654 and the abolitionists during the Civil War period to the founding of the National Association for the Advancement of Colored People and the Civil Rights Movement.

In 1883, Emma Lazarus, a Jewish woman from New York, wrote the sonnet "The New Colossus," which was eventually inscribed at the bottom of the Statue of Liberty. This poem helped define the identity of the United States as a country welcoming of immigrants. Two picturebooks help tell this story: *Emma's Poem: The Voice of the Statue of Liberty* by Linda Glaser (2010) and *Liberty's Voice: The Story of Emma Lazarus* by Erica Silverman (2011).

Jews also played a central role in the American labor movement. Michelle Markel's (2013) picturebook biography *Brave Girl: Clara and the Shirtwaist Makers' Strike of 1909* describes how Clara Lemlich, a young Jewish immigrant, helped lead the largest walkout of women workers in United States history. In *Flesh and Blood So Cheap: The Triangle Fire and Its Legacy*, Albert Marrin (2011) provides a detailed account of the notorious 1911 Triangle Shirtwaist Factory fire, in which 146 workers—mostly young Jewish and Italian immigrant women—perished. Their catastrophic deaths led to changes in working conditions and fueled a campaign for union rights.

Schools of Hope: How Julius Rosenwald Helped Change African American Education (Finkelstein, 2014) tells the story of how the president of the Sears Roebuck Company, the son of German Jewish immigrants, financially supported the building of 5,300 schools in rural African American communities between 1913 and 1932. Several other books depict the role that Jews played in the fight for equal rights for all Americans. *As Good as Anybody: Martin Luther King Jr. and Abraham Joshua Heschel's Amazing March toward Freedom* (Michelson, 2008) is a dual biography of two great Civil Rights leaders. A Jewish immigrant from Poland, Rabbi Heschel, escaped the Nazis and immigrated to America but lost much of his family in the Holocaust. Driven to fight bigotry in all its forms, he became a supporter of King and joined him on the historic march from Selma to Montgomery in 1965. In *Freedom Summer: The 1964 Struggle for Civil Rights in Mississippi*, Susan Goldman Rubin (2014) chronicles the efforts of Civil Rights workers, who flooded some of the most socially oppressive areas of Mississippi, set against the backdrop of the puzzling disappearance of three of these volunteers: Andrew Goodman and Mickey Schwerner, two young Jewish men, and James Chaney, an African American. Their story is also depicted in *Hot Pursuit: Murder in Mississippi* by Stacia Deutsch and Rhody Cohon (2010).

Readers should be exposed to books that "articulate what makes Jews distinct while showing the ways in which Jewish history and thought contribute to the humanities at large," and biographies are the perfect way to illustrate this (Biale et al., 1998, p. 7). An analysis of biographies, autobiographies, and memoirs about American Jews show the remarkable range of contributions in virtually every field and endeavor. While there are countless biographies spanning various formats and age ranges on well-known American Jews like Albert Einstein, Harry Houdini, and Steven Spielberg, lesser-known figures are also being highlighted. For example, several biographies have focused on the Jewish role in the comic industry. Lily Renée Wilheim escaped World War II on the *Kindertransport* to England in 1939, emigrated to the US, and became one of the first female comic book artists, as graphically told in *Lily Renée, Escape Artist* (Robbins, 2011). And while everyone has heard of Superman and Batman, most do not know that the creators behind these superheroes, and many others, were Jewish. Marc Tyler Nobleman chronicles how writer Jerry Siegel and illustrator Joe Shuster created the character of Superman in *Boys of Steel* (Nobleman, 2008) and how Bill Finger was the secret cocreator of Batman and never received credit for or recognition in *Bill the Boy Wonder* (Nobleman, 2012). *Who Was Stan Lee?* (Edgers, 2014) is a brief, accessible biography of the son of Romanian-born Jewish immigrants who made Marvel Comics a household name. The popular Who Was. . .? series also includes other famous American Jews such as Levi Strauss, Harvey Milk, Ruth Bader Ginsburg, Judy Blume, the Three Stooges, and more.

Jewish baseball stars like Hank Greenberg and Sandy Koufax have long served as role models for Jewish readers but can also help remind all readers of the importance of hard work, determination, and remaining true to yourself. Greenberg's life, baseball career, and legacy are detailed in Shelley Sommer's (2011) *Hammerin' Hank Greenberg: Baseball Pioneer*. For younger readers, we suggest Yona Zeldis McDonough's (2006) picturebook biography, *Hammerin' Hank: The Life of Hank Greenberg*. In an unusual and welcome new slant on a well-covered era in American sports history, Cathy Goldberg Fishman (2012) describes the first time Jackie Robinson met Hank Greenberg (when they collided at first base in a 1947 game) in *When Jackie and Hank Met*. The dual biography parallels the racism the two athletes encountered. While Robinson had to break the color barrier, Greenberg faced anti-Semitism and prejudice as one of the few Jewish ballplayers. Sandy Koufax became a hero to American Jews when he refused to pitch in the 1965 World Series on Yom Kippur, one of the holiest and most important days on the Jewish calendar. Jonah Winter's (2009) picturebook biography *You Never Heard of Sandy Koufax?!*, with spectacular illustrations and cover art by André Carrilho, featuring a lenticular three-dimensional inset that, when tilted, sends Koufax through a pitch, tells the story of arguably the greatest left-handed pitcher in baseball history. A lesser-known Jewish baseball player, who helped intelligence officers during World War II, was Moe Berg. Steve Sheinkin's (2012) *Bomb* includes several riveting stories about him in a book for older readers, while the picturebook *The Spy Who Played Baseball* (Jones, 2018) is appropriate for younger readers. But before Berg, Greenberg, and Koufax, there was Lipman Pike, known as America's first professional ballplayer. *Lipman Pike: America's First Home Run King* (Michelson, 2011) mixes the Jewish immigrant experience with the US national pastime in a picturebook biography.

Building a Collection in Libraries, Schools, and Classrooms

While discussions about the lack of diversity in children's books date back more than a century, more recent American Library Association, National Council for the Social Studies, and National Council of Teachers of English statements explicitly focus on the impact of the lack of diverse books for children and the

need to encourage publishers to support more varied texts. For educators looking to build their print resources, one beginning place for reviewing a school
or classroom library is the Lee & Low Classroom Library Questionnaire (Lee &
Low Books, 2020). This tool helps educators "evaluate how culturally responsive and diverse" a library is and identify gaps (Schneider, 2017). While this
questionnaire doesn't explicitly mention Jewish identity or experience, it does
address questions of religious diversity, and many of the types of questions
could apply when considering Jewish nonfiction texts.

Identifying and accessing quality nonfiction depicting the Jewish experience can actually be more difficult than finding books about other populations.
Depending on the focus and purpose, the aspect of Jewish identity may play a
major or very minor role in the text itself. In selecting and using nonfiction about
Jews or Judaism, there are some culturally inappropriate "red flags" that could
potentially eliminate texts from use in a classroom. These markers are provided
here to help educators approach nonfiction texts connected to religion as critical
evaluators: the use of biased terms like *Jesus Christ*, *AD*, and *BC* are often inappropriate; *Jesus*, *CE*, and *BCE* should be used instead. Also, watch carefully for
bias and inaccuracy in books about Israel, recognizing that it is a very controversial place historically, geographically, and politically, both for Jews and non-
Jews.

Final Recommendations

Building a classroom or library collection of nonfiction should be a deliberate
and mindful process for educators at all grade levels. Creating a diverse collection includes many aspects of identity, and religion should not be excluded. Take
the time required to consider representation of diverse religious groups and fill
omissions and inaccuracies in an existing collection. Cull out texts that mischar-
acterize religious communities, populations, and historical events; remember
that, just because a book has a more recent publication date, it is not necessarily better. When in doubt, ask questions and seek resources from experts in the
field. Consider authorship and time period in use of primary source documents,
as perspectives, understandings, and even word usage can change over time.
These documents or texts may still be included in a library; however, they may
require context, educator support, and expertise to explore.

There is a rich body of children's literature portraying the Jewish experience in America, and educators should not hesitate to use these books with all
readers, both Jewish and non-Jewish. If Judaism, Jewish culture, and history are
absent or excluded from the body of multicultural literature available to stu-

dents, stereotypes, prejudices, and misconceptions will persist. This sentiment is strongly echoed by Cummins and Toder (2000), who write:

> If intellectuals and educators decide that Jews are no longer worthy of consideration because they have gained the status and privilege of white, Christian people in our society, then they will glibly overlook the very real exclusion and discrimination many Jews have experienced. (p. 40)

The books we read as children shape our understandings of ourselves and the world in which we live, and we must acknowledge that the multicultural discourse should expand to include the Jewish experience. Meeting people of different religions in books will better prepare children to approach real-life encounters with greater understanding.

Practical Strategies

- Cultivate respect for and awareness of religions by introducing students to differences in beliefs, practices, architecture, and traditions through picturebooks and other nonfiction, secular sources.
- Intentionally include information about Jewish holidays and celebrations throughout the school year, not just as a special unit or in conjunction with Christmas.
- Curate Holocaust selections to make certain they do not all concentrate on the tragedies experienced by the Jews or have Jews presented exclusively as victims.
- Seamlessly integrate Jewish biographies into genre studies of music or literature, or a unit on biographies at large.
- When studying American history, ensure that time periods include the presence and contributions of Jewish Americans and Jewish immigrants.

Ten Additional Nonfiction Books about Jewish Americans

1. Ades, A., & Mildenberger, V. (2020). *Judah Touro didn't want to be famous* (V. Mildenberger, Illus.). Kar-Ben.
2. Blumenthal, D., & D'yans, M. (2019). *Parrots, pugs and pixie dust: A book about fashion designer Judith Leiber* (M. D'yans, Illus.). Little Bee Books.

3. Krasner, B., & Garrity-Riley, K. (2014). *Goldie takes a stand! Golda Meir's first crusade* (K. Garrity-Riley, Illus.). Kar-Ben.

4. Macy, S. (2019). *The book rescuer: How a mensch from Massachusetts saved Yiddish literature for generations to come* (S. Innerst, Illus.). Paula Wiseman Books.

5. Marshall, L. E. (2020). *The polio pioneer: Dr. Jonas Salk and the polio vaccine* (L. Anchin, Illus.). Alfred A. Knopf.

6. Newman, T. (2020). *Itzhak: A boy who loved the violin* (A. Halpin, Illus.). Harry N. Abrams.

7. Nuchi, A. (2018). *God bless America: The story of an immigrant named Irving Berlin* (R. Polivka, Illus.). Hyperion.

8. Ortiz, V. (2019). *Dissenter on the bench: Ruth Bader Ginsburg's life and work.* Clarion Books.

9. Pinkney, A. D. (2016). *A poem for Peter: The story of Ezra Jack Keats and the creation of* The snowy day (L. Fancher & S. Johnson, Illus.). Viking/ Penguin.

10. Raisman, A. (2017). *Fierce: How competing for myself changed everything.* Little, Brown and Company.

Five Online Resources

1. Anti-Defamation League. (n.d.). *Children's literature.* Books Matter. http:// www.adl.org/education-and-resources/resources-for-educators-parents- families/childrens-literature

2. Association of Jewish Libraries. (2018, October). *Love your neighbor: AJL recommends Jewish books for all readers.* https://jewishlibraries.org/Love_ Your_Neighbor

3. Jewish Women's Archive. (n.d.). *Living the Legacy.* https://jwa.org/teach/ livingthelegacy

4. *SJL* Reviews Editors. (2017). *Books on democracy & citizenship.* https://www .facinghistory.org/sites/default/files/SLJ_DemocracyBooklist_2017.pdf

5. United States Holocaust Memorial Museum (2017, December 11). *Teach.* https://www.ushmm.org/teach

Book Awards

- National Jewish Book Awards—see http://www.jewishbookcouncil.org/awards/national-jewish-book-award.html
- Sydney Taylor Book Award—see https://jewishlibraries.org/Sydney_Taylor_Book_Award

Children's Books Cited

Ajmera, M., Nakassis, M., & Pon, C. (2009). *Faith*. Charlesbridge.

Borden, L. (2005). *The journey that saved Curious George: The true wartime escape of Margret and H. A. Rey* (A. Drummond, Illus.). Houghton Mifflin Harcourt Books for Young Readers.

Boritzer, E. (1990). *What is God?* (R. Marantz, Illus.). Firefly Juvenile.

Cooper, I. (2002). *Jewish holidays all year round: A family treasury* (E. Savadier, Illus.). Harry N. Abrams.

Deutsch, S., & Cohon, R. (2010). *Hot pursuit: Murder in Mississippi* (C. Orback, Illus.). Kar-Ben.

Edgers, G. (2014). *Who was Stan Lee?* (J. Hinderliter, Illus.). Penguin Young Readers.

Finder, R. (with Greene, J. M.) (2019). *My survival: A girl on Schindler's list*. Scholastic.

Finkelstein, N. H. (1997). *Heeding the call: Jewish voices in America's civil rights struggle*. Jewish Publication Society.

Finkelstein, N. H. (2002). *Forged in freedom: Shaping the Jewish-American experience*. Jewish Publication Society.

Finkelstein, N. H. (2014). *Schools of hope: How Julius Rosenwald helped change African American education*. Calkins Creek.

Fisher, L. E. (1998). *To bigotry, no sanction: The story of the oldest synagogue in America*. Holiday House.

Fishman, C. G. (2012). *When Jackie and Hank met* (M. Elliott, Illus.). Marshall Cavendish Children.

Glaser, L. (2010). *Emma's poem: The voice of the Statue of Liberty* (C. A. Nivola, Illus.). Houghton Mifflin Books for Children.

Heiligman, D. (2006). *Celebrate Hanukkah: With light, latkes, and dreidels*. National Geographic Kids.

Heiligman, D. (2007a). *Celebrate Passover: With matzah, maror, and memories*. National Geographic Kids.

Heiligman, D. (2007b). *Celebrate Rosh Hashanah & Yom Kippur: With honey, prayers, and the shofar*. National Geographic.

Hoffman, A. (2019). *The brave cyclist: The true story of a Holocaust hero* (C. Fedele, Illus.). Capstone Editions.

Hopkinson, D. (2015). *Courage and defiance: Stories of spies, saboteurs, and survivors in World War II Denmark*. Scholastic.

Jones, C. (2018). *The spy who played baseball* (G. Cherrington, Illus.). Kar-Ben.

Kacer, K. R. (2011). *To hope and back: The journey of the St. Louis* (3rd ed.). Second Story Press.

Kimmelman, L. (2000). *Dance, sing, remember: A celebration of Jewish holidays* (O. Eitan, Illus.). HarperCollins.

Krinitz, E. N., & Steinhardt, B. (2005). *Memories of survival* (E. N. Krinitz, Illus.). Hyperion Books for Children.

Lehman-Wilzig, T. (2007). *Passover around the world* (E. Wolf, Illus.). Kar-Ben.

Lehman-Wilzig, T. (2009). *Hanukkah around the world* (V. Wehrman, Illus.). Kar-Ben.

Levine, K. (2002). *Hana's suitcase: A true story*. Second Story Press.

Markel, M. (2013). *Brave girl: Clara and the shirtwaist makers' strike of 1909* (M. Sweet, Illus.). HarperCollins.

Marrin, A. (2011). *Flesh and blood so cheap: The Triangle fire and its legacy*. Random House.

Marrin, A. (2019). *A light in the darkness: Janusz Korczak, his orphans, and the Holocaust*. Knopf Books for Young Readers.

Meltzer, M. (1976). *Never to forget: The Jews of the holocaust*. Harper & Row.

Michelson, R. (2008). *As good as anybody: Martin Luther King Jr. and Abraham Joshua Heschel's amazing march toward freedom* (R. Colón, Illus.). Knopf Books for Young Readers.

Michelson, R. (2011). *Lipman Pike: America's first home run king* (Z. Pullen, Illus.). Sleeping Bear Press.

Mochizuki, K. (1997). *Passage to freedom: The Sugihara story* (D. Lee, Illus.). Lee & Low Books.

Newman, L. (2014). *Here is the world: A year of Jewish holidays* (S. Gal, Illus.). Abrams Books for Young Readers.

Nobleman, M. T. (2008). *Boys of steel: The creators of Superman* (R. MacDonald, Illus.). Alfred A. Knopf.

Nobleman, M. T. (2012). *Bill the boy wonder: The secret co-creator of Batman* (T. Templeton, Illus.). Charlesbridge.

Robbins, T. (2011). *Lily Renée, escape artist: From Holocaust survivor to comic book pioneer* (A. Timmons & M. Oh, Illus.). Graphic Universe.

Rubin, S. G. (2005). *The flag with fifty-six stars* (B. Farnsworth, Illus.). Holiday House.

Rubin, S. G. (2014). *Freedom summer: The 1964 struggle for civil rights in Mississippi*. Holiday House.

Ruelle, K. G., & DeSaix, D. D. (2008). *The Grand Mosque of Paris: A story of how Muslims rescued Jews during the Holocaust* (D. D. DeSaix, Illus.). Holiday House.

Sheinkin, S. (2012). *Bomb: The race to build and steal the world's most dangerous weapon*. Roaring Brook Press.

Silverman, E. (2011). *Liberty's voice: The story of Emma Lazarus* (S. Schuett, Illus.). Dutton Books for Young Readers.

Sommer, S. (2011). *Hammerin' Hank Greenberg: Baseball pioneer*. Calkins Creek.

Sturges, P. (2000). *Sacred places* (G. Laroche, Illus.). G. P. Putnam's Sons.

Winter, J. (2009). *You never heard of Sandy Koufax?!* (A. Carrilho, Illus.). Schwartz & Wade Books.

Zeldis McDonough, Y. (2006). *Hammerin' Hank: The life of Hank Greenberg* (M. Zeldis, Illus.). Walker.

References

Biale, D., Galchinsky, M., & Heschel, S. (Eds.) (1998). *Insider/outsider: American Jews and multiculturalism*. University of California Press.

Botelho, M. J., & Rudman, M. K. (2009). *Critical multicultural analysis of children's literature: Mirrors, windows, and doors*. Routledge.

Codell, E. R. (2019, October 1). You don't have to be Jewish. *Planet Esme*. http://planet esme.blogspot.com/2019/10/you-dont-have-to-be-jewish.html

Conference on Jewish Material Claims Against Germany & Schoen Consulting. (2018). *Holocaust knowledge and awareness study*. Claims Conference. http://www.claimscon .org/wp-content/uploads/2018/04/Holocaust-Knowledge-Awareness-Study_ Executive-Summary-2018.pdf

Crisp, T. (2015). A content analysis of Orbis Picture Award-winning nonfiction, 1990–2014. *Language Arts*, *92*(4), 241–255. http://www.jstor.org/stable/24577511

Cummins, J., & Toder, N. D. (2000). The Jewish child in picturebooks. *Five Owls*, *15*(2), 38–40.

Fang, Z., Fu, D., & Lamme, L. L. (2003). The trivialization and misuse of multi-cultural education: Issues of representation and communication. In D. L. Fox & K. G. Short (Eds.), *Stories matter: The complexity of cultural authenticity in children's literature* (pp. 284–303). National Council of Teachers of English.

Founders Online. (n.d.). *From George Washington to the Hebrew Congregation in Newport, Rhode Island, 18 August 1790*. National Archives and Records Administration. https://founders.archives.gov/documents/Washington/05-06-02-0135

Fox, D. L., & Short, K. G. (2003). *Stories matter: The complexity of cultural authenticity in children's literature*. National Council of Teachers of English.

Gopalakrishnan, A. (with Persiani-Becker, K.) (2011). *Multicultural children's literature: A critical issues approach*. SAGE.

Harris, V. J. (1997). *Using multiethnic literature in the K–8 classroom*. Christopher-Gordon.

Ingall, M. (2019, October 28). The Holocaust book we need right now. *Tablet*. https://www.tabletmag.com/jewish-life-and-religion/292591/the-holocaust-book-we-need-right-now

Lee & Low Books. (2020). Classroom library questionnaire (English and Spanish eds.). https://www.leeandlow.com/educators/grade-level-resources/classroom-library-questionnaire

Liu, J. (2013, September 30). *A portrait of Jewish Americans*. Pew Research Center. http://www.pewforum.org/2013/10/01/jewish-american-beliefs-attitudes-culture-survey

Rabinowitz, H. (2019, October 7). Diversity needs Jewish books. *The Book of Life*. https://jewishbooks.blogspot.com/2019/10/diversity-needs-jewish-books.html

Schneider, V. (2017, May 22). Classroom library assessment: How culturally responsive is your library? *The Open Book Blog*. http://blog.leeandlow.com/2017/05/22/classroom-library-assessment-how-culturally-responsive-is-your-classroom-library

Silver, L. R. (2010). *Best Jewish books for children and teens*. The Jewish Publication Society.

Silvey, A. (1996). *Children's books and their creators*. Houghton Mifflin.

Totten, S. (Ed.) (2001). *Teaching Holocaust literature*. Allyn and Bacon.

Weiss, B. (2019). *How to fight anti-Semitism*. Crown Publishing.

Muslim American Nonfiction Literature

KARLA J. MÖLLER, *University of Illinois at Urbana–Champaign*
LEILA TARAKJI, *Sunset Ridge School*
DEBORAH J. MARGOLIS, *Michigan State University*

People may tell you that you can't do something because of the way you look, dress, or pray. Your name may sound different. Never forget that you are extraordinary.

—SAIRA MIR, *Muslim Girls Rise: Inspirational Champions of Our Time*

As a counterpoint to pervasive Islamophobia and inaccurate media portrayals of Muslims and Islam in the United States, this chapter provides recommendations of children's nonfiction literature, including single-subject and collective biographies, narrative nonfiction, and traditional informational texts. Foregrounding the voices of cultural insiders, the authors discuss a range of books that demonstrate the diverse experiences, histories, and cultures of Muslim people.

Chapter Guiding Questions

- What insights can educators and students gain by studying nonfiction literature through the added lens of "Muslim" when texts may otherwise be classified as "African," "Arab," or "Asian"?

- What questions should educators consider when evaluating nonfiction texts featuring representations of Muslims and Muslim Americans in classrooms and school libraries?

- How do educators ensure that the nonfiction books they include in their classrooms and libraries reflect the plurality of ethnic and racial backgrounds, cultures, and experiences of Islam and Muslims?

- How can the study of children's nonfiction literature by and about Muslim people counter the stereotyped portrayals of Muslims in media and culture?

According to the Institute for Social Policy and Understanding's "American Muslim Poll 2017" (Mogahed & Chouhoud, 2017), nearly two in five American Muslim families with school-age children reported that their children experienced bullying due to their faith. A quarter of these bullying incidents were perpetrated by a teacher or administrator. Additionally, among all faith communities, Muslims are the most likely to experience some form of religious discrimination. Subsequent Institute for Social Policy and Understanding (2019) surveys over the past several years further indicate that Islamophobia and anti-Muslim sentiment in America are rising. Because of the troubling ties between rising incidences of bullying and discrimination, including in classrooms and schools, it is critical that educators examine what they know (or think they know) and be open to learning more. The K–8 classroom is a critical space for addressing the growing problems of Islamophobia and anti-Muslim sentiment, and Muslim American children's nonfiction literature can be a valuable resource for educators.

Americans who know a Muslim personally reportedly are much less likely to hold negative attitudes toward Islam and Muslim people. Those who do *not* know a Muslim—about half of all Americans (Mogahed & Mahmood, 2019)—must rely instead on the media for their information. However, "reliance on media for information about Muslims was positively associated with stereotypic beliefs, negative emotions, and support for harmful policies" that target Muslims both in the US and abroad (Saleem et al., 2016, p. 604). Media and popular culture often perpetuate an image of uniformity across all Muslims (often referred to as a "Muslim monolith"), overlooking the complexities, rich cultures, and histories of the 1.8 billion Muslims around the world. Media representations of Muslims also largely characterize them as a foreign threat, associating them with a perpetual possibility of terror (Rana, 2011). The cultural and historical contributions of American Muslims, who constitute about one percent of the total American population, often are ignored and their loyalties constantly are questioned.

Representations of Islam and Muslims are widely available. However, too often, they offer essentialized and distorted depictions of the Muslim faith and those who follow it. As Bayoumi (2008) observed, the problem is not so much a lack of representation but that the available representations are "all abstractions" (p. 5). Bayoumi highlighted an underlying problem, that Muslims are "constantly talked about but almost never heard from" (p. 5). To counter this, there is a strong need for Muslim nonfiction that is written and/or illustrated *by* Muslims ("insider" or #OwnVoices authors and illustrators) and that highlights Muslim contributions to American culture throughout history. Such literature illustrates the rich diversity of Muslim and Muslim American communities, which encompass a vast number of national origins, ethnic and racial backgrounds, cultural traditions, beliefs, and practices. Inclusion of informed nonfiction texts in K–8 classrooms can help counter the racialization (Meer, 2013) and essentialization of Muslim people by infusing reality, highlighting the complexities and humanity of their experiences, into their representations.

The present chapter's writing team consists of Leila, an insider scholar of Muslim American literature and doctoral candidate, and outsider scholar allies Karla, a professor of children's literature, and Deborah, a librarian in Middle East studies. We are united advocates for a more complete and complex picture of Muslims in American life and nonfiction literature. For this chapter, our goal is to introduce books that will support educators and students in understanding more deeply how Muslim Americans negotiate, express, and represent their multifaceted identities. The texts discussed in this chapter foreground the voices and perspectives of cultural insiders and #OwnVoices (Duyvis, 2015; Yorio, 2018) book creators. We also include some carefully vetted quality texts by outsider authors and illustrators that offer valuable material for use in classrooms.

Countering Misconceptions and Nonfiction Text Selection

Including nonfiction books in classrooms and libraries that depict Muslims in a variety of ways can help dispel ingrained stereotypes about Muslim heritage and/or Islamic faith. Educators must engage themselves and their students in the process of identifying and questioning biases and inaccuracies in historical, political, and cultural representations.

In order to do so, it is essential to counter the stereotype of the Muslim monolith by having a better understanding of who Muslim American people are. According to Mogahed and Chouhoud (2017), the Muslim American community is America's most ethnically diverse faith community (25 percent Black, 24 percent white, 18 percent Asian descent, 18 percent Arab, 7 percent multiracial, 5 percent Hispanic and Latinx). Around half of this population was born outside of the US and emigrated from regions across the world, including the Middle East, North Africa, South Asia, sub-Saharan Africa, Europe, and other continents and regions. Muslim Americans' roots and traditions from across the world illustrate the global pan-ethnic nature of the Muslim population.

A common misconception by cultural and religious outsiders is the notion that Islam is foreign to America and that Muslims residing in the US are largely noncitizen immigrants, when in fact about 86 percent are American citizens through birth or naturalization (Mogahed & Chouhoud, 2017). Furthermore, a Muslim presence in the US extends back to America's earliest days, with estimates that 15 to 30 percent of the enslaved people who were brought from Africa to America were of Muslim heritage (Beydoun, 2014).

Often, Muslims are associated with being Arab and vice versa, when in actuality the vast majority of Muslims are non-Arab and do not live in the Middle East. Citing Suleiman (2000), Al-Hazza and Lucking (2005) wrote that, while "Islam is the predominant religion of the Middle East, and most Arab countries are located in the Middle East . . . only 20 percent of Muslims are Arabs" (p. 32). If not examined critically, terms like *Muslim* and *Muslim American* can serve to racialize a wide range of languages, cultures, and ethnicities into a singular category. It is important, therefore, to highlight the plurality of the Muslim community in the US. It is also important that nonfiction books shared with children address Muslim Americans *as* Americans, centering their belonging and contributions to America's national fabric. Many works of Muslim American nonfiction for children can highlight the rich diversity of what is known as the *Umma*, an Arabic word that refers to the community of believers of Islam.

When selecting children's nonfiction for discussion in this chapter, we prioritized books featuring a wide array of Muslim people throughout history, and we consciously included titles featuring both secular and religious perspectives. Such an approach to literature selection aligns well with our theoretical approach, which is grounded in scholarship focused on culturally relevant (Ladson-Billings, 1992, 1995) and culturally sustaining (Ladson-Billings, 2014; Paris, 2012; Paris & Alim, 2014) pedagogies ("CRP" and "CSP," respectively). Educators who engage in CRP recognize and value students' (in Ladson-Billings's earlier work, specifically African American urban students') knowledge, lived experiences, and cultural practices, drawing from those elements as rich pedagogical resources in support of learning that builds academic success, cultural competence, and sociopolitical consciousness in their students.

Those teachers who also foreground CSP expand upon that cultural synergy in ways that center "a fluid understanding of culture, and a teaching practice that explicitly engages questions of equity and justice" (Ladson-Billings, 2014, p. 74). Further, they embrace the heterogeneity of cultural experiences that students bring with them. CSP continually repositions students as active subjects and participants, rather than as objects of teaching and learning. To Paris and Alim (2014), the "two most important tenets [of CSP] are a focus on the plural and evolving nature of youth identity and cultural practices and a commitment to embracing youth culture's counterhegemonic potential" (p. 85). Building upon the tenets of CRP and CSP, nonfiction books that feature diverse representations of Muslim Americans are essential. Although we occasionally weave in additional texts, we have chosen to illuminate nonfiction books that generally fit within four categories: (1) biographies of Muslim people, with a special emphasis on women and girls; (2) narrative nonfiction that offers readers opportunities to see Muslims in books about everyday lives that are not dominated by a focus on war; (3) nonfiction books about the sacred, including religious observations, celebrations, and pilgrimages; and (4) nonfiction texts that focus on visual representations of culture, including art and architecture.

Creating a quality, balanced collection of books for classroom use requires that educators consider literature from multiple angles. This means analyzing selections for quality of content and illustration (e.g., accuracy, authenticity, respectfulness, and inclusion from cultural, ethnic, and religious viewpoints), from literary and aesthetic stances (e.g., literary elements, genre, text features, and illustrations), and from the standpoint of reader engagement (e.g., age, knowledge, and experience-appropriateness). Balance in presentation and approach is also necessary. In an effort to ensure that no single book will serve as a generalized or essentialized depiction, we have taken these elements into account in our selection of children's nonfiction discussed below.

Biography: Representations of Muslim People

It is important to consider gender stereotypes when selecting biographies portraying Muslim and Muslim American people. In our selection, we purposefully identified historical and contemporary depictions of women and girls so that females are not solely depicted as being either "Muslim girls in distress" (Sensoy & Marshall, 2010, p. 295) or as the "stereotype of the oppressed Muslim girl" (Khan, 2009, p. 502). To avoid these stereotypes, literature must show Muslim women making meaningful choices about a wide range of life activities—including education, careers, partners, and clothing—in joyful ways. Rukhsana Khan's (2006) elation over a comic strip that depicted students in a school cafeteria reminded us of this:

> In the background, standing in line, was a Muslim girl in hijab. It gave me a ridiculous sense of joy—of validation—to see "myself" reflected in a cartoon strip. Especially since this Muslim wasn't doing anything bad. No bombs. No threats. No screaming headlines. She was just getting lunch. And she was pretty, too! (p. 36)

Such essential joy should not be so limited. Nor should it be limited only to females. So, in an attempt to combat inflammatory stereotypes of Muslim men often reinforced in US media and politics, we searched for books that showed males as deep and complex individuals and caring parents and partners. A final goal in our selection was to find nonfiction texts that offered historical knowledge, featured contemporary inclusion, and highlighted the various locations Muslims call home. Below, we discuss collective and single-subject biographies of people who exemplify empowerment, leadership, and accomplishment across history and countries.

Collective Biographies

Three collective biographies for younger readers that feature strong Muslim females are *Muslim Girls Rise: Inspirational Champions of Our Time* (Mir, 2019), *Extraordinary Women from the Muslim World* (Maydell & Riahi, 2007), and *First Generation: 36 Trailblazing Immigrants and Refugees Who Make America Great* (Wallace & Wallace, 2018).

Mir's (2019) picturebook, *Muslim Girls Rise: Inspirational Champions of Our Time*, features nineteen contemporary women and girls who have made huge impacts in a wide range of professions, including as activists and politicians, scientists, judges, comedians, authors, sports figures, cartoonists, and more. This picturebook defies stereotypes of Muslim women, what they look like, what they wear, where they come from, and how they practice Islam. For example, the book includes images of women of various nationalities, ethnicities, and races, including some who wear a diverse array of head coverings in public or who wear none at all. The book also includes images of women who came to the Islamic faith through birth or through conversion.

This diverse group of contemporary Muslim women offers essential models for today's youth. In fact, many of them began their activism and careers as young girls or teenagers. Among the women and girls featured in this collection are education activist Malala Yousafzai (who became an education activist and blogger by the age of eleven); tech entrepreneur Amani al-Khatahtbeh (who cofounded MuslimGirl.com at age seventeen); and Olympic fencing medalist, sports clothing entrepreneur, and political activist Ibtihaj Muhammad (who became the first American female Olympian to compete in a hijab and began fencing at age thirteen).

Maydell and Riahi's (2007) *Extraordinary Women from the Muslim World* provides in-depth portraits of thirteen Muslim women across history, starting with the Prophet Muhammad's wives Khadija and Aisha. Five of the women featured live(d) in recent times, including Turkish novelist and emancipation activist Halide Edib Adivar; Egyptian singer Umm Kulthum; Turkish military pilot and Istanbul International Airport namesake Sabha Gökçen; Moroccan painter Chaïbia Talal; and Iranian lawyer, judge, and human rights activist Shirin Ebadi. As in Mir's (2019) text, *Extraordinary Women* depicts both women who wear a head covering and those who do not, reinforcing the important point that this is a woman's choice in Islam. *Extraordinary Women* is exquisitely illustrated by richly hued realistic oil paintings that add personal depth to all the focal women for whom an image is available and appropriate.

Finally, Wallace and Wallace's (2018) *First Generation: 36 Trailblazing Immigrants and Refugees Who Make America Great* features historical and modern first-generation American men and women of various religious and ethnic backgrounds, including LGBTQ+ activists and people who are either known to be Muslim or who are from countries with significant Muslim populations. While its primary focus is on immigrants and refugees, its representations are broadly inclusive. In *First Generation*, readers will encounter profiles similar to (and sometimes featuring the same women as) those in *Muslim Girls Rise* (Mir, 2019) and *Extraordinary Women* (Maydell & Riahi, 2007). For example, Fatimah Hussein's work founding a company that produces sports hijabs and modest activewear for Muslim girls and women is highlighted, and education activist Razia Jan's efforts to establish a woman's college and the free Zabuli Education Center for Girls outside of Kabul are described. All three collective biographies highlighted in this section offer readers and educators multiple opportunities to confront and question stereotypes through their realistic and varied portrayals of Muslim and Muslim American girls and women.

Single-Subject Picturebook Biographies

While we found a number of single-subject picturebook biographies about Muslims, only a small subset is by Muslim authors or illustrators. Below, we highlight examples that focus on historical figures, civil rights leaders, musicians, and athletes.

Lebanese author Fatima Sharafeddine and Iraqi illustrator Intelaq Mohammed Ali are the creators of excellent single-subject biographical picturebooks about two historically important Muslim individuals. In *The Amazing Discoveries of Ibn Sina* (Sharafeddine, 2015), they explore the life of their subject, a polymath (someone who is an expert in many areas) who was both a philosopher and a skilled physician. This biography emphasizes its subject's love of reading and how, through reading, he found a cure for a sultan's illness when other physicians could not effectively treat him. For his service, Ibn Sina subsequently was rewarded with access to the sultan's library. Sharafeddine's (2014) *The Amazing Travels of Ibn Battuta* depicts its subject's life as an explorer who gained extensive international knowledge and then shared what he learned upon returning home to Tangier, Morocco. The book begins with Ibn Battuta's first trip, to Mecca, in 1325 at the age of twenty-one and concludes with his final return to Morocco in 1354.

Both narratives are accompanied by authentic and detailed colorful pencil drawings with stylized, large-eyed depictions of humans as well as intricate page borders that invoke historic Persian miniature art forms. To further enrich readers' knowledge bases, these texts can be paired with other nonfiction books by outsider authors, such as the highly regarded picturebook biography *Traveling Man: The Journey of Ibn Battuta, 1325–1354* (Rumford, 2001), which is told in an accessible first-person narrative. Additionally, more detail can be found in *Ibn Battuta: The Journey of a Medieval Muslim* (Albert, 2018). Students could then explore another important historical figure, the prince and warrior Saladin, in books such as *Saladin: The Muslim Warrior Who Defended His People* (Geyer, 2006) and *Saladin: Noble Prince of Islam* (Stanley, 2002).

In a more contemporary context, Ilyasah Shabazz's (2014) *Malcolm Little: The Boy Who Grew Up to Become Malcolm X* is a heartfelt and informative picturebook biography about her father's childhood. The book also includes details about the lives of X's parents, who were passionate about working toward equity and justice, and their work with the Marcus Garvey movement to position X's later activism within his family's values. Illustrator A. G. Ford's realistic oil paintings, in warm shades that feature rich brown and yellow tones, extend the text, with colors linking across pages to emphasize love and closeness, shifts from joyfulness to despair, and other emotional connections and progressions. As only one example, the orange of Malcolm's blanket used when playing with his siblings bleeds into the orange of the flames devouring the family home on the following page.

Throughout, the text and images unite to emphasize how the loss of Malcolm X's parents, the fierceness of his spirit, and the love and advocacy examples his family set influenced and inspired him to become a leader. The book ends on a hopeful note for young Malcolm and with a detailed, personal author's note that will encourage people to read further about his exceptional life. Other books to pair with this one could include *Malcolm X: A Fire Burning Brightly* (Myers, 2000), *The Book Itch: Freedom, Truth, and Harlem's Greatest Bookstore* (Nelson, 2015), and *28 Days: Moments in Black History That Changed the World* (Smith, 2015).

Contemporary Somali Canadian poet and musician K'naan (2012) tells (with Sol Guy) his own story and the story of his well-known reggae-fusion song in *When I Get Older: The Story behind "Wavin' Flag."* Readers are introduced to his early life in Mogadishu, including information about his close relationship with his grandfather, who wrote the poem upon which the uplifting song "Wavin' Flag" is based. K'naan describes his mother's determined bravery in securing immigration papers after the violence of the Somalian Civil War hit close to their home. In the back matter, K'naan includes a reproduction of his sheet music and song lyrics, along with additional information about his life and Somalia. Illustrator Rudy Gutierrez's swirling, energetic paintings capture the pain and joy of the family's journey, as well as K'naan's music, blending realistic images of people's faces with richly hued expressionistic background compositions. Readers who want to explore K'naan's experiences further can engage with primary sources, such as his other music and writings, including his brief account of his return visit to Mogadishu after two decades (K'naan, 2011) and interviews about his songs and reflections on his work and life (e.g., Smith, 2010). Some of K'naan's more politically infused writing and music can open doors for older students to consider world events and national actions as interconnected and to reflect on large-scale inequities and perceptions.

Finally, while there are a number of quality single-subject picturebook biographies about Muslim athletes such as boxer Muhammad Ali and basketball player Kareem Abdul Jabar, here we chose to focus on a Muslim athlete who may be less well known: Maria Toorpakai Wazir. The picturebook *A Girl Called Genghis Khan: How Maria Toorpakai Wazir Pretended to Be a Boy, Defied the Taliban, and Became a World Famous Squash Player* was written by Michelle Lord (2019), a cultural outsider. Wazir's parents' willingness to engage in subterfuge to support their daughter's passion for sports exemplifies challenges girls face in their struggles for equity while also debunking stereotypes about Muslims and how they live their faith. Throughout her squash training, Wazir still "honored her traditions by praying five times a day" (p. 13). Wazir does not wear a hijab in her daily life, but she is depicted with her head covered while praying, showing her combination of religious respect and personal choice beautifully.

This biography is compelling in text and image, with language that lends itself to being read aloud and with an engaging visual progression that supports the story. The vivid cartoon-style illustrations by Pakistani Muslim feminist and digital design artist Shehzil Malik add energy and emotion. For example, the playful endpapers change from the beginning of the book (squash racquets and balls) to the end (Wazir playing squash in six different action shots). Although Lord (2019) does not include an author's note with information about her research and writing processes, the volume does include back matter that provides recommendations for additional reading, a selective bibliography, and a timeline of "female firsts" in sports.

Narrative Nonfiction

Narrative nonfiction constitutes nonfiction content that is written like a story. These books often include elements typically associated with fiction, including literary elements, such as plot, theme, and character, and story structures like rising tension, a climax, and falling action. Although commonly used in biographies, the narrative nonfiction we highlight here has a broader scope and includes such topics as family histories and important world events.

Nonfiction featuring Muslims and Muslim Americans often tells the stories of immigrants and refugees, particularly people who have had to flee from war-torn homelands. While these are both important and necessary narratives, it is essential to offer readers additional nonfiction narratives that focus on lives and relationships without the heartache of war and other injustices. The heart-warming picturebook *My Grandma and Me* (Javaherbin, 2019) describes the loving bond between a grandmother and her granddaughter who are living in Iran. Written by the granddaughter, the story illuminates aspects of their close relationship that will appeal to all readers who have been close to their grandparents, while also depicting elements of Islamic faith throughout (e.g., mosques, Ramadan) that will offer personal reflections to Muslim readers and information to religious outsiders.

Coming to America: A Muslim Family's Story (Wolf, 2003) is a photo essay that describes the daily and weekly life of a family who immigrated from Egypt to the United States after the father received a green card during the 1995 Diversity Immigrant Visa program. The children—two girls and a boy—are depicted with their parents at home and in the mosque, as well as at school and at play with both Muslim and non-Muslim friends. The family members are successful and happy in the US, but they still value and miss Egypt. The adults are depicted as having a strong partnership and the children are depicted with love and hope for their lives and careers. Tricia Brown's (2006) *Salaam: A Muslim American Boy's Story* makes the important contribution of depicting a mixed-faith family. This nonfiction photo essay highlights the impact of the main character's mother's conversion to Islam when she married. The book discusses prejudice, including some initial resistance to the mother's religious conversion. However, this is not the primary focus of the text. Instead, inclusion, family joy, and facts about Muslims and Muslim life are centered. The Five Pillars of Islam are also described and a glossary is included.

We turn now to two quality narrative nonfiction texts that do focus upon war and its impact. *Lost and Found Cat: The True Story of Kunkush's Incredible Journey* (Kuntz & Shrodes, 2017) is the true story of Kunkush, a cat who is lost during his family's journey from Iraq to Greece. When the family (a widow and her five children) is forced to flee violence in Iraq, they bring their beloved cat with them. En route to Greece, Kunkush's carrier breaks and he is lost. The book highlights the efforts of aid workers who find Kunkush and, recognizing the sacrifices and hardships the family has already endured, work with a world-wide community using social media to reunite Kunkush with his family. The reunion of the family and their cat is an important small moment of light and human kindness during a time of tremendous hardship.

The Grand Mosque of Paris: A Story of How Muslims Rescued Jews during the Holocaust (Ruelle & DeSaix, 2009) recounts the brave Muslims who took enormous personal risks to shelter Jews in the mosque during the 1940–1944 Nazi occupation of Paris. Through gripping narration and arresting images, the authors have recounted a vital piece of interfaith history for upper elementary readers. The text also includes seven pages of back matter that educators will find useful as a model for the kinds of research that go into the creation of well-documented nonfiction books.

The Sacred: Religious Observations, Celebrations, and Pilgrimages

A number of high-quality nonfiction books about religious observations, celebrations, and pilgrimages written or illustrated by Muslims and Muslim Americans are available today. Many refer to the Five Pillars of Islam, the religion's core beliefs and practices, including the declaration of faith (*shahada*), prayer (*salah*), alms (*zakat*), the fasting of Ramadan (ending with the Islamic holiday Eid al-Fitr, which is the festival of the breaking of the fast), and the Hajj Pilgrimage. Also frequently highlighted is the hijab, the head covering worn in public by many Muslim women as an expression of love for Islam. Additional faith-based concepts referenced in these books include respecting parents, demonstrating Prophetic manners, and treating others well. Many, too, emphasize the importance of family and community.

One book that highlights Muslim family and community celebrations is *Mabrook! A World of Muslim Weddings* (Robert, 2016). This picturebook presents a range of styles, practices, traditions, and ways of celebrating weddings and marriages amongst Muslim people. It covers ceremonies and celebrations held across a large span of geographic areas, including Pakistan, Morocco, Somalia, and the United Kingdom. Shirin Adl's illustrations are colorful, eclectic, and joyful—completed through various artistic methods (3D collage embellishments, drawings, and paintings) and extensive use of multimedia (paper, fabric, and what appear to be pastels, watercolors, crayons, acrylic, and ink). The book is a beautiful union of diversity in text and image and includes consciously interracial illustrations. No same-sex marriages are included, however, so the text could be expanded with use of online information, such as the news from the United Kingdom about one of their first same-sex Muslim weddings (e.g., Bruner, 2017).

A number of books that highlight Muslim religious traditions include a focus on Ramadan, a holy month of fasting, reflection, and prayer for Muslim people. To offer a nonfiction text set that is informative and inclusive, we highlight three books here, each intended for readers of different ages or reading levels. *Ramadan* (Eliot, 2018), part of Simon & Schuster's Celebrate the World series, is a board book for very young readers that includes simplistic, straightforward descriptions of the traditions that occur during the month of observance. The text is accompanied by Iranian-born artist Rashin Kheiriyeh's illustrations, brilliant gouache paintings featuring traditional Islamic floral flourishes and designs.

Suhaib Hamid Ghazi's (1996) *Ramadan* follows the experiences of a young boy, Hakeem, as he and his family observe Ramadan. Much of the book conveys information about the practices involved in Ramadan, such as fasting, attending the mosque, reflecting, and spending time with family. Illustrator Omar Rayyan uses watercolor in both realistic and impressionistic styles to convey various practices of Ramadan and highlight associated phases of the moon throughout the month. Some pages sport ornate designs with Islamic design geometry or Arabic words.

Finally, for older readers, *Ramadan: The Holy Month of Fasting* (Khan, 2018) offers the most detailed information of the three and includes important nonfiction text features such as modern photographs, text boxes, and other informational inserts within the body of the book, as well as a glossary, index, and resource list at the back. It covers basic information about Islam and Ramadan and shares details and images of Ramadan celebrations in thirteen countries.

Design: Books Featuring Art and Architecture Design

When selecting children's nonfiction depicting Muslims and Muslim Americans, careful consideration of the art is paramount. In current Islamic artistic tradition, for example, the face and body of prophets, particularly Muhammad, "cannot be drawn and cannot be produced in pictures because they are, according to Islamic faith, infallible individuals, role models and therefore should not be presented in any manner that might cause disrespect for them" (Dr. Azzam Tamimi, former head of the Institute of Islamic Political Thought, quoted in McManus, 2015, para. 28). For example, in Demi's (2003) biography, Muhammad is depicted as a golden silhouette, but no explicit imagery of his features is included.

Along with the cautionary note about what should(n't) be included in Islamic art, it is also paramount to acknowledge the great contributions Muslim people have made to the world of art and design. One way this can be accomplished is through sharing nonfiction texts that feature or highlight important works of art created by Muslim individuals. Lizann Flatt's (2012) *Arts and Culture in the Early Islamic World* describes art through calligraphy, textiles, literature, movement, painting, pottery, glass- and metalware, and various forms of architecture. The book is part of the currently six-book Life in the Early Islamic World series and presents information in a concise and well-organized manner. In addition to the primary text, the book also includes a glossary, index, timelines, and biographies of focal artists and historical figures. The other books in the series are also recommended. Na'ima bint Robert's (2005) *Journey through Islamic Art* incorporates an element of fantasy by framing the text as a young girl's fictionalized journey through enticingly painted (gouache) illustrations of actual locations, including cities, mosques, and gardens, starting in historical Sarmakand and Baghdad and ending with the building of the Taj Mahal. Through engagement with this text, readers are introduced to the rich heritage and art and architecture of Islamic civilization. The book is written in both Arabic and English, with the Arabic text foregrounded on either the left-hand page or above the English translation throughout the book.

Ritu Khoda and Vanita Pai's (2016) *Raza's Bindu* introduces readers to influential Indian Muslim painter Sayed Haider (S. H.) Raza, who was born before the 1947 partition of India and later lived in France. This biography offers only minimal details of the artist's life as a child, focusing on Raza's love of nature and a singular event in elementary school in which his teacher asked him to stare intently at a dot for an extended period of time. This event inspired Raza's *bindu* paintings, varied visual reflections on dots. The majority of the book shares artistic and philosophical principles in Raza's art and encourages readers to try painting in the style of Raza's bindus.

These books are only three of many available nonfiction titles that explore the lives and contributions of Muslims and Muslim Americans artists, designers, and architects. They range from standard informational text to those that blur the boundaries between fiction and nonfiction.

In Closing

Incorporating Muslim and Muslim American nonfiction literature in classrooms and libraries is important for all students. Muslim-focused nonfiction offers a vital alternative to the distorted information that is propagated by popular culture and media. To study and teach Muslim and Muslim American nonfiction is to acknowledge Muslims and their roles in American life and within larger national and global communities. Perhaps more important, it emphasizes the complexity and humanity of Muslim people and allows all readers to connect with Muslim and Muslim Americans' experiences on an intimate level. Engagement with these texts in classrooms or libraries may provide non-Muslim students with their first or only experiences with positive depictions of Islam and Muslims. For Muslim students, the opportunity to see their faith and communities represented in a positive light can be valuable and empowering. These experiences can create a wonderful space for cross-cultural dialogue and understanding. It is our hope that this chapter provides material that encourages educators to share these books with students and to engage with their students in critically analyzing and questioning representations of Muslim people in media and popular culture.

Practical Strategies

- Provide students with single-subject biographies written by cultural insiders. Engage them in a critical comparative study by then examining other biographies and nonfiction resources, including primary sources, to add complexity and richness to their understandings. Vary this activity by including Muslims who lived historically and in the present day, or by focusing on specific professions and considering who is represented and who is not.

- Provide students with collective biographies about Muslim and Muslim American women. Engage them in an analysis of who is represented in these books and how they are depicted in word and image.

- Have students read and explore a variety of children's nonfiction books about Muslims and Muslim Americans. Lead them in a discussion of what surprises and is new to them. Working together, investigate the points they raise to establish accuracy and examine assumptions. For example, what marks a book as being inclusive of Muslims? Why?

- Provide groups of students with copies of nonfiction books that have been selected to receive an award for Muslim youth literature (see Book Awards, below). Look for patterns and question whether any particular geographical location, cultural practice, or religious observant is over- or underrepresented. Compare these patterns with literature not selected by the awarding agencies.

- Examine winners and honorees of other major book awards for nonfiction, such as the Robert F. Sibert Informational Book Medal (see http://

www.ala.org/alsc/awardsgrants/bookmedia/sibertmedal) and the Orbis Pictus Award (see https://ncte.org/awards/orbis-pictus-award-nonfiction-for-children). Consider whether any books by and featuring Muslim people and characters are represented.

Ten Additional Nonfiction Books about Muslims

1. Al-Hassani, S. T. S. (Ed.). (2012). *1001 inventions: The enduring legacy of Muslim civilization* (3rd ed.). National Geographic.

2. Ali-Karamali, S. (2013). *Growing up Muslim: Understanding the beliefs and practices of Islam*. Ember.

3. Barnard, B. (2011). *The genius of Islam: How Muslims made the modern world* (B. Barnard, Illus.). Knopf Books.

4. Khan, S. (2000). *Tell me about the Prophet Mohammad: What the Prophet's message is, why his life is so important, and what he teaches me*. Goodword.

5. Mann, E. (2008). *Taj Mahal: A story of love and empire* (A. Witschonke, Illus.). Mikaya.

6. Mileham, R. (Ed.) (2012). *1001 inventions & awesome facts from Muslim civilization*. National Geographic Kids.

7. Romero, L. (2016). *Ibn al-Haytham: The man who discovered how we see* (A. Amro, Illus.). National Geographic Kids.

8. Wilkinson, P. (2018). *DK Eyewitness books: Islam*. DK Children.

9. Winter, J. (2017). *The world is not a rectangle: A portrait of architect Zaha Hadid* (J. Winter, Illus.). Beach Lane.

10. Yousafzai, M. (2017). *Malala's magic pencil* (Kerascoët, Illus.). Little, Brown Books for Young Readers.

Five Online Resources

1. Girls of the Crescent. (n.d.). *Empowering Muslim girls through books*. https://www.girlsofthecrescent.org

2. Institute for Social Policy and Understanding. (2018, September). *Educators' toolkit: Resources for teachers, instructors, and administrators*. https://www.ispu.org/educators

3. Islamophobia is Racism. (n.d.). *Resource for teaching & learning about anti-Muslim racism in the United States.* https://islamophobiaisracism.word press.com

4. Robinson, R. (2019, January 2). *An elementary-level annotated bibliography of Middle East and Arab World themed literature.* Middle East Outreach Council. http://www.meoc.us/resources/an-elementary-level-annotated-bibliogra phy-of-middle-east-and-arab-themed-world-literature

5. TeachMideast. (2019, March 20). *For educators.* https://teachmideast.org/for-educators

Book Awards

- Arab American Book Awards—see https://arabamericanmuseum.org/book-awards
- Children's Africana Book Award—see http://africaaccessreview.org/childrens-africana-book-awards
- Middle East Book Award—see http://www.meoc.us/book-awards.html
- South Asia Book Award—see https://southasiabookaward.wisc.edu

Children's Books Cited

Albert, E. (2018). *Ibn Battuta: The journey of a medieval Muslim.* Kube.

Brown, T. (2006). *Salaam: A Muslim American boy's story* (K. Cardwell, Illus.). Henry Holt and Company.

Demi. (2003). *Muhammad* (Demi, Illus.). Margaret K. McElderry Books.

Eliot, H. (2018). *Ramadan* (R. Kheiriyeh, Illus.). Little Simon.

Flatt, L. (2012). *Arts and culture in the early Islamic World.* Crabtree.

Geyer, F. (2006). *Saladin: The Muslim warrior who defended his people.* National Geographic.

Ghazi, S. H. (1996). *Ramadan* (O. Rayyan, Illus.). Holiday House.

Javaherbin, M. (2019). *My grandma and me* (L. Yankey, Illus.). Walker Books.

Khan, A. Z. (2018). *Ramadan: The holy month of fasting.* Orca Book Publishers.

Khoda, R., & Pai, V. (2016). *Raza's bindu* (K. Shanbhag, Illus.). Art1st.

K'naan (with Guy, S.) (2012). *When I get older: The story behind "Wavin' Flag"* (R. Gutierrez, Illus.). Tundra.

Kuntz, D., & Shrodes, A. (2017). *Lost and found cat: The true story of Kunkush's incredible journey* (S. Cornelison, Illus.). Crown.

Lord, M. (2019). *A girl called Genghis Khan: How Maria Toorpakai Wazir pretended to be a boy, defied the Taliban, and became a world famous squash player* (S. Malik, Illus.). Sterling.

Maydell, N., & Riahi, S. (2007). *Extraordinary women from the Muslim world* (H. Amin, Illus.). Global Content Ventures.

Mir, S. (2019). *Muslim girls rise: Inspirational champions of our time* (A. Jaleel, Illus.). Salaam Reads/Simon & Schuster Books for Young Readers.

Myers, W. D. (2000). *Malcolm X: A fire burning brightly* (Leonard Jenkins, Illus.). Amistad.

Nelson, V. M. (2015). *The book itch: Freedom, truth, and Harlem's greatest bookstore* (R. G. Christie, Illus.). Carolrhoda Books.

Robert, N. b. (2005). *Journey through Islamic art* (D. Mayo, Illus.). Mantra.

Robert, N. b. (2016). *Mabrook! A world of Muslim weddings* (English–Arabic ed.) (S. Adl, Illus.; S. Fawzi, Arabic trans.). Frances Lincoln Children's Books.

Ruelle, K. G., & DeSaix, D. D. (2008). *The Grand Mosque of Paris: A story of how Muslims rescued Jews during the Holocaust* (D. D. DeSaix, Illus.). Holiday House.

Rumford, J. (2001). *Traveling man: The journey of Ibn Battuta 1325–1354* (J. Rumford, Illus.). Houghton Mifflin Harcourt.

Shabazz, I. (2014). *Malcolm Little: The boy who grew up to become Malcolm X* (A. G. Ford, Illus.). Atheneum Books for Young Readers.

Sharafeddine, F. (2014). *The amazing travels of Ibn Battuta* (I. M. Ali, Illus.). Groundwood.

Sharafeddine, F. (2015). *The amazing discoveries of Ibn Sina* (I. M. Ali, Illus.). Groundwood.

Smith, Jr., C. R. (2015). *28 days: Moments in Black history that changed the world* (S. W. Evans, Illus.). Roaring Brook Press.

Stanley, D. (2002). *Saladin: Noble Prince of Islam* (D. Stanley, Illus.). HarperCollins.

Wallace, S. N., & Wallace, R. (2018). *First generation: 36 trailblazing immigrants and refugees who make America great* (A. Nowicka, Illus.). Little, Brown Books for Young Readers.

Wolf, B. (2003). *Coming to America: A Muslim family's story* (B. Wolf, Photog.). Lee & Low Books.

References

Al-Hazza, T., & Lucking, B. (2005). The minority of suspicion: Arab Americans. *Multicultural Review, 14*(13), 32–38. https://doi.org/10.1598/RT.62.3.3

Bayoumi, M. (2008). *How does it feel to be a problem?: Being young and Arab in America.* Penguin Press.

Beydoun, K. A. (2014, July 3). African slaves were the 1st to celebrate Ramadan in America. *The Root.* https://www.theroot.com/african-slaves-were-the-1st-to-celebrate-ramadan-in-ame-1790876253

Bruner, R. (2017, July 11). This history-making couple just had one of the U.K.'s first same-sex Muslim weddings. *Time.* https://time.com/4853939/gay-muslim-marriage/

Duyvis, C. (2015). FAQ. *#OwnVoices.* https://www.corinneduyvis.net/ownvoices

Khan, R. (2006, September 2). Muslims in children's books: An author looks back and at the ongoing publishing challenges. *School Library Journal.* https://www.slj.com/?detailStory=muslims-in-childrens-books

Khan, R. (2009). It's how you say it. *The Horn Book Magazine, 85*(5), 499–505.

K'naan. (2011, September 24). A son returns to the agony of Somalia. *The New York Times.* https://www.nytimes.com/2011/09/25/opinion/sunday/returning-to-somalia-after-20-years.html

Ladson-Billings, G. (1992). Reading between the lines and beyond the pages: A culturally relevant approach to literacy teaching. *Theory Into Practice, 31*(3), 312–320. https://doi.org/10.1080/00405849209543558

Ladson-Billings, G. (1995). Toward a theory of culturally relevant pedagogy. *American Educational Research Journal, 32*(3), 465–491. https://doi.org/10.31022F00028312032003465

Ladson-Billings, G. (2014). Culturally relevant pedagogy 2.0: a.k.a. the remix. *Harvard Educational Review, 84*(1). https://doi.org/10.17763/haer.84.1.p2rj131485484751

McManus, J. (2015, January 15). Have pictures of Muhammad always been forbidden? *BBC News Magazine.* https://www.bbc.com/news/magazine-30814555

Meer, N. (2013). Racialization and religion: Race, culture and difference in the study of antisemitism and Islamophobia. *Ethnic and Racial Studies, 36*(3), 385–398. https://doi.org/10.1080/01419870.2013.734392

Mogahed, D., & Chouhoud, Y. (2017). *American Muslim poll 2017: Muslims at the crossroads.* Institute for Social Policy and Understanding. https://www.ispu.org/american-muslim-poll-2017

Mogahed, D., & Mahmood, A. (2019). *American Muslim poll 2019: Predicting and preventing Islamophobia.* Institute for Social Policy and Understanding. https://www.ispu.org/public-policy/american-muslim-poll

Paris, D. (2012). Culturally sustaining pedagogy: A needed change in stance, terminology, and practice. *Educational Researcher, 41*(3), 93–97. https://doi.org/10.3102/0013189X12441244

Paris, D., & Alim, H. S. (2014). What are we seeking to sustain through culturally sustaining pedagogy? A loving critique forward. *Harvard Educational Review, 84*(1), 85–100. https://doi.org/10.17763/haer.84.1.982l873k2ht16m77

Rana, J. (2011). *Terrifying Muslims: Race and labor in the South Asian diaspora.* Duke University Press.

Saleem, M., Yang, G. S., & Ramasubramanian, S. (2016). Reliance on direct and mediated contact and public policies supporting outgroup harm. *Journal of Communication, 66*(4), 604–624. https://doi-org.proxy2.cl.msu.edu/10.1111/jcom.12234

Sensoy, Ö., & Marshall, E. (2010). Missionary girl power: Saving the "Third World" one girl at a time. *Gender and Education, 22*(3), 295–311. https://doi.org/10.1080/09540250903289451

Smith, C. L. (2010, February 27). K'naan: "My success is their success." *The Guardian.* https://www.theguardian.com/music/2010/feb/28/knaan-interview

Suleiman, M. (2000). *Teaching about Arab Americans: What social studies teachers should know* (ED442714). https://files.eric.ed.gov/fulltext/ED442714.pdf

Yorio, K. (2018, October 23). #OwnVoices not familiar to all. *School Library Journal.* https://www.slj.com/?detailStory=ownvoices-not-familiar-all

10 Reflecting, Observing, Participating: Nonfiction Books Depicting Individuals with Disabilities

SHARON BLACK, *Brigham Young University*
TERRELL A. YOUNG, *Brigham Young University*
MARY ANNE PRATER, *Brigham Young University*
TINA M. TAYLOR, *Brigham Young University*

"My name is Julia. Sometimes I wiggle or make sounds that I can't control, because I have Tourette's syndrome. People may look at me funny because they think I am not paying attention or just acting out. But it's not true; I am listening. I don't always like having to explain—it frustrates me—but it helps when I tell people that it's just what my body does."

—SONIA Sotomayor, *Just Ask! Be Different, Be Brave, Be You*

Individuals with disabilities have been widely neglected in children's nonfiction books. When these books are used in inclusive classrooms, students with disabilities benefit as they reflect on their own needs, challenges, strengths, and potential victories. Their peers better understand circumstances of these classmates' lives. Further understanding and compassion come with deeper thought and vicarious involvement. This chapter discusses current trends, selection criteria, specific recommended books, and suggestions for deepening young readers' involvement with nonfiction literature by and about people with disabilities.

Chapter Guiding Questions

- How can educators assess the accuracy of content and images in nonfiction books depicting people with disabilities? What stereotypes should be avoided?

- What sorts of outside research by educators and students can ensure that nonfiction books present the actual realities and lives of people with disabilities?

- How are interpersonal relationships including individuals with disabilities portrayed in nonfiction for children and youth? Why are reciprocal relationships so important?

Julia is one of ten children introduced in *Just Ask! Be Different, Be Brave, Be You* by Sonia Sotomayor (2019), illustrated by Rafael López, a pair who together have created a seamless text that works to dismiss ableism (mistreatment or neglect of those with disabilities) and racism for young readers. Framed by a context of creating a garden, each child explains their disability, demonstrating strengths that contribute to making them the strong vibrant individuals they are. Some, like Julia, along with Anthony who uses a wheelchair, Madison and Arturo who are blind, Vijay who is deaf, and Grace who has Down syndrome, have disabilities that are visible to observers. In contrast, Rafael who has asthma, Bianca who has dyslexia, Anh who stutters, and Nolan who has an occasionally life-threatening nut allergy may not seem to have disabilities until others know them well. Two friends in the book who have autism—Jordan, who speaks, and Tiana, who does not—share their disability as they play together.

López, a native of Mexico who specializes in portraying diverse children, and Sotomayor, who grew up in Puerto Rican areas of East and South Bronx in New York, USA, are familiar with the experiences of children of diverse backgrounds. Children depicted in this book are not generic; they have a variety of facial and physical characteristics, skin pigmentations, hairstyles and textures, and clothing. The characters, who are racially diverse and have a variety of disabilities, work together with excitement and enthusiasm. Anthony in his wheelchair is involved in everything. Anh also is central, although her mouth is closed and she has a shy little smile. Vijay, whose deafness makes him quiet as well, can be seen beside her. The children who are blind run alongside the rest, each carrying a large plant in one hand, with the other hand on their service dog or cane. All these children have different strengths and cultural traits, and they are one tightly unified big happy group.

In her letter introducing the book, Sotomayor (2019) explains:

> I hope by seeing yourself or your friends in this story, you will understand that we're all different, and you will find that notion comforting and empowering.... Instead of fearing our differences or ignoring them, we can shed light on them and explore them together. (p. 1)

Although a fictional picturebook, *Just Ask* is a factual text. It packs a great deal of information about abilities and disabilities into one short book. The children are composites with realistic voices that make them seem authentic for readers.

Classrooms and libraries may not have this number or diversity of students with disabilities. But Sotomayor's goal in portraying these children as positively interacting with one another should be the goal of every educator, therapist, or administrator who works with children: to promote confidence, acceptance, appreciation, friendship, and inclusion. The use of books depicting children with disabilities as diverse, capable, contributing, and accepting individuals can contribute significantly to these goals. The other books highlighted in this chapter relate experiences of real individuals. It is our hope that educators will share these books to (a) help children with disabilities see themselves as happy, capable, strong, contributing individuals; (b) help nondisabled classmates, peers, and others appreciate these individuals as friends and treat them equitably; and (c) promote compassion, understanding, and unity among all people (see Grow et al., 2019).

The coauthors of this chapter identify as persons who are nondisabled, but we teach with and study, research, write, and care deeply about individuals with disabilities, especially in regard to the ways they are portrayed in children's literature. Mary Anne Prater and Tina M. Taylor have devoted their professional careers to teaching students with disabilities, preparing future special educators, and studying the characterization of disability in books for young readers. They are also cofounders of the Dolly Gray Children's Literature Award honoring these books (see also Book Awards, below), and have served as chair or committee members collectively for this award for over thirty years. Terrell Young has spent many years as a classroom teacher and has devoted his academic career to literature written for children and young adults. His specialty area is quality nonfiction. Sharon Black has studied and written about portrayals of disabilities in children's literature. Her work is motivated by a close family member with autism who has benefited significantly from warm, nurturing inclusion in diverse early childhood classrooms.

Current Trends

Books portraying people with disabilities are becoming more widely available as school inclusion increases in number and quality. In 1975, United States federal legislation mandated special education services for all school-age children with disabilities. Since that time, students with disabilities have received services in increasingly more inclusive settings with their peers. In 2016, 94.9 percent of them were educated in classrooms where they were included with their peers for at least part of the day, a 59 percent increase from 2008 (US Department of Education, 2019). In 2018, 63.1 percent of students with disabilities were educated in classrooms with these peers for 80 percent or more of the day (US Department of Education, 2019).

As increasing numbers of students with disabilities are being included in general education classrooms, teachers and other educators need to select books with specific students in mind, including (a) those who need to see depictions of their own experiences and challenges, (b) those who share background experiences or interests with their classmates or schoolmates with disabilities, and (c) all other students—who should be involved in this unification (Crawford & Calabria, 2018; Prater et al., 2006).

Laminack and Kelly (2019) explain that books enable readers to "view a reality beyond what is known through personal experience" (p. xvi). For some, this may include the reality of those close to them. For example, when Jayanth Uppaluri, an upper elementary student, read Sharon Draper's (2010) fictional book *Out of My Mind*, she was able to see Melody, the protagonist with cerebral palsy who is unable to speak, as a bright and capable person. Because of this, she was then able to see her own brother with autism in a new light. After encountering this text, Jayanth's relationship with her brother became more meaningful. In a letter to the author, Jayanth wrote:

> Before I read your book, I thought my brother didn't understand me. Because he couldn't talk that well, I didn't think he could understand anyone. After I read your book, I realized something. I was wrong. He understands me. The only person who didn't understand anything was me. (quoted in Allen, 2014, para. 10; see also Uppaluri, 2017)

Most of the recently published children's nonfiction books about or featuring people with disabilities are life stories—biographies, autobiographies, and memoirs. Although traditionally these genres feature well-known historical figures, such as Louis Braille and Helen Keller, many biographies today feature well-known contemporary people with disabilities. One notable example is Sy Montgomery's (2014) *Temple Grandin: How the Girl Who Loved Cows Embraced Autism and Changed the World*. This biography focuses on Grandin, a person on the autism spectrum who is well known for her scientific contributions surrounding the treatment of livestock. For older readers, Jim Ottaviani's (2019) *Hawking* is a graphic biography of Stephen Hawking, the brilliant physicist with amyotrophic lateral sclerosis (also known as Lou Gehrig's disease).

Another recent trend is for biographies and autobiographies to feature less widely known individuals with disabilities (Young et al., 2020). In *Born Just Right* (Reeves & Reeves, 2019), readers meet Jordan Reeves, a middle school student who was born with a limb difference—her left arm stops right above the elbow.

Jordan notes that her arm does not define her but gives her "many opportunities to see the world in a different way" (p. 2). Shane Burcaw's (2017) *Not So Different: What You REALLY Want to Ask about Having a Disability* is the autobiography of an individual with spinal muscular atrophy who has gained recognition through his books and social media presence.

Some quality nonfiction books are not biographical; many of these are narrative nonfiction, which provide accounts of well-researched factual stories or events. Narrative nonfiction texts convey information by using literary styles and techniques often found in fiction. As Stewart and Young (2018) write, "Narrative nonfiction appeals to fiction lovers because it includes real characters and settings, narrative scenes, and ideally a narrative arc with rising tension, a climax, and denouement" (p. 12). One example, *All the Way to the Top: How One Girl's Fight for Americans with Disabilities Changed Everything* (Pimentel, 2020), describes the efforts of a child with cerebral palsy, Jennifer Keelan, who participated from her wheelchair in demonstrations for the disability rights movement. The book includes a moving description of the Capital Crawl, a protest involving many individuals who use wheelchairs, including Jennifer, who rode to the US Capitol Building, climbed out of their chairs, and pulled themselves to the top of the Capitol steps. As noted in Pimental's book, the visibility of this event contributed greatly to Congress's subsequent passage of the Americans with Disabilities Act.

Selection Criteria

Several researchers have described and advocated for the use of criteria when depicting individuals with disabilities in literature for children (Beckett et al., 2010; Blaska, 2003; Grow et al., 2019). Some criteria include evaluations of personal portrayal, interactions and relationships, and exemplary practices. Below, we use and adapt these criteria, applying them to children's nonfiction.

Personal Portrayal

Portrayals of people with disabilities need to be realistic and accurate. An individual with a disability should not be portrayed as exclusively a hero or a victim, or as identical to or completely different from their nondisabled peers. To acknowledge the personhood that all humans share, person-first language should generally be used (e.g., not a "disabled person" but a "person with a disability"). Shane Burcaw, the individual with spinal muscular atrophy mentioned previously, has a body as small as a child's and a head that is the same size as an adult's. In his book for adult readers, *Laughing at My Nightmare* (Burcaw, 2014), he explains, "I desperately wanted to show the world that I was normal despite my disability" (p. 83). Burcaw's self-acceptance strategy is reflected in the book's title: he uses genuine humor, though with acerbic undertones.

Interactions and Relationships

Although an individual may have a variety of interpersonal experiences, their portrayal in nonfiction should emphasize reciprocal relationships: shared humanity—not pity—and respect. Although severely limited physically, Burcaw (2014) has a close, loving, and highly supportive family, many friends with whom he shares a variety of activities (including sports), and a girlfriend. His dependence on a complex motorized wheelchair and his need for personal assistance—even for brushing his teeth—do not preclude him from these relationships.

With a contrasting but equally engaging tone, in *Proud to Be Deaf: Discover My Community and My Language* (Beese et al., 2019), seven-year-old Ava Beese, who is deaf, tells of good friends at her school who have learned sign language in order to communicate with her. Communication is not always easy or totally accurate, but Ava loves her friends and appreciates their efforts. Ava is depicted as joining her friends in doing what seven-year-old children do.

Exemplary Practices

Portrayals of inclusion, citizenship, valued occupations, and self-determination for individuals with disabilities should be represented in contemporary settings. But depictions and characterizations in biographies and all nonfiction must be accurate to and reflect the time period. Two examples of this represented in children's biographies include Louis Braille's hunger to read books before he created braille and Temple Grandin's difficulties when her teachers had no knowledge of what she herself would later discover about autism.

Books with contemporary settings should portray inclusiveness in schools and communities. As detailed later in this chapter, two African children with disabilities, Rebeka Ueiyonze in Rwanda and Emmanuel Ofosu Yeboah of Ghana, were forbidden at first to attend school, and both had to take extreme measures to prove they could keep up with their classmates. Ava Beese, mentioned previously, has been fully included in her school in London, accompanied by a sign language interpreter. She notes, "I'm the only deaf child at my primary school—at first, I didn't notice that I was different from the other students, but as I've got older, I've learned that I'm unique" (Beese et al., 2019, p. 14).

Awards as Criteria

Another way to select children's nonfiction books depicting people with disabilities is to examine lists of books that have received national or international awards. As many have noted, award-winning books have undergone critical scrutiny. Three major awards recognize books for children and young adults featuring people with disabilities.

The annual Schneider Family Book Awards (see Table 10.1 for a list of recent nonfiction award winners), administered by the American Library Association, honor an author or illustrator for an outstanding artistic expression of the disability experience for child or adolescent audiences.

The biennial Dolly Gray Children's Literature Award emphasizes authenticity over artistry in the portrayal of the individual with a disability. Administered by the Division on Autism and Developmental Disabilities of the Council for Exceptional Children, this award focuses on developmental disabilities, such as autism, intellectual disabilities, and developmental delays. Authors, illustrators, and publishers of high-quality fiction and biography for children and young adults are honored (see Table 10.2 for a list of recent nonfiction awardees).

Outstanding Books for Young People with Disabilities is a book list compiled by the International Board on Books for Young People (IBBY) in odd-numbered years, including fiction and nonfiction texts for and about children and young adults with disabilities. These books may be produced in braille, sign language,

TABLE 10.1. Schneider Family Book Award Nonfiction Winners since 2005

Year Awarded	Book Title, Author, Illustrator	Disability
2005	*My Thirteenth Winter: A Memoir*, written by Samantha Abeel	Specific learning disability
2010	*Django: The World's Greatest Jazz Guitarist*, written and illustrated by Bonnie Christensen	Orthopedic impairment (hand)
2014	*A Splash of Red: The Life and Art of Horace Pippin*, written by Jen Bryant and illustrated by Melissa Sweet *	Orthopedic impairment (arm injury)
2015	*A Boy and a Jaguar*, written by Alan Rabinowitz and illustrated by Cátia Chien	Speech impairment
2016	*Emmanuel's Dream: The True Story of Emmanuel Ofosu Yeboah*, written by Laurie Ann Thompson and illustrated by Sean Qualls *	Orthopedic impairment (leg)
2017	*Six Dots: A Story of Young Louis Braille*, written by Jen Bryant and illustrated by Boris Kulikov	Blindness
2018	*Silent Days, Silent Dreams*, written and illustrated by Allen Say	Autism, deafness, and mutism
2020	*Just Ask! Be Different, Be Brave, Be You*, written by Sonia Sotomayor and illustrated by Rafael López *	Various

Note: * Indicates the book features Black, Indigenous, or people of color.

or pictographs; some are in a format that provides readers with a tactile experience (see Table 10.3 for nonfiction books listed by IBBY).

TABLE 10.2. Dolly Gray Children's Literature Award Nonfiction Winners since 2006

Year Awarded	Book Title, Author, Illustrator	Disability
2006	*Keeping Up with Roo*, written by Sharlee Glenn and illustrated by Dan Andreasen	Intellectual disability
2012	*My Brother Charlie*, written by Holly Robinson Peete and Ryan Elizabeth Peete and illustrated by Shane W. Evans *	Autism
2016	*My Friend Suhana*, written by Shaila Abdullah and Aanyah Abdullah *	Cerebral palsy
2018	*The Girl Who Thought in Pictures: The Story of Dr. Temple Grandin*, written by Julia Finley Mosca and illustrated by Daniel Rieley	Autism

Note: * Indicates the book features Black, Indigenous, or people of color.

TABLE 10.3. IBBY Outstanding Books for Young People with Disabilities Nonfiction Winners since 2011

Year Awarded	Book, Author, Illustrator	Disability
2011	*Signing Smart: My First Signs*, written by Michelle Anthony and Reyna Lindert	Deafness
	I've Got a Feeling, written by Stephanie Owen Reeder *	Autism
	The Lucky One, written by Deborah Cowley with photographs by Kathy Knowles *	Orthopedic impairment
	The Bite of the Mango, written by Mariatu Kamara and Susan McClelland *	Dismembered hands
	Ballerina Dreams: A True Story, written by Lauren Thompson (with Joann Ferrara), and photographs by James Estrin *	Cerebral palsy, Erb's palsy
2013	*Point to Happy: For Children on the Autism Spectrum*, written by Miriam Smith and Afton Fraser, and photographs by Margo Smithwick *	Autism spectrum
2015	*Stir It Up! Recipes & Techniques for Young Blind Cooks*, by National Braille Press, with illustrations by Janet Malone	Blindness
	Out-of-Sight Science Experiments: For Grades 2–5, written by Lillian A. Rankel and Marilyn D. Winograd, with illustrations by Janet Malone	Blindness
	A Splash of Red: The Life and Art of Horace Pippin, written by Jen Bryant and illustrated by Melissa Sweet	Limb impairment
	Emily Included: A True Story, written by Kathleen McDonnell, with photographs from the Eaton family	Cerebral palsy
	Writing with Grace: A Journey beyond Down Syndrome, written by Judy McFarlane	Down syndrome
	Temple Grandin: How the Girl Who Loved Cows Embraced Autism and Changed the World, written by Sy Montgomery (foreword by Temple Grandin), with images and design drawings by Temple Grandin	Autism
2019	*Proud to be Deaf: Discover My Community and My Language*, written by Ava Beese, Lilli Beese, and Nick Beese, illustrated by Romina Martí	Deafness

Note: * Indicates the book features Black, Indigenous, or people of color.

Examining Tables 10.1, 10.2, and 10.3 reveals that autism and orthopedic disabilities are the most frequently represented in these nonfiction award-winning children's books, followed by speech impairment and cerebral palsy. Deafness was treated in only three of the books, and blindness, Down syndrome, and a specific learning disability were treated in only one book each, despite their prevalence in the educational settings.

Books with Personal Portrayals for Classroom Use

Realistic portrayal of disabilities and of the individuals who live with them must be reliable in order to help children with disabilities affirm their own strengths and needs and to guide their peers without disabilities to be accepting and view those who have disabilities in positive ways (Rieger & McGrail, 2015). Books told from multiple perspectives can be particularly enlightening (Azano et al., 2017). Descriptions of recommended books follow.

Books with Accurate and Appealing Portrayals

A Boy and a Jaguar is an autobiographical picturebook by Alan Rabinowitz (2014) in which he recalls his childhood stuttering as so severe that he could not express himself verbally to anyone but animals. He promised his pets and the jaguar in the Bronx Zoo that if he could ever find his voice, he would "be their voice." As an adult who was a world-recognized expert on and advocate for jaguars, Rabinowitz wrote that he was still healing, deriving strength from the jaguars in the jungle and in the preserves that he had developed. He was obviously highly intelligent and capable; he just happened to have a severe stuttering problem. It could be helpful for children who stutter to read about a man whose speech problem did not define who he was and who he became.

Some accounts of young children living with a disability are authored by those individuals who have had the experience themselves. Often, these are coauthored by adults who have shared the experience with them. *My Brother Charlie* (Peete & Peete, 2010) is an appealing picturebook account of early childhood autism written by twelve-year-old Ryan Elizabeth Peete (alias Callie), a neurotypical person, and her mother, Holly Robinson Peete, an international autism advocate. Accompanied by vivid illustrations by Shane W. Evans, the book is written from Ryan's perspective about her life with her twin, R. J. (alias Charlie), who has autism. The moving account of love and support within this African American family is a backdrop for Ryan's (Callie's) complex feelings of love for her brother, which also include the frustration she feels when worrying about and being unable to communicate effectively with him.

Highlighted previously, Ava Beese, who is profoundly deaf, collaborated with her parents, Lilli and Nick Beese (who are also deaf), on *Proud to be Deaf: Discover My Community and My Language* (2010). Beautiful photographs are provided of Ava, who narrates the book, though not in her seven-year-old language. Home, school, friends, and activities are presented as Ava experiences them. For older children, in-depth information is included with abundant illustrations of deaf culture, including the use of sign language, and deaf communities in England and other places in the world. Deafness, as treated by the Beese family, is a prevalent, normal, happy way of living—as deaf communities worldwide know it to be.

Reading or listening to nonfiction books featuring personal portrayals of people with disabilities is not enough. It is also important to encourage discussion and provide opportunities for young readers to ask questions and learn more. Some nonfiction books include discussion questions, but educators can also create questions of their own that enable students to find points of connection, open up, and explore their own experiences and relationships as/with people who have disabilities.

Portrayals of Positive Interactions and Relationships in Children's Nonfiction

Physical therapist Joann Ferrara owns Associated Therapies in Queens, New York. She and a group of young preteen and teen assistants lead weekly ballet classes for little girls with cerebral palsy or Erb's palsy. These girls want to dance and dream of being ballerinas despite being unable to stand erect for very long and having limited use of their limbs. Each girl has a helper who holds and supports her while she dances. The children work very hard on their dancing, which helps them make major progress in strengthening and controlling their muscles and their balance. Because of the close bonds developed between the children and their helpers, the assistants can easily recognize when the dancer needs more or less support. The nonfiction book *Ballerina Dreams* (Thompson, 2007), with stunning photographs by James Estrin, memorably depicts the class's first recital.

In another nonfiction book that has positive portrayals of interactions and relationships between people who are disabled and those who are not, Naoki, who has autism, dreams of writing stories and books. However, he cannot speak, and initially does not interact with others. But because of his ability to memorize word shapes, he learns to read and spell even though he cannot hear or identify phonetics. He attends mainstream school, where he reads and writes obsessively.

At the age of thirteen, Naoki Higashida (2007) authored, *The Reason I Jump: The Inner Voice of a Thirteen-Year-Old Boy with Autism*, which became an international bestseller translated into more than thirty languages. Despite his gifted skills with language, Naoki had meltdowns because of his autism. Classmates and other outsiders saw him flap his hands and arms, stumble awkwardly as his body seemed disconnected from his environment, avoid all social interaction, and often retreat into his own world.

When he was a boy, no one understood who Naoki was or what he was going through. His book (validated and praised by Temple Grandin) has helped young people and adults worldwide avoid the intense loneliness and disconnection that were so much a part of his own school experience and everyday life. As an adult, Higashida still does not speak, but he has become one of Japan's most popular and successful novelists. Educators and students worldwide, as well as individuals with autism and their families, continue to learn a great deal from the realization of his dream.

Emmanuel Ofosu Yeboah, of Ghana, West Africa, had to challenge not only his classmates but an entire country and culture to fulfill his dream. His father left when Emmanuel was born with only one leg, as his country's culture taught that an individual with a disability was useless, even cursed. However, Emmanuel proved they were wrong. As a child, he hopped on one leg two miles to school and back each day, and learned to ride a bike and play soccer with his classmates, winning their friendship as well as respect. When Emmanuel's beloved and devoted mother became ill, he left school and moved to a large city where he worked hard shining shoes and serving drinks to make money to send to his family.

Emmanuel's dream was to ride a bicycle around his country to show people that individuals with disabilities can do unexpected things. With help from the Challenged Athletes Foundation in the USA and a blessing from the ruler of his country, Yeboah rode his bike four hundred miles in ten days, cheered everywhere by people with and without disabilities and forever changing the ways in which disabilities were viewed in Ghana. Yeboah did not write a book to tell his story (as Naoki did); he rode a bike to do this and left the writing to others, including Laurie Ann Thompson (2015), who wrote *Emmanuel's Dream: The True Story of Emmanuel Ofosu Yeboah*.

Another nonfiction book that depicts a young African child with a physical disability who faced serious cultural prejudice is *Her Own Two Feet: A Rwandan Girl's Brave Fight to Walk* (Davis & Uwitonze, 2019). This book, written by the child, Rebeka, and the mother of her US family, shares the dreams of Rebeka and those people in two countries who love her. The book opens in an impoverished part of Rwanda in the middle of the night. Two-year-old Medea awakens to help her four-year-old sister, Rebeka, whose legs and feet are so twisted and her arms so weak that she cannot even crawl. Together, the girls pull themselves across the space between home and their outside toilet. Refusing local pressure to abandon Rebeka, her devoted parents and siblings do all they can for her, despite their struggles to obtain life's necessities. When "cursed" Rebeka cannot go to school, Medea uses her own back, arms, and legs to support Rebeka as she conditions herself to the pain of standing and learns to walk with agony on the tops of her twisted feet. Educators see the child standing outside the school and intervene, and Rebeka is finally able to attend a Rwandan "free school," where she struggles to learn alongside Medea and the other younger children. US sponsors of the school notice her pain and determined spirit and contact medical experts.

Rebeka then travels to the United States for a year to undergo therapy and surgery on her legs and feet. Knowing nothing of the US but the word *hello*, Rebeka lives with the Davis family, but feels agony at leaving her family in Rwanda and facing the unknown. Together, the Davis family and Rebeka learn, love, and laugh. When Rebeka returns to Rwanda, she walks on her own two feet, leaving US friends behind whose lives will never be the same. Meredith Davis later visited Rwanda and conducted extensive observations and interviews to gather the specific and intimate details that bring to life this courageous child and the families and friends who love her (Davis & Uwitonze, 2019). The photographs of Rebeka and her loved ones at all stages and phases of her life are memorable, uplifting, and joyful.

Children of all ages and within all educational contexts need to be exposed to positive relationships between individuals with and without disabilities, reciprocal exchanges in which neither participant is overly dependent on or in all ways stronger than the other. Both the individual(s) with a disability and those who share their lives must be strong partners.

Conclusion

In *Normal: One Kid's Extraordinary Journey* (Newman & Newman, 2019), Nathaniel Newman (who has Treacher Collins syndrome) and his mother describe Nathaniel's life, including information about his family, school, relationships, surgeries, and progress. His voice is fairly light and humorous and expresses that he just wants to be seen "as Nathaniel Newman . . . a normal kid who happens to look different" (p. 166). However, Nathaniel also shares details about what it feels like to have Treacher Collins syndrome:

I could hardly breathe. My nose didn't connect to my airway, and because my jaw was so small, my tongue filled my mouth. There were problems with most of my senses. I couldn't smell because my cheekbones were behind my nose, blocking it. I couldn't eat because my jaw was small and out of alignment. I could barely hear because I didn't have ears to capture the sound and deliver it to my brain. I didn't have bottom eyelids, which meant I couldn't close my eyes fully, and my vision wasn't great. (Newman & Newman, 2019, p. 9)

The way he juxtaposes humor and reality gives readers insight into Nathaniel's experiences. This allows those who may also have Treacher Collins syndrome to see someone like themselves represented in a nonfiction book. It can also help those who do not have Treacher Collins syndrome themselves understand that Nathaniel is a person first and not only a person with a disability. Nathaniel Newman—like Naoki Higashida, Emmanuel Yeboah, Rebeka Uwitonze, Shane Burcaw, Ava Beese, Alan Rabinowitz, R. J. Peete, and a group of young dancers—is just "a normal kid who happens to [be] different" (p. 165).

Practical Strategies

- Develop classroom-based units focusing on the unique contributions of people with disabilities in various content areas. Have students host a poster session where they share and discuss places where these individuals might have been included in or excluded from curriculum content.

- Gather primary sources, such as letters or photographs, to share with students in order to help them learn more about notable historical figures who were also people with disabilities. Read picturebook biographies about those people, as well. Have students compare what they learned from the primary sources with what information is presented in the biographies. Conclude by discussing accuracy and representation.

- Have students read a biography and watch a documentary about one person with a disability. Together, identify information that appears in both texts and lead students in a conversation about how information (particularly information related to the person's disability) is presented—and why.

- After reading nonfiction books that discuss children with disabilities who have had difficulty accessing schools and facilities, have students tour their own educational environment and identify design features that allow or prevent access, thereby introducing concepts of universal design. Students can follow up by writing letters to school officials arguing for changes needed to address issues of design or limitations to access.

• Provide students with sets of award-winning nonfiction books that are included in Tables 10.1–10.3. Ask students to identify the types of disabilities represented in the books. Use their findings to write publishers and request greater diversity in literary representation.

Ten Additional Nonfiction Books about People with Disabilities

1. Barasch, L. (2004). *Knockin' on wood: Starring Peg Leg Bates* (L. Barasch, Illus.). Lee & Low Books.

2. Bell, C. (2014). *El Deafo* (D. Lasky, Illus.). Harry N. Abrams.

3. Burnell, C. (2020). *I am not a label: 34 disabled artists, thinkers, athletes and activists from past to the present* (L. M. Baldo, Illus.). Wide Eyed Editions.

4. Donohue, M. R. (2021). *Stompin' at the Savoy: How Chick Webb became the king of drums* (L. Freeman, Illus.). Sleeping Bear Press.

5. Golio, G. (2020). *Dark was the night: Blind Willie Johnson's journey to the stars* (E. B. Lewis, Illus.). Nancy Paulsen Books.

6. Long, J. (with Long, H.) (2018). *Unsinkable: From Russian orphan to Paralympic swimming world champion.* Houghton Mifflin Harcourt.

7. Pitzer, M. W. (2004). *I can, can you?* (M. W. Pitzer, Photog.). Woodbine House.

8. Scott, J. (2020). *I talk like a river* (S. Smith, Illus.). Holiday House/Neal Porter Books.

9. Seeger, P., & Jacobs, P. D. (2006). *The deaf musicians* (R. G. Christie, Illus.). G. P. Putnam's Sons.

10. Wolfe, H. (2021). *Unstoppable: Women with disabilities* (K. Patkau, Illus.). Second Story Press.

Five Online Resources

1. Disability in Kidlit. (n.d.). *Disability in Kidlit.* https://disabilityinkidlit.com

2. IRIS Center & Prater, M. A. (2018, June 28). *Children's books: Portrayals of people of disability*. Vanderbilt University. https://iris.peabody.vanderbilt.edu/resources/books

3. Kleekamp, M. (2019, May 28). How to critically select children's books with representations of disability experiences. *The Open Book Blog*. https://blog.leeandlow.com/2019/05/28/how-to-critically-select-childrens-books-with-representations-of-disability-experiences

4. National Library Service for the Blind and Print Disabled. (n.d.). *Disability awareness for children pre-K through sixth grade*. Library of Congress. https://www.loc.gov/nls/resources/general-resources-on-disabilities/disability-awareness-children-pre-k-sixth-grade

5. Ray, A. (2016, April 21). *Influential kids' books featuring capable disabled characters*. Books For Littles. https://booksforlittles.com/disability-normalization

Book Awards

- Dolly Gray Children's Literature Award—see https://www.dollygrayaward.com
- IBBY Outstanding Books for Young People with Disabilities—see https://www.ibby.org.uk/awards/outstanding-books-young-people-disabilities
- Schneider Family Book Award—see http://www.ala.org/awardsgrants/schneider-family-book-award

Children's Books Cited

Abdullah, S., & Abdullah, A. (2014). *My friend Suhana: A story of friendship and cerebral palsy*. Loving Healing Press.

Abeel, S. (2003). *My thirteenth winter: A memoir*. Scholastic.

Anthony, M., & Lindert, R. (2009). *Signing smart: My first signs* (M. Berg, Illus.; M. Anthony & R. Lindert, Photog.). Scholastic.

Beese, A., Beese, L., & Beese, N. (2019). *Proud to be deaf: Discover my community and my language* (R. Martí, Illus.). Wayland.

Burcaw, S. (2017). *Not so different: What you REALLY want to ask about having a disability* (M. Carr, Photog.). Roaring Brook Press.

Bryant, J. (2013). *A splash of red: The life and art of Horace Pippin* (M. Sweet, Illus.). Knopf.

Bryant, J. (2016). *Six dots: A story of young Louis Braille* (B. Kulikov, Illus.). Knopf Books for Young Readers.

Christensen, B. (2009). *Django: World's greatest jazz guitarist* (Illus. B. Christensen). Flash Point.

Cowley, D. (2008). *The lucky one* (K. Knowles, Photog.). Osu Children's Library Fund.

Davis, M., & Uwitonze, R. (2019). *Her own two feet: A Rwandan girl's brave fight to walk.* Scholastic.

Draper, S. M. (2010). *Out of my mind.* Athenum.

Glenn, S. (2004). *Keeping up with Roo* (D. Andreasen, Illus.). G. P. Putnam's Sons.

Higashida, N. (2007). *The reason I jump: The inner voice of a thirteen-year-old boy with autism* (K. A. Yoshida & D. Mitchell, Trans.). Random House.

Kamara, M., & McClelland, S. (2008). *The bite of the mango.* Annick Press.

McDonnell, K. (2011). *Emily included: A true story* (Eaton family, Photog.). Second Story.

McFarlane, J. (2014). *Writing with Grace: A journey beyond Down syndrome.* Douglas & McIntyre.

Montgomery, S. (2014). *Temple Grandin: How the girl who loved cows embraced autism and changed the world* (T. Grandin, Illus.). Houghton Mifflin Harcourt.

Mosca, J. F. (2017). *The girl who thought in pictures: The story of Dr. Temple Grandin* (D. Rieley, Illus.). The Innovation Press.

National Braille Press. (2015). *Stir it up! Recipes & techniques for young blind cooks* (J. Malone, Illus.). Author.

Newman, M., & Newman, N. (2020). *Normal: One kid's extraordinary journey* (N. Swaab, Illus.). Houghton Mifflin Harcourt.

Ottaviani, J. (2019). *Hawking* (L. Myrick, Illus.). Roaring Brook Press.

Peete, H. R., & Peete, R. E. (2010). *My brother Charlie* (S. W. Evans, Illus.). Scholastic.

Pimentel, A. B. (2020). *All the way to the top: How one girl's fight for Americans with disabilities changed everything* (N. Ali, Illus.). Sourcebooks.

Rabinowitz, A. (2014). *A boy and a jaguar* (C. Chien, Illus.). Houghton Mifflin Harcourt.

Rankel, L. A., & Winograd, M. D. (2011). *Out-of-sight science experiments: For grades 2–5* (J. Malone, Illus.). National Braille Press.

Reeder, S. O. (2010). *I've got a feeling.* National Library of Australia.

Reeves, J., & Reeves, J. L. (2019). *Born just right.* Aladdin.

Say, A. (2017). *Silent days, silent dreams* (A. Say, Illus.). Arthur A. Levine.

Smith, M., & Fraser, A. (2011). *Point to happy: A book for kids on the autism spectrum* (M. Smithwick, Photog.). Workman.

Sotomayor, S. (2019). *Just ask! Be different, be brave, be you* (R. López, Illus.). Philomel Books.

Thompson, L. (with Ferrara, J.) (2007). *Ballerina dreams: A true story* (J. Estrin, Photog.). Feiwel & Friends.

Thompson, L. A. (2015). *Emmanuel's dream: The true story of Emmanuel Ofosu Yeboah* (S. Qualls, Illus.). Schwartz & Wade Books.

References

Allen, E. (2014, July 11). *Letters about literature: Dear Sharon Draper*. Library of Congress Blog. https://blogs.loc.gov/loc/2014/07/letters-about-literature-dear-sharon-draper

Azano, A. P., Tackett, M., & Sigmon, M. (2017). Understanding the puzzle behind the pictures. *AERA Open, 3*(2), 1–12. https://doi.org/10.1177/233285841770682

Beckett, A., Ellison, N., Barrett, S., & Shah, S. (2010). Away with the fairies? Disability within primary-age children's literature. *Disability and Society, 25*(3), 373–386. https://doi.org/10.1080/09687591003701355

Blaska, J. K. (2004, Winter). Children's literature that includes characters with disabilities or illnesses. *Disability Studies Quarterly, 24*(1). https://doi.org/10.18061/dsq.v24i1.854

Burcaw, S. (2014). *Laughing at my nightmare*. Roaring Brook Press.

Crawford, P. A., & Calabria, K. (2018). Mirrors and windows for all: Nonfiction picture books as tools for understanding disabilities. In V. Venika-Agbaw, R. M. Lowery, L. A. Hudock, & P. H. Ricks (Eds.), *Exploring nonfiction literacies: Innovative practices in classrooms* (pp. 31–43). Rowman & Littlefield.

Grow, H., Black, S., Egan, K., Taylor, T., Moss, K., Wadham, R., & Prater, M. A. (2019). A decade of disability depictions in Newbery Award books. *Education and Training in Autism and Developmental Disabilities: Research to Practice, 6*(1), 58–71.

Laminack, L. L., & Kelly, K. (2019). *Reading makes a difference: Using literature to help students speak freely, think deeply, and take action*. Heinemann.

Prater, M. A., Taylor, T. M., & Johnstun, M. L. (2006). Teaching students about learning disabilities through children's literature. *Intervention in School and Clinic, 42*(1), 14–24. https://doi.org/10.1177/10534512060420010301

Rieger, A., & McGrail, E. (2015). Exploring children's literature with authentic representation of disability. *Kappa Delta Pi Record, 51*(1), 18–23.

Stewart, M., & Young, T. A. (2018). Defining and describing expository literature. In V. Yenika-Agbaw, L. A. Hudock, & R. M. Lowery (Eds.), *Does nonfiction equate truth?: Rethinking disciplinary boundaries through critical literacy* (pp. 11–24). Rowman & Littlefield.

Uppaluri, J. (2017). The only person who didn't understand anything was me. In C. Gourley (Ed.), *Journeys: Young readers' letters to authors who changed their lives* (pp. 21–25). Library of Congress Center for the Book.

US Department of Education. (2019). *41st annual report to Congress on the implementation of the Individuals with Disabilities Education Act, Parts B and C.* Office of Special Education and Rehabilitative Services. https://www2.ed.gov/about/reports/annual/osep/2019/parts-b-c/index.html

Young, T. A., Bryan, G., Jacobs, J. S., & Tunnell, M. O. (2020). *Children's literature, briefly* (7th ed.). Pearson.

From the Sidelines to the Stonewall: LGBTQ+ Nonfiction for Early and Middle Grade Readers

JON M. WARGO, *Boston College*
JOSEPH MADRES, *Boston College*

All invited, all excited / This day in June, we're all united!

—GAYLE PITMAN, *This Day in June*

This chapter draws on a series of diverse nonfiction texts—Stonewall awardee and honor books in particular—to examine how lesbian, gay, bisexual, transgender, and queer (LGBTQ+) peoples and histories are documented, discussed, and displayed in children's nonfiction. Using a form of critical content analysis and thinking with queer theory, three questions guide this inquiry: (1) Whose/ what story is told?; (2) Who, in the text, has power, voice, and agency?; and (3) How does the text close and with what assumptions (as they pertain to LGBTQ+ issues, topics, and/or people) are readers left? Through a close reading, insights about contemporary LGBTQ+ nonfiction and Stonewall awardee/honor books are shared. More specifically, we detail and discuss how the bulk of the LGBTQ+ children's nonfiction featured in this chapter renders queer life as normative and apolitical. Arguing for the importance of mobilizing LGBTQ+ nonfiction for social justice, we close with implications for a more radical practice.

Chapter Guiding Questions

- Whose and/or what stories are represented and portrayed in diverse nonfiction books by and about LGBTQ+ people?
- How, and to what degree, are the lived conditions and experiences of LGBTQ+ life reflected in children's nonfiction?
- What might it mean and look like to read children's nonfiction through a queer lens? What role might a culturally sustaining queer pedagogy play in K–8 classrooms?

• How do LGBTQ+ nonfiction texts challenge conditions of inequity? How can they help promote social justice?

In a *Huffington Post* article, contributor Harry Lewis (2017) highlighted how Betsy DeVos went on record during her US Secretary of Education confirmation hearing arguing that safeguarding lesbian, gay, bisexual, transgender, and queer (LGBTQ+) students and other protected minority classes was "unsettled law" and not under her or her department's purview (para. 1). DeVos's statement, no matter how unsettling, is not unique. Take, for example, Maya Dillard Smith's resignation as executive director of Georgia's chapter of the American Civil Liberties Union. Questioning the Obama administration's directive to allow transgender students to use the bathroom that matches their gender identity, she stated that she "philosophically" differed in opinion (Jenkins, 2016). These so-called philosophical tensions are deeply social and imbued in the lived realities that are combatted every day by LGBTQ+ people, a term we use to acknowledge the presence and persistence of all expressions, identities, and sexualities, inclusive of race, ethnicity, and language rendered in broader conceptions of LGBTQ+-identifying communities.

For many LGBTQ+-identifying children, the daily encounter of school is no better. Curricular and pedagogical decision making is influenced not only by the sociopolitical context within which it is situated, but also by the curricular resources made available. According to the GLSEN *2017 National School Climate Survey* (Kosciw et al., 2017), elementary and middle grade gender-nonconforming students are more likely to experience harassment and are less likely to have access to LGBTQ+ resources. This, coupled with data that indicate that "67.6 percent of LGBTQ[+] students in schools with an inclusive curriculum said their peers were accepting of LGBTQ[+] people, compared to 36 percent of those without an inclusive curriculum," suggests that behavior toward LGBTQ+ individuals is more welcoming with the presence of an inclusive curriculum (GLSEN, 2019, p. 1). So, what are educators to do? How do LGBTQ+ issues and representation come to matter in inclusive curricula and in literature more specifically? This essay provides answers to some of these questions and considers the role of LGBTQ+ nonfiction and informational texts.

Critically analyzing children's and young adult Stonewall awardee and honor books, this chapter explores what it may mean to develop a "[q]ulturally sustaining pedagogy," with "[Q]SP" being a re-theorization of culturally sustaining pedagogies that centers LGBTQ+ youth (Wargo, 2016). Divided into three sections, the chapter traces LGBTQ+ representation across early and middle grades nonfiction. It first provides an overview of nonfiction, highlighting the continued dearth of queer-inclusive themes in the early and middle grades nonfiction corpus. Then, through a critical content analysis of nonfiction recipients of the Mike Morgan and Larry Romans Children's and Young Adult Literature Award (a subcategory of the Stonewall Book Awards; see also Book Awards, below), we interrogate the themes presented in these books and examine how and what they represent to young learners. Last, we talk across this analysis to further envision a [q]ulturally sustaining English language arts approach in PreK–8 classrooms. We suggest that children's nonfiction, represented through the awardee and honor books included, has an important and political role to play in forwarding queer conversations and developing more LGBTQ+-inclusive classrooms.

Why Nonfiction?

Despite recent educational initiatives such as the Common Core State Standards (National Governors Association Center for Best Practices & Council of Chief State School Officers, 2010), wherein increased attention to informational texts has subtly secured their spot in elementary classrooms, texts utilized in PreK–8 English language arts curricula remain largely composed of children's fiction (Duke, 2000; Jeong et al., 2010). The lack of use and the scarcity of nonfiction may be due, in large part, to the fact that it is a text style that is hard to define (Maloch & Bomer, 2013). Notwithstanding its slippery signification, for the purposes of this chapter, we define nonfiction by the ways in which it emphasizes facts, its presumed accuracy (historical and otherwise) of information, and the ways in which it conveys information about the world (see Duke & Bennett-Armistead, 2003). Although this text type largely allows readers to readily access information that may fall outside of their everyday personal experience, its focus on LGBTQ+ topics remains lackluster.

At the close of 2013, there were more than 150 picturebooks featuring LGBTQ+ characters. This is quite different from the underwhelming visibility texts offered this group in the 1970s and 1980s. According to Cart and Jenkins (2015), the first US young adult nonfiction text with LGBTQ+ content was first published in 1969. While others chart earlier nonfiction explorations into LGBTQ+ topics and themes (e.g., see Tribunella, 2012), these first texts were largely focused on the diversity of families and served the didactic purpose of increasing tolerance and inclusion. While still prominent themes and issues today, the focus of nonfiction texts is now more dynamic. Topics include continuums of romantic desire, LGBTQ+ pride, and tumultuous histories of queer resistance and activism. With a growing openness in the US cultural landscape, the need for responsive and LGBTQ+-inclusive texts is now greater than ever. Since 2011, for example, several states (including California, Colorado, Illinois, New Jersey, and Oregon) have passed LGBTQ+-inclusive curriculum bills. Requiring public schools to teach LGBTQ+-inclusive social studies, these bills underscore that social studies instruction must be nondiscriminatory and include the roles and contributions of all peoples included under the Human Rights Act.

Despite a noted scarcity of LGBTQ+ peoples and topics in award-winning nonfiction (see, e.g., Crisp, 2015; Crisp et al., 2017), their prominence in other award categories, such as the American Library Association's Stonewall Book Awards, illuminates their place and purpose in the English language arts classroom.

Charting Queer Visibility in Diverse Children's and Young Adult Literature: Why the Stonewall Book Awards?

Launched in 1971, the Stonewall Book Award is the first and most enduring set of literary awards for LGBTQ+ texts. Sponsored by the American Library Association's (ALA) Gay, Lesbian, Bisexual, and Transgender Round Table, the award is given across three categories: the Barbara Gittings Literature Award, the Israel Fishman Non-Fiction Award, and the most recent category, the Mike Morgan and Larry Romans Children's and Young Adult Literature Award. Honor awards in each category are also given. We chose to focus upon the Stonewall Book Award as it is often seen as highlighting for readers the "best-of-the-best" texts for queer-inclusive themes. According to the ALA, the primary criterion for awardee and honor texts is that they have "exceptional merit" relating to the LGBTQ+ experience (American Library Association, 2009, para. 1). These books—vetted by a rotating panel of experts—have received the seal of approval from the ALA, a reputable organization for educators and families.

Since its inception in 2010, the Mike Morgan and Larry Romans Children's and Young Adult Literature Award has recognized forty-six texts (fifteen winners and thirty-one honorees). All fifteen awardees thus far have been fiction, with the exception that the 2015 winner, *This Day in June* (Pitman, 2014), has facets of nonfiction and also pedagogical resources embedded at the end of the book. Out of the forty-six total texts, only five are classified as nonfiction. Historically, this lackluster response to nonfiction, as a genre, is common. Meltzer (1976) and Kiefer and Wilson (2011), for example, have documented that other major children's literature awards (e.g., Newbery Medal, Boston Globe–Horn Book Award) have a history of not recognizing this text type.

The five nonfiction Stonewall Book Award honor recipients include Stevenson's (2016) *Pride: Celebrating Diversity and Community*, Silverberg's (2015) *Sex*

Is a Funny Word: A Book about Bodies, Feelings, and YOU, Kuklin's (2014) *Beyond Magenta: Transgender Teens Speak Out*, Setterington's (2013) *Branded by the Pink Triangle*, and Alsenas's (2008) *Gay America: Struggle for Equality*. These texts are examined here and serve as primary units of analysis. Given this small sample, however, we also include an array of nonfiction texts we regularly see in classroom spaces and libraries. Taken together, our text set works to highlight both the "award-winning" books as well as those more regularly seen across early and middle grade educational spaces.

Mobilizing Critical Content Analysis to Think with Queer Theory

In this chapter, we use a critical content analytic lens to investigate how and in what ways LGBTQ+ peoples are portrayed, talked about, and featured in focal nonfiction texts. Content analysis encompasses an array of research methods used to describe and interpret written artifacts. Critical, here, is a "stance of locating power in social practices in order to challenge conditions of inequity" (Short, 2017, p. 1). As an apparatus and tool, in critical content analysis, "the researcher uses a specific critical lens as the frame from which to develop the research questions and to select and analyze the texts" (Short, 2017, p. 5). Queer theory became a frame through which we analyzed texts. We use queer in this work, like Meyer (2010), to "challenge traditional understandings of gender and sexual identity by deconstructing the categories, binaries, and language that support them" (p. 20). Reading across these books, three units of analysis guided the inquiry: (1) focalization (whose/what story is told?), (2) social characteristics/traits of subjects (who has power, voice, and agency?), and (3) closure (how does the nonfiction text end and with what assumptions [concerning LGBTQ+ difference and diversity] are readers left?).

Positionality, Analysis, and Evaluation

As a research team including a gay professor (Jon) and gay doctoral student (Joseph), both of whom identify as cisgender (meaning our gender identity aligns with the biological sex we were assigned at birth), our own interests in examining early childhood and elementary nonfiction texts featuring LGBTQ+ topics and peoples emerged from our own histories. Jon is a former primary grades teacher and Joe is a former arts educator. In examining the focal texts, however, we tried to divorce ourselves from our own presuppositions concerning representation in LGBTQ+ children's texts. We did, however, note tensions and dissonances that emerged in our readings. Our analytic process involved reading and analyzing all nonfiction texts included under the PreK–8 umbrella that were featured on the Stonewall Book Award list.

After we located the books used in this project, we first examined all text contained within the book itself (e.g., forewords, authors' notes, indexes). In our analysis of representative topics and themes across the Stonewall awardees, we also examined additional materials included with the books (e.g., a gender identity wheel in Pessin-Whedbee's [2017] *Who Are You? The Kid's Guide to Gender Identity*).

In the following section, we read across subjects and events to categorize major themes in the texts included in our analysis. It is important to acknowledge here that our own readings could limit the engagement others might have with these same texts or the utility of these texts and materials in classroom and library spaces. Our approach to critical content analysis calls us to recognize how early and middle grade texts position their readers, the ideologies and particular persons for which they advocate, and the worlds of progress they imagine.

A Not-So-Queer List: Examining the Nonfiction World of the ALA Stonewall Book Awards

Guided by our critical content analysis, we present three overarching insights found across the selected texts. These categories—"Heroes and Heroic Nonfiction Texts," "Sex, Her-Stories, and Other Gender-Bending Narratives of Self-Expression," and "Holidays for Gays? Examining Pride as a Celebration of Diversity and Community"—reveal tensions in how difference and diversity are maintained and discussed in children's LGBTQ+-inclusive nonfiction.

Heroes and Heroic Nonfiction Texts

Contemporary biographies and narrative nonfiction texts reign as those books most readily visible in diverse LGBTQ+ children's nonfiction. Kuklin's (2014) *Beyond Magenta: Transgender Teens Speak Out*, for example, provides a series of nonfiction vignettes that highlight the lived experiences of diverse transgender adolescent and genderqueer (a person who does not subscribe to conventional gender identities) youth. Beautifully designed to include portraits of transition coupled with family photographs documenting this personal journey, this 2015 Stonewall Honor book adds nuance to representations of the transgender experience in a way that is readable for early adolescent readers. Of particular importance to this chapter, however, is the text's supplemental material. The "About the Callen-Lorde Community Health Center" and the "Q&A with Dr. Manel Silva, Clinical Director of the HOTT [Health Outreach to Teens] Program" are important features in the text to include for early learners and caregivers interested in what it means to *be* transgender. Although oriented perhaps too specifically on the "parts" and "health" features, the resources are important pedagogical tools for parents, caregivers, and allies who are working to better understand the personal journeys of trans teens.

While not a Stonewall awardee, *I Am Jazz* (Herthel & Jennings, 2014) is a grade-level appropriate nonfiction picturebook that examines a young child's experiences and explorations with gender identity and expression. A somewhat autobiographical tale about Jazz's personal and family-based journey with gender dysphoria, the book concludes with a resource from the TransKids Purple Rainbow Foundation, an organization recognizing Jennings as an honorary cofounder. While at first glance the book is seemingly problematic in the way it reinscribes the gender binary (masculinity/femininity), the book is readily accessible to students who are aware of the now-popular celebrity of Jazz Jennings.

Taken together, *Beyond Magenta* (Kuklin, 2014) and *I Am Jazz* (Herthel & Jennings, 2014) represent an interesting finding from our critical analyses of texts. When considering *whose* voices are amplified, transgender youth and adolescents are centered. While we find incredible merit in focusing on this minoritized population, the texts skirt the possibility of discussing and confronting issues of sexuality. In *Beyond Magenta*'s glossary, for example, we found it quite startling that more colloquial terms that many transgender youth find problematic (e.g., metrosexual) were highlighted while more inclusive terms like *queer* and *gender creative* were sidelined. Similarly, by highlighting how it was, in short, a story about a "girl brain but a boy body" (p. 8), *I Am Jazz* misses opportunities to signal that this is a single story (Adichie, 2009) and that others may not share Jazz's journey.

Outside of the texts presented here on the Stonewall shortlist, we also highly recommend Krakow's (2002) *The Harvey Milk Story*, Winter's (2009) *Gertrude Is Gertrude Is Gertrude Is Gertrude*, Christensen's (2011) *Fabulous! A Portrait of Andy Warhol*, and Burgess's (2020) *Drawing on Walls: A Story of Keith Haring*. These biographies, unlike the two above, examine historical heroes that advanced the visibility of many LGBTQ+ peoples. Similarly, Pitman's (2017) *When You Look Out the Window: How Phyllis Lyon and Del Martin Built a Community* (2017) and

Sewing the Rainbow: The Story of Gilbert Baker and the Rainbow Flag (2018) are also quite important additions to the LGBTQ+ body of nonfiction. Skirting issues of desire, these books provide nice segues into talking across same-sex partnership and also amplify the contributions of some LGBTQ+ heroes directly. However, like the larger body of LGBTQ+ children's literature more generally, the people profiled in these biographies are overwhelmingly white.

Sex, Her-Stories, and Other Gender-Bending Narratives of Self-Expression

In addition to nonfiction books about heroic LGBTQ+ people and/or books that allow readers to witness the stories of identities-in-transition, another category (this one queerer than the first) emerged when we examined the Stonewall Award winners and honor books. Beyond biographies, the larger corpus of LGBTQ+ children's nonfiction also included stories that documented queer histories and knowledge about sex and gender in particular.

One relatively recent children's history of gay and lesbian rights is *Gay and Lesbian History for Kids: The Century-Long Struggle for LGBT Rights* (Pohlen, 2016). Through a timeline divided into ten subsections (Two Moms, A Brief History, The Birth of a Movement, In the Shadows, Out of the Closets, Into the Streets, AIDS and a Conservative Backlash, Setbacks and Victories, Things Get Better, and Everyday Heroes), Pohlen creates a powerful historical primer that details a century-long struggle for LGBTQ+ progress. Featured in Pohlen's photographic archive of queer activism and resistance are small call-out activities that work to equate some of the larger historical actions (e.g., designing the Pride flag) to more kid-friendly practices. Pohlen's text also features a number of diverse LGBTQ+ heroes—Barbara Jordan, for example—to highlight the voices of history that worked toward increased human rights for LGBTQ+ communities.

Although rich in detail, Pohlen's (2016) history comes up short in its attempt to do too much. By watering down the more political dimensions of LGBTQ+ history with activities (e.g., creating a flag, going on a ribbon hunt), readers leave the text without a critical understanding of how LGBTQ+ people of color came to inform and simultaneously promote intersectional justice in the late twentieth century. Similarly, in the Stonewall honor book *Pride: Celebrating Diversity and Community* by Robin Stevenson (2016), history is quite localized and centered in US issues. While marked as a trusted text in promoting LGBTQ+ issues and themes in children's nonfiction, Pohlen's text presents only one side of a many-sided, and indeed complicated, history. For a more detailed and diverse account of some of these events—namely the Stonewall Uprising—read Sanders's (2019) *Stonewall: A Building, an Uprising, a Revolution.*

In contrast to Pohlen's (2016) sometimes didactic account of LGBTQ+ history, *Branded by the Pink Triangle*, a 2014 Stonewall honor text by Ken Setterington (2013), provides an in-depth history of gay persecution in Nazi Germany during World War II. Setterington's book provides a rich nonfiction account of personal stories of "homosexual men" imprisoned in concentration camps. Names of real men, like Josef and Gad, stick with the reader as the horror of Hitler's "final solution" provides a backdrop to LGBTQ+ persecution. This book provides a detailed account of the history of the pink triangle, an icon that still means a great deal for many LGBTQ+ people today.

A positive aspect of the nonfiction Stonewall honor awardees is that they include rich resources for developing a shared language about sex and gender more broadly. Silverberg's (2015) *Sex Is a Funny Word* is one example of this type of text. Divided into six parts, *Sex Is a Funny Word* includes sections focused on bodies, touch, crushes, love, relationships, and talking about sex. At the beginning of the book, readers are introduced to four culturally diverse characters who lead them through the exploration.

Beautifully illustrated by Fiona Smyth, the overarching text truly includes all the colors of the rainbow when talking about sex, gender, and other sometimes-sticky issues with educators. *Sex Is a Funny Word* (Silverberg, 2015) positions itself as a conversation guide for young readers. The first page includes a description of the book titled "To the Grown-Up Reader." Trigger warnings for certain sections (e.g., "Touch") are provided, as well as a quick overview of how to access, teach, and engage with the book in conversations that might otherwise seem uncomfortable. This introductory page is complemented by later pages that continue the conversation. For example, at the end of the introduction, readers discover one of the book's guides asks questions such as: "Have there ever been times you have heard the word sex and not understood what it meant?" and "Who are some people in your life who you trust? How can you tell if you trust someone?" Simple in nature, this is one of the first texts we've seen that provides this level of dialogic scaffolding for conversations between learners and potentially uneasy educators and caregivers.

In addition to being an excellent resource for inquisitive young readers, *Sex Is a Funny Word* (Silverberg, 2015) is also one of the few texts that focuses on body parts, touch, and desire. Accompanied by visuals regarding the varied appearances of top, bottom, and middle parts, *Sex Is a Funny Word* includes diagrams and glossaries. Similarly, in a section titled "Touch," Silverberg examines not only how touch is something that continuously needs to be negotiated, but also how norms regarding touch differ for various cultural and religious groups. By investigating the politics of touch, *Sex Is a Funny Word* also explores self-touch (masturbation), as well as sexual abuse. While noticeably intended to encourage conversation, *Sex Is a Funny Word* is one of the few texts that examines sex, gender, and romantic desire in meaningful ways. The book is a key resource for classrooms and libraries.

Taken together, histories and how-to resource guides are emerging text types on the Stonewall honor award list. If, however, educators are seeking more child-friendly ways to discuss issues of gender identity and desire, we highly recommend Maya Gonzalez's (2017) *The Gender Wheel: A Story about Bodies and Gender for Everybody* and Brooke Pessin-Whedbee's (2017) *Who Are You? The Kid's Guide to Gender Identity*. Including notes for adult readers, a page-by-page guide to key concepts, and an "about gender" wheel resource, Pessin-Whedbee's nonfiction picturebook is a riff of Gonzalez's earlier text. Richly colored with various peoples exploring the question of "Who am I?," each book walks young readers through gender identity from birth to early childhood. Tackling concepts like "cisgender" directly, both texts' merit lies in their ability to continuously encourage readers to ask themselves, "Who [am I]?" Attached in the back of the Pessin-Whedbee book, and a major resource to consider engaging within your reading of the text, is a rotating pin-wheel that quite literally encourages young children to highlight their body, identity, and expression alongside declarative statements that start with "I have . . . ," "I am . . . ," and "I like . . ." Valuable tools for teaching LGBTQ+ themes and issues, *Who Are You? The Kid's Guide to Gender Identity* and *The Gender Wheel: A Story about Bodies and Gender for Everybody* are among the best books we have seen for encouraging nuanced conversations about gender identity.

Holidays for Gays? Examining Pride as a Celebration of Diversity and Community

Some of the most popular LGBTQ+-inclusive nonfiction texts for children today revolve around the global phenomena that constitute Pride. *Pride: Celebrating Diversity and Community* (Stevenson, 2016) is an exemplar text for teaching many components of the LGBTQ+ experience and celebration of Pride. Divided into four sections, the larger text is organized around the history of Pride, Pride and identity, celebrating Pride today, and Pride around the world. While, at first glance, readers may be wary that the annual event and parade might be glossed over as an apolitical event devoid of its own history, the book does an excellent job describing its origins and activist beginnings.

In addition to sections that detail a wide array of information about Pride's global appeal and terminology, this nonfiction text is layered with primary source photographs, small asides highlighting personal stories of resistance (rightly called "proud moments"), queer facts as page headers and footers, and a glossary that includes terminology like *gender identity* and *sexual orientation*. *Pride* (Stevenson, 2016) is one of the few nonfiction texts for young readers that helps them acquire a shared language. While the text can be used as a pedagogical resource for need-to-know information about LGBTQ+ peoples' histories, rights, and contemporary issues, it can also be used as a call to action. Stevenson closes the text by asking readers to write about justice and inclusion in celebrating diversity and community.

Pride's visual iconography also makes it an exemplar for teaching LGBTQ+ topics. Through stunning images of people, places, and parades, Stevenson (2016) highlights all hues of the rainbow, illustrating racially diverse families and people and amplifying the diversity of queer experiences. That said, and in line with other texts for young readers, the book disavows talking about desire directly and instead sidelines it to stories of the AIDS crisis and gay marriage.

In addition to this more sophisticated history of Pride, Pitman's (2014) *This Day in June* provides a fictive narrative of a young child exploring the Pride parade. The book is notable, in part, because it is the only picturebook to date selected as a winner of the Stonewall Book Award. This text includes resources like a glossary that highlights many of the same terms that are featured in Stevenson's (2016) text. Featuring bright and colorful drag queens and leather daddies, the text is a portrait of many types of people who participate in this LGBTQ+ celebration. For this reason, alongside its award status, we include it as a recommended text to pair with others that examine queer Pride.

Fictive Futures and Possibilities of Progress?
Reading across These Texts

Reading across the nonfiction books we examined to identify themes, we now want to return to the primary analytic units of content analysis that guided our inquiry: *focalization* (whose story is told?), *social characteristics/traits of characters* (who has power, voice, and agency?), and *closure* (how does the nonfiction text end and with what assumptions are readers left?). In terms of focalization, books from a range of perspectives were included as Stonewall nonfiction texts. From Indigenous perspectives on Pride (as an event) to depictions of the lives of gay Jewish men who survived Nazi persecution, these books clearly discussed LGBTQ+ issues and themes. This, however, comes as no surprise, due to the fact that the queer readers of the ALA Stonewall Book Award Round Table are the individuals who select the LGBTQ+ honor and award books.

When examining the social characteristics and traits of people and histories represented in these books, however, we found that an overarching vision of normativity is presented and guides the factual information included. Whether reifying the gender binary, narrowly portraying family units, privileging white lesbian and gay historical figures, or promoting marriage as a one-size-fits-all end result of queer liberation, the Stonewall Book Award's vision of what LGBTQ+ life entails is limited. Thus, while a narrative of progress is painted for young readers, we question the stock image of LGBTQ+ experience that it represents.

The category of closure, like the focal characteristics and histories presented, also left us with more questions than answers. While some of the books leave conversation and engagement with caregivers, families, and educators as endpoints, others promote a vision of progress that is reminiscent of the "It Gets Better" campaign, a large-scale effort to share personal stories of hope in response to devastating statistics of suicides among LGBTQ+ youth. While we recognize the pedagogical value of advocating that things get better, we also encourage educators to use nonfiction texts to ask, "For *whom* does it get better?" and "*Why* must it get better?"

Instructional Recommendations and Provocations

In closing, we want to step away from these specific nonfiction texts to look more broadly at the ways in which engaging LGBTQ+ issues in the early and middle grades is a political act for educators. As we have argued elsewhere, resource-based pedagogies (Paris, 2012) leave much to be desired when it comes to considering the roles of gender, sexuality, and their intersections with other identities-in-difference. As an approach to pedagogy, [Q]SP "encourages educators to both understand the multiplicity of experiences [LGBTQ+] . . . students bring with them into the classroom while simultaneously working to cultivate a reimagining of our world and the democratic endeavor of cultural pluralism" (Wargo, 2017, p. 40). Thus, we end this chapter with a more political question: Is the purpose of LGBTQ+ children's nonfiction to normalize the queer experience?

As educators, we have a responsibility to fulfill the promise of inclusion for all children and families. That said, we need to better support education, library, and literature professionals in locating, accessing, assessing, and using books that feature LGBTQ+ people and themes. Moreover, we need to examine the ways in which desire and sex come to be named and represented in nonfiction texts that highlight the history and lived experiences of LGBTQ+ people. If nonfiction is "literature of fact," then educators must be steadfast in their quest to truthfully represent a multitude of queer experiences. Reading nonfiction through a [Q]SP lens is one way educators can be responsive to tensions that undergird gender diversity, issues of sexual difference, and investigations into LGBTQ+ identities. As educators work to locate LGBTQ+ resources and nonfiction texts, they can also remain cognizant of which histories, identities, relationships, and events are made visible.

Practical Strategies

- Have students engage in book club discussions about nonfiction texts featuring diverse people, including LGBTQ+ people, in order to supplement what is missing in history and social studies textbooks.
- Use diverse LGBTQ+ nonfiction to engage in inquiry-based investigations about how broader social justice movements have intersected and advanced equity.
- Have students examine LGBTQ+ nonfiction for possible gender stereotypes. Follow up by helping students locate counterexamples to read and discuss.
- Provide students with several nonfiction books about Pride. Ask them to analyze the various texts to try to fully appreciate the significance and history of this annual holiday.
- Work with students to gather all of the representations of LGBTQ+ people in children's nonfiction that you can locate. Then do the same thing for nonfiction books depicting people identified in the text as heterosexual. Guide students in discussing the implications of your findings.

Ten Additional Nonfiction Books Depicting LGBTQ+ People

1. Beer, S. (2018). *Love makes a family* (S. Beer, Illus.). Dial Books.
2. Genhart, M. (2019). *Rainbow: A first book of pride* (A. Passchier, Illus.). Magination Press.
3. Lamé, A. (2017). *From prejudice to pride: A history of the LGBTQ+ movement.* Wayland.

4. Medina, N. (2019). *What was Stonewall?* (J. Murray, Illus.). Penguin.

5. Prager, S. (2020). *Rainbow revolutionaries: Fifty LGBTQ+ people who made history* (S. Papworth, Illus.). HarperCollins.

6. Rotner, S., & Kelly, S. M. (2016). *Families* (S. Rotner, Photog.). Holiday House.

7. Sanders, R. (2020). *Mayor Pete: The Story of Pete Buttigieg* (L. Hastings, illus.). Henry Holt & Company.

8. Sicardi, A. (2019). *Queer heroes: Meet 53 LGBTQ heroes from past and present!* (S. Tanat-Jones, Illus.). Wide Eyed Editions.

9. Stevenson, R. (2019). *Pride colors*. Orca Book Publishers.

10. Thorn, T. (2019). *It feels good to be yourself: A book about gender identity* (N. Grigni, Illus.). Henry Holt and Company.

Five Online Resources

1. Alfred, R. (n.d.). *The Gay Life* [Radio broadcast archive]. KSAN. https://diva.sfsu.edu/collections/glbt/12616

2. GLSEN. (n.d.). *Who we are: Championing LGBTQ issues in K–12 education since 1990*. http://www.glsen.org

3. Human Rights Campaign. (n.d.). *Glossary of terms*. HRC. www.hrc.org/resources/glossary-of-terms

4. ONE National Gay & Lesbian Archives at the USC Libraries. (2018). *ONE archives*. University of Southern California. https://one.usc.edu

5. The Trevor Project. (2021, February 18). *Saving young LGBTQ lives*. https://www.thetrevorproject.org

Book Awards

- Lambda Literary Awards—see https://www.lambdaliterary.org/awards
- Mike Morgan and Larry Romans Children's and Young Adult Literature Award—see http://www.ala.org/awardsgrants/stonewall-book-awards-mike-morgan-larry-romans-children%E2%80%99s-young-adult-literature-award

- Rainbow Book List—see https://glbtrt.ala.org/rainbowbooks
- Stonewall Book Awards—see http://www.ala.org/rt/rrt/award/stonewall/honored

Children's Books Cited

Alsenas, L. (2008). *Gay America: Struggle for equality*. Amulet Books.

Burgess, M., & Cochran, J. (2020). *Drawing on walls: A story of Keith Haring* (J. Cochran, Illus.). Enchanted Lion Books.

Christensen, B. (2011). *Fabulous! A portrait of Andy Warhol* (B. Christensen, Illus.). Henry Holt and Company.

Gonzalez, M. (2017). *The gender wheel: A story about bodies and gender for everybody* (M. Gonzalez, Illus.). Reflection Press.

Herthel, J., & Jennings, J. (2014). *I am Jazz* (S. McNicholas, Illus.). Penguin.

Krakow, K. (2002). *The Harvey Milk story* (D. Gardner, Illus.). Two Lives.

Kuklin, S. (2014). *Beyond magenta: Transgender teens speak out* (S. Kuklin, Photog.). Candlewick Press.

Pessin-Whedbee, B. (2017). *Who are you? The kids guide to gender identity* (N. Bardoff, Illus.). Jessica Kingsley Publishers.

Pitman, G. E. (2014). *This day in June* (K. Litten, Illus.). Magination Press.

Pitman, G. E. (2017). *When you look out the window: How Phyllis Lyon and Del Martin built a community* (C. Lyles, Illus.). Magination Press.

Pitman, G. E. (2018). *Sewing the rainbow: The story of Gilbert Baker and the rainbow flag* (H. Clifton-Brown, Illus.). Magination Press.

Pohlen, J. (2016). *Gay & lesbian history for kids: The century-long struggle for LGBT rights* (J. Spence, Illus.). Chicago Review Press.

Sanders, R. (2019). *Stonewall: A building, an uprising, a revolution* (J. Christoph, Illus.). Random House.

Setterington, K. (2013). *Branded by the pink triangle*. Second Story Press.

Silverberg, C. (2015). *Sex is a funny word: A book about bodies, feelings, and YOU* (F. Smyth, Illus.). Seven Stories Press.

Stevenson, R. (2016). *Pride: Celebrating diversity and community*. Orca Book Publishers.

Winter, J. (2009). *Gertrude is Gertrude is Gertrude is Gertrude* (C. Brown, Illus.). Atheneum Books for Young Readers.

References

Adichie, C. N. (2009, July). *The danger of a single story* [Video]. TED Conferences. https://www.ted.com/talks/chimamanda_adichie_the_danger_of_a_single_story.html

American Library Association. (2009). *Stonewall book awards list*. Rainbow Round Table. http://www.ala.org/rt/rrt/award/stonewall/honored

Cart, M., & Jenkins, C. (2015). *Top 250 LGBTQ books for teens: Coming out, being out, and search for community*. American Library Association.

Crisp, T. (2015). A content analysis of Orbis Pictus Award-winning nonfiction, 1990–2014. *Language Arts, 92*(4), 241–253.

Crisp, T., Gardner, R. P., & Almeida, M. (2017). The all-heterosexual world of children's nonfiction: A critical content analysis of LGBTQ identities in Orbis Pictus Award books. *Children's Literature in Education, 49*(4), 1–18.

Duke, N. K. (2000). 3.6 minutes per day: The scarcity of informational texts in first grade. *Reading Research Quarterly, 35*(2), 202–224. https://doi.org/10.1598/RRQ.35.2.1

Duke, N., & Bennett-Armistead, S. (2003). *Reading and writing informational text in the primary grades*. Scholastic.

GLSEN. (2019). *Curricular standards that include LGBTQ+ representation promote student achievement and wellbeing*. https://www.glsen.org/sites/default/files/2020-08/Curricular-Standards-Statement-2020-3.pdf

Jenkins, C. (2016, June 2). *ACLU's Georgia director resigns over transgender bathroom debate*. Reuters. https://www.reuters.com/article/georgia-lgbt/aclus-georgia-director-resigns-over-transgender-bathroom-debate-idUSL1N18U2FG

Jeong, J., Gaffney, J. S., & Choi, J. O. (2010). Availability and use of informational texts in second-, third-, and fourth grade classrooms. *Research in the Teaching of English, 44*(4), 435–456.

Kiefer, B., & Wilson, M. (2011). Nonfiction literature for children: Old assumptions and new directions. In S. Wolf, K. Coats, P. Enciso, & C. Jenkins (Eds.), *Handbook of research on children's and young adult literature* (pp. 290–299). Routledge.

Kosciw, J. G., Greytak, E. A., Zongrone, A. D., Clark, C. M., & Truong, N. L. (2017). Executive summary. In *The 2017 national school climate survey: The experiences of lesbian, gay, bisexual, transgender, and queer youth in our nation's schools* (p. xiii–xxviii). GLSEN. https://www.glsen.org/sites/default/files/2019-10/GLSEN-2017-National-School-Climate-Survey-NSCS-Full-Report.pdf

Lewis, H. (2017, June 6). *Betsy DeVos won't protect LGBT students, so we have to*. HuffPost. https://www.huffpost.com/entry/betsy-devos-wont-protect-lgbt-students-so-we-have_b_593712e3e4b06bff911d7ba0

Maloch, B., & Bomer, R. (2013). Informational texts and the common core standards: What are we talking about, anyway? *Language Arts, 90*(3), 205–213.

Meltzer, M. (1976). Where do all the prizes go? The case for nonfiction. *The Horn Book Magazine, 52*, 17–23. https://www.hbook.com/?detailStory=where-do-all-the-prizes-go-the-case-for-nonfiction-2

Meyer, E. J. (2010). *Gender and sexual diversity in schools*. Springer.

National Governors Association Center for Best Practices & Council of Chief State School Officers. (2010). *Common Core State Standards for English language arts & literacy in history/social studies, science, and technical subjects.* http://www.corestandards.org/assets/CCSSI_ELA%20Standards.pdf

Paris, D. (2012). Culturally sustaining pedagogy: A needed change in stance, terminology, and practice. *Educational Researcher, 41*(3), 93–97. https://doi.org/10.3102%2F0013189X12441244

Short, K. (2017). Critical content analysis as research methodology. In H. Johnson, J. Mathis, & J. G. Short (Eds.), *Critical content analysis of children's and young adult literature: Reframing perspective* (pp. 1–27). Routledge.

Tribunella, E. (2012). Between boys: Edward Stevenson's *Left to themselves* (1891) and the birth of gay children's literature. *Children's Literature Association Quarterly, 37*(4), 374–388. https://doi.org/10.1353/chq.2012.0055

Wargo, J. M. (2016). Queer, quare, and [q]ulturally sustaining. In Brockenbrough, E., Ingrey, J., Martino, W., and N. Rodriguez. (Eds.), *Queer studies and education: Critical concepts for the twenty-first century* (pp. 299–307). Palgrave Macmillan.

Wargo, J. M. (2017). Hacking heteronormativity and remixing rhymes: Enacting a [q]ulturally sustaining pedagogy in middle grades English language arts. *Voices from the Middle, 24*(3), 39–43.

Coda

When I was younger, I was taught that fiction was fake, and nonfiction was real. It was a simplistic way of describing the two writing forms, but, for elementary-age me, it was an easy way to distinguish what was real from what was imagined. As an adult, that knowledge was always resting within the dark recesses of my mind, influencing how I approached the texts situated within each genre. Fiction was untrue, a collection of words that created a simulated reality. Nonfiction was truth, an accurate depiction of events that occurred within the past or present, a precise account unencumbered by the ideological forces that permeate this world. Ideologies are systems of ideas that influence how we think about the world, how we engage with the world, and how we view others who exist in the world. Because of this, it would seem that ideological influence would only affect how we understand things that are open to interpretation. Ideology impacts everything, however, even the truths we tell, and *Reading and Teaching with Diverse Nonfiction Children's Books* challenges us to consider how our truths can be manipulated by ideology.

Specifically, each of the authors asks us to reflect on how the truths of minoritized populations are often overlooked, omitted, or obliterated because dominant truths are considered more important. They ask us to question what happens when truth telling is incomplete and what happens when harsh realities are glossed over to protect adult-defined notions of childhood innocence. They ask us to examine what happens when those same children are forced to see stereotypical depictions of their pasts and presents consecrated by dominant society as accurate portrayals. Ultimately, these authors highlight the importance of questioning, of looking into the nonfiction texts we read and asking ourselves whose truths aren't included and who benefits from those truths being dismissed.

Throughout my reading of this book, I was continuously reminded of my time as a high school English language arts teacher, for although this book says it's written for K–8 teachers, there are lessons for us all. The Common Core State

Standards for English language arts highlight the reading of informational text, and, across each grade band, analyzing key ideas, examining the author's craft and writing structure, and exploring the integration of knowledge and ideas are centered. Yet there is no standard for the analysis of how ideology can influence each of these components. There is no standard that asks us how ideological underpinnings can influence the main purpose, the author's point of view, or even which key details are included. This book calls our standards into question, as it challenges us to consider how our pedagogical choices in the teaching and selection of nonfiction texts can go against culturally sustaining pedagogies simply by refusing to acknowledge the various ways that the authors of informational texts choose which aspects of the truth to tell.

Utilizing the various strategies presented across the chapters, though, can help educators of all grade levels to better align with culturally sustaining practices, as we center more inclusive portrayals of all people, no matter their ability, religion, ethnicity, nationality, language, or race. We can employ the frameworks and reflect upon the guiding questions to ensure that we are critically engaging with text and acknowledging the truths of people whose pasts and presents have been muted behind "truths" that are considered more marketable in the traditional publishing arena. We can use the nonfiction exemplars listed in each chapter to better identify which stories we may have overlooked when we were stocking our shelves. We can apply what this book teaches us to how we select books for our future classrooms, but we can also share these processes with students, so they, too, can critically examine the nonfiction texts they read, whether the standards ask them to or not.

When I was younger, I believed that fiction was fake and nonfiction was true, but it was not until I reached adulthood that I understood how much this simplistic belief could have negatively influenced how I viewed others and how I viewed myself. I did not understand how the ideology present within nonfiction texts narrowed my view of history and the present. This book, however, can ensure that teachers and students have more tools to use as they interrogate the partiality of nonfiction. It can ensure that students learn that sometimes nonfiction does not always equate to fact. It can help all educational stakeholders reflect on the partiality of nonfiction, especially as we work to create a more pluralistic schooling experience for every student.

Stephanie Renee Toliver
Boulder, Colorado

Index

. *See also* Asian American
Jewish American nonfiction, 130–46
   baseball stars, 139
   collections, 139–40
   exclusions of from multiculturalism, 131
   Holocaust, 134–36
   Jewish contributions to American culture, 136–39
   Jews as insiders and outsiders, 131–32
   list of titles, 141–42, 143–45
   multiculturalism through food and holidays, 133–34
   online resources, 142
   practical strategies, 141
Jewish Holidays All Year Round: A Family Treasury (Cooper), 134
Journey for Justice: The Life of Larry Ithong (Mabalon & Romasanta), 58
   primary sources, 65, 66–67
Journey That Saved Curious George, The: The True Wartime Escape of Margret and H. A. Rey (Borden), 136
Journey through Islamic Art (Robert), 159
Just Ask! Be Different, Be Brave, Be You, 166, 167–68

Kahlo, Frida, 24
Kamin, Rachel, 130, 212
Keelan, Jennifer, 170
Kelly, K., 169
Khadjia (wife of Muhammad), 152
Kid's Guide to Asian American History, A: More Than 70 Activities (Petrillo), 69
Kim, Esther June, 58, 62–63, 66, 212
K'naan, 154
Koufax, Sandy, 139
Kulthum, Umm, 152

labor movement, 137–38
Laminack, L.L., 169
Larrick, N., 82
Latinx nonfiction, 21–40
   accuracy, 27–29
   activities for reading, 34–35
   biographies, 29–30
   cultural content, 27–29
   digital platforms, 24–25

   expository nonfiction, 30–31
   illustrations, 25–26
   insider vs. outsider authors, 28
   lists of titles, 35, 36–39
   memoirs, 29–30
   nonfiction poetry, 31–32
   online resources, 36
   practical strategies, 34–35
   selection criteria, 25–28, 35
   series books, 32–33
   Spanish text, 26–27
   trends in children's books, 23–25
   writing quality, 26–27
Lázaro, Georgina, 32
Lazarus, Emma, 137
Lectorum, 32
Lee & Low Books, 43
   Classroom Library Questionnaire, 140
Lemlich, Clara, 137–38
letter writing, 179
Leung, Julie, 68
Lewis, Harry, 185
Lewis, John, 86
LGBTQ+ nonfiction, 24, 184–200
   critical analysis, 188–94
   lists of titles, 190–91, 196–97, 198
   online resources, 197
   practical strategies, 196
   Pride holidays, 193–94, 196
   progress theme, 194–95
Liberty's Voice: The Story of Emma Lazarus (Silverman), 137
library activity, 71
Lightning Dreamer: Cuba's Greatest Abolitionist, The (Engle), 31
Lily Renée: Escape Artist (Robbins), 138
Lin, Maya, 67–68
Lipman Pike: America's First Home Run King (Michelson), 139
Liston, Melba Doretta, 84
Little House series, 54
Little Leaders: Bold Women in Black History (Harrison), 84
Little Legends: Exceptional Men in Black History (Harrison), 84
Little Melba and Her Big Trombone (Russell-Brown), 84

Editors

Thomas Crisp is an associate professor of children's literature and literacy in the Department of Early Childhood and Elementary Education in the College of Education and Human Development at Georgia State University. His scholarly work focuses on issues of justice and representation in children's and young adult literature, media, and culture. He is concerned primarily with literature by and about people who self-identify as LGBT or queer. He is currently the president of the Children's Literature Associa-  tion and is coeditor of the *Journal of Children's Literature*. Crisp previously served on the board of directors for the Children's Literature Association and NCTE's Children's Literature Assembly, and serves on the editorial board of *Children's Literature in Education*, along with a number of editorial review boards for distinguished journals. He is an International Youth Library fellow and the recipient of the International Literacy Association's Elva Knight Research Grant and the International Research Society for Children's Literature's Research Grant.

Roberta Price Gardner is an assistant professor of reading and literacy education at Kennesaw State University, where she teaches both literacy methods and children's, adolescent, and culturally relevant literature courses. She served as an elementary school librarian before earning her doctorate at the University of Georgia. Her research interests center on the relationships among literature, literacy, social positioning, and educational equity, especially at the elementary school levels. She has been the chair of NCTE's Elementary Section Steering Committee

(2018–2020), and is a former NCTE Cultivating New Voices Among Scholars of Color Fellow (2014–2016 cohort).

Suzanne M. Knezek is an associate professor of literacy education in the School of Education and Human Services at the University of Michigan–Flint, where she teaches both literacy methods and children's, adolescent, and multicultural literature courses. She taught elementary school in rural Texas before earning her doctorate at Michigan State University. Her scholarship focuses on representations of diversity in children's books and the preparation of preservice and practicing literacy teachers in field settings. Knezek serves as director of the University of Michigan–Flint School of  Education and Human Services Reading Center and is coeditor of the Teachers' Voices column in the *Journal of Children's Literature*.

Contributors

Kathryn H. Au became a professor at the University of Hawai'i, where she was the first person to hold an endowed chair in education. Au focused her efforts on establishing the Ka Lama Teacher Education Initiative to assist Native Hawaiians to become teachers in their own communities. She worked for twenty-three years at the Kamehameha Elementary Education Program as a teacher in grades K–2, and then as a researcher and teacher educator. Au serves or has served on the editorial advisory boards of many journals, including *Reading Research Quarterly*, *The Reading Teacher*, *Journal of Adolescent and Adult Literacy*, and *Journal of Literacy Research*. She served as president of the International Reading Association in 2009–2010. She has been president of the National Reading Conference and vice president of the American Educational Research Association.

Sharon Black is an associate professor who is editor and writing consultant for the McKay School of Education at Brigham Young University. She loves the diversity and variety of her work. Sharon is coeditor of *Systematic and Engaging Early Literacy: Instruction and Intervention*, and sole author of chapters on foundations, print awareness, and arts integration. Her research and writing in children's literature includes classroom use of children's books featuring characters with disabilities to help children with and without disabilities develop positive and healthy perspectives for themselves and for one another. She has authored and coauthored journal articles and book chapters on literacy education and children's literature extended to focus on gifted/talented education, folklore, mythology, storytelling, early expository text structures, and speech language pathology, as well as various classroom strategies for teaching reading and writing. She has also published several journal articles and an extensive book chapter involving linguistic analysis.

Amina Chaudhri is an associate professor in the Teacher Education department at Northeastern Illinois University, where she teaches courses in literacy, social studies, and children's and YA literature. She is a longtime reviewer and contributor to Booklist and served on the Orbis Pictus Book Award Committee. She is the author of the book *Multiracial Identity in Children's Literature.*

Denise Dávila is an assistant professor of language and literacy studies at the University of Texas at Austin. She is a graduate of The Ohio State University, where she earned a PhD in teaching and learning with a specialization in literature for children and young adults. She was the committee chair of NCTE's Orbis Pictus Award for Outstanding Nonfiction for Children, 2020–2021, and is a member of the national committee for the Tomás Rivera Mexican American Children's Book Award. Her scholarship examines (a) the use of children's literature to discuss diverse religious perspectives among children, families, and educators and (b) the role of linguistically and culturally inclusive books in community-based early literacy programs for families.

Sarah Elovich holds an MA in early childhood education. She is a writer, speaker, and communications coach. Her work has advanced out-of-school educational opportunities for children and families.

Rachel Kamin has been a synagogue librarian for over twenty years and is currently director of the Joseph and Mae Gray Cultural & Learning Center at North Suburban Synagogue Beth El in Highland Park, Illinois. She has served as the chair of the Sydney Taylor Book Award Committee, a national committee of the Association of Jewish Libraries that presents awards to the best Jewish children's books each year, and was the book review editor for children and teens for the Association of Jewish Libraries Reviews. She writes articles and book reviews for *School Library Journal, BookLinks, Judaica Librarianship, Library Journal,* and *Jewish Book Council.* Kamin holds a BA in history from Grinnell College and a master's degree in library and information science from the University of Michigan.

Esther June Kim is an assistant professor in the School of Education at William & Mary. Her research focuses on civic education and how race and religion shape students' civic agency. Specifically, using the work of Sylvia Wynter, she explores the potential for ideological transformation in traditional and nontraditional school spaces. Prior to her work as a teacher educator, she taught secondary history and humanities in South Korea and California.

Joseph Madres is a doctoral student in the Curriculum and Instruction program in the Lynch School of Education and Human Development at Boston College. A former arts educator and community artist, Madres's scholarship documents how the arts can be mobilized in building critical democratic futures.

Deborah J. Margolis is Middle East studies librarian at Michigan State University (MSU). For the past six years, she has served as project director of MSU's Muslim Journeys scholar-led campus-community book discussion series. Margolis organizes and leads educational programming in the areas of Muslim, Jewish, Middle East, and genocide studies. She curates literary-based exhibitions, most recently "Jordan's Bedouins: Deeply Rooted" and "Forms of Activism: Sahar Khalifeh's Palestine." In 2019 she received the Charles A. Gliozzo International Award for Public Diplomacy from MSU. Margolis has worked in a variety of settings, including as youth services coordinator at the Maryland State Library for the Blind and Physically Handicapped, and has been a leader and trainer of the Mother Goose on the Loose early literacy program. She holds a master of library science and a master of arts in Jewish studies.

Betsy McEntarffer spent most of her working life in libraries, university, public, elementary school, and school district centralized libraries. She was born in conservative midwestern America in an all-white neighborhood with little contact with other cultures. During her years as an elementary school library paraeducator, she became involved in volunteer work with a fair-trade company now called Ten Thousand Villages. That opened her eyes to the rest of the world—its inequities and its diversity. She subsequently became involved with her school district's MOSAIC book review committee—a group of like-minded educators that seeks to detect bias in books for youth and children and to provide schools with examples of the best in multicultural literature. These experiences have been instrumental in her own cultural proficiency journey. In the process, she became acquainted with Debbie Reese, who has been a mentor and friend in this journey. She is still learning.

Karla J. Möller is an associate professor of children's literature in the Curriculum and Instruction department at the University of Illinois at Urbana–Champaign. Her career has offered her varied experience as an educator, including as a first-grade paraprofessional and elementary school teacher in Georgia, USA, and an ESL and social studies teacher in Schleswig-Holstein and Bremen, Germany. Her research focuses on culturally sustaining literature and literacy practices in the elementary and middle grades—including attention to access, availability, and use of print and digital resources—for all students. She works collaboratively with teachers, who invite her into their classrooms and schools for long-term projects related to response to culturally diverse literature. Her research is grounded in the notion of literacies for social justice that address a range of equity issues affecting students within the educational system, as well as societal issues that students and teachers seek to change through social activism. For three years, she coedited *Journal of Children's Literature*. Now, she happily just reads and reviews for it.

Jamie Campbell Naidoo is the Foster-EBSCO Endowed Professor at the University of Alabama School of Library and Information Studies in Tuscaloosa. He has worked as both elementary school librarian and public children's librarian, and was the 2018–2019 president of the Association for Library Service to Children. Naidoo is active in the American Library Association as well as the United States Board on Books for Young People, serving on numerous book award committees and in various leadership roles. He publishes and presents frequently on topics related to diversity in children's literature and library services to diverse populations, particularly LGBTQ+ families and Latinx families. His website is http://jcnaidoo.people.ua.edu.

Mary Anne Prater is a professor of special education and dean of the McKay School of Education at Brigham Young University. She has taught as a special educator in the public schools and as a teacher educator for thirty-six years. Prater's research interests include how disability is portrayed in children's literature. She is cofounder of the Dolly Gray Children's Literature Award, which celebrates positive portrayals of developmental disabilities in children's and young adult literature.

Ruth E. Quiroa is an associate professor of reading, language, and literacy at National Louis University, and a former kindergarten and bilingual (Spanish–English) second-grade educator. She teaches courses (undergraduate, graduate) in youth literature, preservice literacy methods, comprehension, and teaching writing. Quiroa's research focuses on how teacher engagement with Indigenous Peoples' and people of color's literature influences their instructional practices; trends and issues in Latinx youth literature; magical realism in Latinx picturebooks; and immigrant-themed graphic novels. She has served as a selection committee member and chair for the Américas Book Award for Children and Adolescents (2010–2012) and a selection committee member for the Pura Belpré Award (2013), the Randolph Caldecott Award (2019), and the Jane Addams Award (2020–2022).

Debbie Reese is tribally enrolled at Nambé Owingeh, a sovereign Native Nation in what is currently called New Mexico. Her articles and book chapters are used across the United States and Canada in English, library science, and education courses, but she is most well known for her blog, *American Indians in Children's Literature*. She launched it in 2005, believing in the impact that open access research can have on practitioners and their work with children. A former schoolteacher and assistant professor, she was selected to give the American Library Association's prestigious 2019 Arbuthnot Lecture. She holds a PhD in education from the University of Illinois and an MLIS from San Jose State University.

Noreen Naseem Rodríguez is an assistant professor of teacher learning, research, and practice in the School of Education at the University of Colorado Boulder. She studies Asian American education, teachers of color, the teaching of difficult histories, and critical uses of diverse children's literature. Her research has been published in practitioner and scholarly journals and she is the coauthor of *Social Studies for a Better World: An Anti-Oppressive Approach for Elementary Educators* (2021) with Katy Swalwell. She received the 2019 Early Career Award from the Children's Literature Assembly of NCTE and the 2021 Early Career Award from the Research on the Education of Asian Pacific Americans Special Interest Group of the American Educational Research Association. Prior to her work in teacher education, she served in AmeriCorps Literacy First and was a bilingual elementary teacher in Austin, Texas.

Leila Tarakji is a PhD candidate in the Department of English at Michigan State University. Her research focuses on multicultural ethnic literature and she is particularly committed to the development of Muslim American literary studies. She explores how Muslims in the United States use literature to (re) imagine and express their identity as members of their respective communities and to illustrate the rich dynamics of Muslim (American) culture and history. Her work also considers how Muslim texts define Islam in America and engage with representations of their faith and community in US media and culture. Tarakji's dissertation project investigates expressions of *Umma* or community that transcend historical and geographical boundaries in contemporary Muslim American literature.

Tina M. Taylor is a professor and associate dean in the McKay School of Education at Brigham Young University. She has worked in the field of education for more than thirty years as a special educator, professor, and administrator. She has written several articles and has coauthored three books about using children's literature that includes characters with special needs. She is one of the founders and current chair of the Dolly Gray Children's Literature Award, which recognizes high-quality children's books that portray characters with developmental disabilities.

Ebony Elizabeth Thomas was born and raised in Detroit and taught elementary language arts, high school English, and creative writing in public schools for several years after graduating from Florida A&M University. She earned her PhD from the University of Michigan in 2010 and is currently an associate professor at Penn GSE in the Division of Literacy, Culture, and International Education. Thomas's program of research is most keenly focused on children's and adolescent texts (broadly construed); the teaching of African American literature, history, and culture in K–12 classrooms; and the roles that race, class, and gender play in classroom discourse and interaction. Her most recent book is *The Dark Fantastic: Race and the Imagination from Harry Potter to the Hunger Games* (2019). She is also coeditor of the 2012 anthology *Reading African American Experiences in the Obama Era: Theory, Advocacy, Activism* (with Shanesha R. F. Brooks-Tatum).

Stephanie Renee Toliver is an assistant professor of literacy studies and secondary humanities at the University of Colorado Boulder. She is also a 2019 NAEd/Spencer Dissertation Fellow. Her current research is based in the critical tradition, analyzing young adult speculative fiction in an effort to promote social justice and equity in the English classroom. Within this research area, she focuses on representations of and responses to people of color in speculative fiction texts to discuss the implications of erasing youth of color from futuristic and imaginative contexts. Toliver's research interests include speculative fiction, social justice education, and Black girl literacies.

Jon M. Wargo is a 2020 NAEd/Spencer postdoctoral fellow and an assistant professor in the Lynch School of Education and Human Development at Boston College. Using feminist, queer, and poststructural modes of inquiry, he examines how historically minoritized children and youth use literacy and technology to design more just social futures. Publishing extensively across the areas of digital literacy, children's literature, civic and social education, and qualitative research, his scholarship can be found in the pages of *Jour-*

nal of Literacy Research, *Voices from the Middle, Journal of Children's Literature, Qualitative Inquiry, New Media & Society, Learning, Media, and Technology*, and *Language Arts*. A former Denver Public Schools teacher, Wargo holds a BA in English and gender studies from Indiana University–Bloomington and a PhD in curriculum, instruction, and teacher education from Michigan State University. At Boston College, Wargo teaches undergraduate and graduate courses in digital literacies, social studies, qualitative research methods, and arts-based inquiry.

Michele Widdes is an avid reader and currently teaches eighth-grade English language arts at Sunset Ridge School in Northfield, Illinois, where she has been an educator for over twenty years. Her work has appeared in *Best Practice: New Standards for Teaching and Learning in America's Schools* (2nd ed.) by Smokey Daniels and Steve Zemelman and *Gifted Child Today*. She has a BA in English and Jewish studies from Tulane University and a master of arts in teaching from National Louis University.

Vivian Yenika-Agbaw is a professor of children's literature at Pennsylvania State University, University Park, where she teaches children's and young adult literature. Prior to that, she taught children's literature and other literacy courses at Bloomsburg University and Clarion University of Pennsylvania. She is the author of *Taking Children's Literature Seriously: Reading for Pleasure and Social Change* and coeditor of *Does Nonfiction Equate Truth? Rethinking Disciplinary Boundaries through Critical Literacy* and *Adolescents Rewrite Their Worlds: Using Literature to Illustrate Writing Forms*.

Terrell A. Young is a professor of children's literature at Brigham Young University. His publications include many journal articles and thirteen books, including the coedited *Deepening Students' Mathematical Understanding with Children's Literature* (2018) and the coauthored seventh edition of *Children's Literature, Briefly* (2020). He has served as president of the International Literacy Association's Children's Literature and Reading Special Interest Group, the NCTE Children's Literature Assembly, and the United States Board on Books for Young People. Young has enjoyed serving on numerous book award committees, including the 2019 John Newbery Award, the American Folklore Society Aesop Prize, the USBBY Outstanding International Books, the NCTE Excellence in Poetry for Children Award, the NCTE Orbis Pictus Award for Outstanding Nonfiction for Children, the Notable Children's Books in the Language Arts, the Notable Books for a Global Society, the Washington Children's Choice Picture Book Award, and the YALSA Nonfiction Award.

This book was typeset in TheMix and Palatino by Barbara Frazier.

Typefaces used on the cover include Typo Grotesk and Gotham.

The book was printed on 50-lb. White Offset paper by Seaway Printing Company, Inc.